# Bernard Shaw and His Contemporaries

Series Editors
Nelson O'Ceallaigh Ritschel
Massachusetts Maritime Academy
Pocasset, MA, USA

Peter Gahan
Independent Scholar
Los Angeles, CA, USA

The series *Bernard Shaw and His Contemporaries* presents the best and most up-to-date research on Shaw and his contemporaries in a diverse range of cultural contexts. Volumes in the series will further the academic understanding of Bernard Shaw and those who worked with him, or in reaction against him, during his long career from the 1880s to 1950 as a leading writer in Britain and Ireland, and with a wide European and American following.

Shaw defined the modern literary theatre in the wake of Ibsen as a vehicle for social change, while authoring a dramatic canon to rival Shakespeare's. His careers as critic, essayist, playwright, journalist, lecturer, socialist, feminist, and pamphleteer, both helped to shape the modern world as well as pointed the way towards modernism. No one engaged with his contemporaries more than Shaw, whether as controversialist, or in his support of other, often younger writers. In many respects, therefore, the series as it develops will offer a survey of the rise of the modern at the beginning of the twentieth century and the subsequent varied cultural movements covered by the term modernism that arose in the wake of World War 1.

More information about this series at
http://www.palgrave.com/gp/series/14785

Christopher Wixson

# Bernard Shaw and Modern Advertising

Prophet Motives

Christopher Wixson
Eastern Illinois University
Charleston, IL, USA

Bernard Shaw and His Contemporaries
ISBN 978-3-030-08749-4         ISBN 978-3-319-78628-5  (eBook)
https://doi.org/10.1007/978-3-319-78628-5

© The Editor(s) (if applicable) and The Author(s) 2018
Softcover re-print of the Hardcover 1st edition 2018
This work is subject to copyright. All rights are solely and exclusively licensed by the Publisher, whether the whole or part of the material is concerned, specifically the rights of translation, reprinting, reuse of illustrations, recitation, broadcasting, reproduction on microfilms or in any other physical way, and transmission or information storage and retrieval, electronic adaptation, computer software, or by similar or dissimilar methodology now known or hereafter developed.
The use of general descriptive names, registered names, trademarks, service marks, etc. in this publication does not imply, even in the absence of a specific statement, that such names are exempt from the relevant protective laws and regulations and therefore free for general use.
The publisher, the authors and the editors are safe to assume that the advice and information in this book are believed to be true and accurate at the date of publication. Neither the publisher nor the authors or the editors give a warranty, express or implied, with respect to the material contained herein or for any errors or omissions that may have been made. The publisher remains neutral with regard to jurisdictional claims in published maps and institutional affiliations.

Cover illustration: Lebrecht Music and Arts Photo Library/Alamy Stock Photo

Printed on acid-free paper

This Palgrave Macmillan imprint is published by the registered company Springer International Publishing AG part of Springer Nature
The registered company address is: Gewerbestrasse 11, 6330 Cham, Switzerland

# Acknowledgements

Every monograph is fundamentally a collaborative venture, and I am humbled by the network of benevolent individuals that animated this one and sustained its author intellectually, emotionally, and creatively at various moments throughout the process.

I am incredibly beholden to series editors Peter Gahan and Nelson O'Ceallaigh Ritschel, for their kindness, enthusiasm, and deep repository of Shavian knowledge. I am also sincerely appreciative of all of the fine editorial work done by Tomas René and Vicky Bates at Palgrave MacMillan on behalf of this project. Special thanks too to Debra Rae Cohen, R. Darren Gobert, and three anonymous reviewers whose critical feedback was perceptive and insightful. A section of Chapter 1 and Chapter 2 first appeared as "Looking After the Drainage: Health, Marketing, and the Turkish Bath in Bernard Shaw's *Misalliance*" in *Modern Drama* (60:1). That material is reprinted with permission from University of Toronto Press, with thanks to Meaghan Lloyd for her help securing it.

I also wish to thank Dr. John Boneham, Jane McGuinness, and Sue Waterhouse (British Library), Eve Read (History of Advertising Trust), Joshua Rowley and Pete Moore (Hartman Center, Duke University), Sarah Johnson (Eastern Illinois University), the Council on Faculty Research (Eastern Illinois University), and the librarians at Eastern Illinois University and the University of Illinois at Urbana-Champaign who all provided invaluable research assistance during the process.

Warm gratitude is due to fellow members of the International Shaw Society, whose support and guidance have been exceptional along the way, especially Jennifer Buckley, Leonard Conolly, Richard Dietrich, Ellen Dolgin, Brad Kent, Gustavo A. Rodríguez Martín, Michael O'Hara, Michel Pharand, Sally Peters, Lawrence Switzky, Jay Tunney, and Matthew Yde, all of whom I admire as scholars and as people.

I also want to recognize colleagues at Eastern Illinois University and its environs whose commitment to research and creative activity has been nourishing and inspirational: Melissa Ames, Melissa Caldwell, Kevin Doolen, Christopher Gadomski, Anne Thibault Geen, Frank Monier, Robin Murray, Linda Peete, Christina Peter, Dana Ringuette, Nick Shaw, Anita Shelton, Jad Smith, Leslie Sweet-Myrick, Tim Taylor, and Angela Vietto.

A quarter-century ago, Austin Briggs introduced me to Shaw with *Heartbreak House* and modeled gracefully and passionately how to be a teacher-scholar. For decades, the Shaw Festival directors Tadeusz Bradecki, Jackie Maxwell, Neil Munro, and Christopher Newton, along with their superb design teams and companies of actors, profoundly deepened my understanding of the stage life of Shaw's brilliant and complex plays.

My mother, Donna Wixson, first cultivated in me the habit of theatergoing and thus engendered what have become lifelong personal and professional conversations with plays, playwrights, and theater practitioners. During the process of writing, advice and encouragement from my father, Neal Wixson, were thoughtful and impactful, as was the vitality drawn from a community of family members: Lindsey Wixson, Lois Worthington, Roland Worthington, and Valerie Worthington.

I am ineffably indebted to Marjorie for her love and support; her commitment to the mission of the academy is remarkable and galvanizing.

Finally, I wish to thank especially Maisie and Charlie Wixson who as toddlers reaffirmed for me the importance of sustained, undaunted curiosity and risk-taking in play and now in their middle childhood make me grateful, happy, and proud to be engaged in meaningful, lifelong conversations with them.

## Contents

1 Introduction: "Press as Corrected, G.B.S."     1

2 Prescription and Petrifaction: Proprietary Medicine, Health Marketing, and *Misalliance*     31

3 "The Shadow of Disrepute": G.B.S. and Testimonial Marketing     59

4 "The Biggest Scoop in Advertising History": Personality Marketing, G.B.S., and the Near-Testimonial     93

5 "Those Magic Initials, G.B.S.": Copywriting for the Irish Clipper     133

Bibliography     163

Index     177

# List of Figures

| | | |
|---|---|---|
| Fig. 1.1 | Turkish bath advertisement, *The Windsor Magazine* 35:204 (December 1911), p. xviii | 4 |
| Fig. 3.1 | Formamint advertisement, from *Collier's Magazine* (5 December 1914), p. 26 | 74 |
| Fig. 3.2 | Formamint advertisement, digital collections at the New York Public Library | 75 |
| Fig. 4.1 | Cartoon, *Advertiser's Weekly* (March 15, 1929), p. 441 | 104 |
| Fig. 4.2 | Simmons advertisement, *Time* 13:18 (May 6, 1929), p. 29 | 120 |
| Fig. 5.1 | Irish Clipper advertisement, *The New Yorker* (July 17, 1948) | 140 |
| Fig. 5.2 | Irish Clipper advertisement, *The Saturday Review* (July 17, 1948), p. 6 | 141 |
| Fig. 5.3 | Irish Clipper travel poster, ca. 1940s | 151 |

CHAPTER 1

# Introduction: "Press as Corrected, G.B.S."

> *Should you set out to extol or to advertise Bernard Shaw,*
> *you know that this has already been done with incomparable*
> *energy and talent, and that it has been done by one who knows.*[1]
> —John Palmer

In its November 18, 1950 issue, *The New Yorker* reported that Scribner's bookstore, the day after Bernard Shaw's death, "threw together a window display made up of a number of his works and a sign reading, 'G.B.S. 1846–1950.'" The short article went on to recount how "Scribner's Shaw remained a hundred and four years old until the next day, when the year of his birth was moved up to 1856. It was Scribner's that was born in 1846."[2] The bookseller's mistake actually produced an ideal piece of marketing in which the writer (Shaw) is obscured by the client (Scribner's) and the brand ("G.B.S."). It also creates two competing pictures of Shaw—an author transfigured into a commodity by marketing over which he had little control and a copywriter who expertly deployed self-advertising to market his work and a larger political, ethical, and aesthetic vision.

Raymond Williams maintains that "the half-century between 1880 and 1930 [saw] the full development of an organized system of commercial information and persuasion, as part of the modern distributive system in conditions of large-scale capitalism."[3] For Roy Church, this apogee had its roots in "the late seventeenth century when, to strengthen sales appeal, rhetoric was added to information in the form of announcement concerning the availability of goods," coextensive "with the appearance of newspapers which proliferated during the eighteenth-century in London and also in the provinces."[4] Most accounts of the advent of *modern* British advertising identify the abolition of the advertisement tax (1853) and the newspaper stamp (1855) as the impetus for its proliferate growth, contemporaneous to the swell of commodity culture. In *Advertising in Britain: A History*, T. R. Nevett additionally attributes the expanding circulation growth of magazines and newspapers (hence advertising) to a decrease in prices, an increase in wages, and advancements in transportation and mass production.[5] Indeed, "the publishing trade was one of the most highly industrialized sectors of British manufacturing [and,] using modern systems of production, communication, and distribution, publishers created a mass public for their products" and a showcase for those of their advertisers.[6] If this network initially sought to promote goods and services, it evolved quickly to focus on the registering of brands on the public consciousness in order "to build long-term reputation … [and] guarantees [of] the consistent quality of the branded product."[7] An enormous uptick in the amount and visibility of press advertising and agencies occurred in Britain in the middle of the nineteenth century, and Shaw was born into "a widespread culture of brand advertising in Ireland": "From the period of the Famine onwards … the Irish press, from north to south, and from supposedly non-partisan and widely distributed freesheets to paid-for newspapers of various political hues, was inextricably wedded to advertising."[8] He would observe in the 1890s that, "in the present century of universal progress, no art, perhaps, has attained to such subtly-varied developments, as that of advertising."[9]

Concurrent with the rise of modern advertising, Shaw's prolific campaign to create and sustain his "G.B.S." persona in the public consciousness endured for more than seventy years. As Brad Kent has argued, the "self-fashioning and creation of a public personality was an integral element of literary culture in the modern period,"[10] and, beginning in the 1880s, Shaw skillfully brokered print appearances by "G.B.S." in newspapers and periodicals to enhance the visibility of his literary writing and dovetail with his Fabian interests in getting important ideas into public discourse for debate. Although he wrote to Otto Kyllman in 1903 of an intention to "give [his] mind to the whole business of advertising one of these days," Shaw indeed was already and always a consummate salesman.¹¹ As shrewdly as he could imitate professional marketing strategies, though, Scribner's shop window is indicative of how "G.B.S." could be a marketing tool for other hands besides his own. Alice McEwan has observed that the brand he created "was so successful that it was co-opted by the marketplace, assuming its role within a myriad of advertising gimmicks and promotional strategies in mass culture," eventually surpassing its creator.¹²

Advertising's double-edge for Shaw is pointedly displayed in his 1910 play *Misalliance* by the characters of Gunner and Lina Szczepanowska. Arriving in the play to exact revenge on Tarleton, Gunner musters no resistance to the lure of commodity upon entering the Tarleton household when he is suddenly and mysteriously arrested by the sight of the unwrapped Turkish bath unit, one of the most widely recognized and advertised home-cure contraptions: "his attention is caught by the Turkish bath. He looks down the lunette, and opens the panels."¹³ His preoccupation is disrupted by the arrival of Hypatia and Joey, and he quickly takes refuge *inside* the bath. As the lovers banter, Shaw writes that "the head of the scandalized man in the Turkish bath has repeatedly risen from the lunette, with a strong expression of moral shock."¹⁴ The humor of Gunner's head popping up through the bath is not derived solely from the farce of unexpected and undesired eavesdropping. E. S. Turner reminds that "hardly any magazine or store's catalogue of the 'eighties and 'nineties was without an illustration of one of these domestic sweat-boxes, with the patient's head protruding from the top."¹⁵ Original audiences would surely and immediately have recalled the ubiquitous image of the disembodied head atop the Turkish bath contraption from decades of periodical advertisements (see Fig. 1.1). The man depicted is wholly absorbed by commerce, his individual agency fully co-opted by the marketplace.

A more empowering relationship to advertising is illustrated by another unexpected visitor to the Tarleton home, Polish acrobat Lina Szczepanowska who, with her speeches and demonstrations, proves to be a master copywriter, styling herself like a patent medicine that sells an entire lifestyle, a vision of robust health and well-being. As such, Lina is an incarnation of the figure Shaw promoted throughout his life, animated solely by individual will but operating under the auspices of "a dynamic ever-moving biological Life Force."¹⁶ Like Lina, Shaw was his own copywriter marketing salubrious Shavian physical, mental, and spiritual fitness via "G.B.S." Throughout his life, Shaw endeavored to

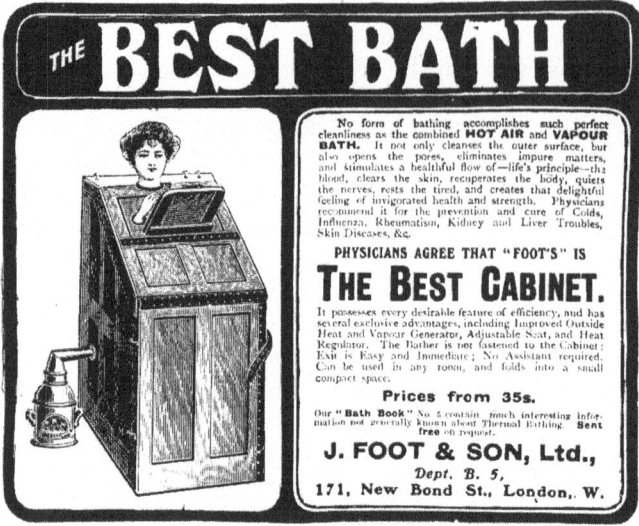

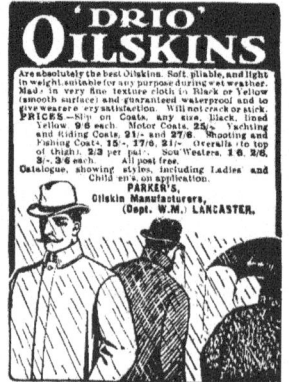

**Fig. 1.1** Turkish bath advertisement, *The Windsor Magazine* 35:204 (December 1911), p. xviii

harness marketing successfully as a vehicle towards individual and collective advancement and to fend off as much as possible *being* harnessed like Gunner into a mere hoarding, complicit with oppressive economic forces. His eventual forays into commercial campaigns were always fraught with anxious negotiation to retain integrity apart from client and product.

Advertising's double-edged potential informs Shaw's understanding of the word itself and governs his usage of it in his literary work. Actually, the meanings gathered during the etymological journey of the word "advertising" seem themselves very Shavian indeed, beginning with a provocative amalgam of promulgation and admonishment. Derived from Old French, "advertising" initially meant to "give notice of (something)" or "to make generally known," often as a formal and sincere warning. It referred to the action of both taking and giving note, announcing information for consideration and the heeding of counsel. This sense certainly endured, as newspapers even into the modern period retained the title of "advertiser." Surprisingly, it is another great playwright (William Shakespeare in *Much Ado About Nothing*) who provides the earliest recorded usage of the word to mean "calling public attention to." By the early eighteenth century and the advent of print media, "advertisement" gains further texture as publicity transfigures to promotion, announcement to a means of selling services or commodities, arriving closer to our contemporary definition. At that point, in practice, the word thus embarked upon what Shaw calls its "adventures in Capitalism in pursuit of profits."[17]

The word "advertising" and its variants appear more than forty times in Shaw's plays and prefaces, and, while its usage threads his entire playwriting career, there is a clear concentration during its first half, up to the First World War. The word's journey through his writing follows an evolution in which connotative and denotative meanings accrue, and his choices of when to use it provide a clue as to Shaw's developing understandings of the concept. Among the novels, the word only appears in *Cashel Byron's Profession, Love among the Artists*, and *The Irrational Knot*, all written in the early 1880s. In four of six instances, the word is used to denote benign newspaper publicity for artistic endeavors (theater productions, novel publication). The other two refer to solicitation notices, in one case for a "comfortable husband [that] need not be handsome, as the lady is short sighted." When he turns to playwriting in the

1890s, "advertising" begins to appear more frequently and with an edge. The meaning of the word expands beyond simply informational notices to include rhetorical craft on the part of their creators. In act three of *Widowers' Houses*, for instance, Lickcheese reveals that Cokane helps him by infusing a "literary style" into the former's "letters and draft prospectuses and advertisements."[18] In *Getting Married*, Mrs. George indicates to Hotchkiss that "Mr. Collins was looking out for a clever young man [like him] to write advertisements."[19] That cleverness in turn intends to exert an effect on readers, as, at the beginning of act two of *You Never Can Tell*, Finch McComas is described as having "exhausted all the news in his papers and is at present reduced to the advertisements, which are not sufficiently succulent to induce him to persevere with them."[20]

There is always an agenda of course behind the manufactured succulence, and Shaw's continued use of the word indicates that for him "advertising" denotes a staging of authority. The most vulgar example occurs in a set description for the public marketplace in *The Devil's Disciple*:

> The gallows which hangs there permanently for the terror of evildoers, with such minor advertizers and examples of crime as the pillory, the whipping post, and the stocks, has a new rope attached, with the noose hitched up to one of the uprights, out of reach of the boys.[21]

The various punishment apparati are both symbols of state power as well as criminal in and of themselves, all threatening the individual's autonomy. With that meaning, "advertising" provides Shaw with a vocabulary for various critiques. Vivie, in act four of *Mrs. Warren's Profession*, uses it when she confronts her mother, designating the difference between them:

> I know very well that fashionable morality is all a pretence, and that if I took your money and devoted the rest of my life to spending it fashionably, I might be as worthless and vicious as the silliest woman could possibly be without having a word said to me about it. But I don't want to be worthless. I shouldn't enjoy trotting about the park to advertize my dressmaker and carriage builder, or being bored at the opera to shew off a shopwindowful of diamonds.[22]

Similarly, Shaw describes Hector Malone's father in *Man and Superman* as "not having the stamp of the class which accepts as its life-mission the advertising and maintenance of first rate tailoring and millinery."[23]

Both instances loudly evoke Shaw's famous critique of a theater corrupted by commercial forces, producing plays consisting of "a tailor's advertisement making sentimental remarks to a milliner's advertisement in the middle of an upholsterer's and decorator's advertisement."[24] The enslavement of consumers to marketed taste to such an extent that they become advertisement pops up in *Misalliance* not only in Gunner's refuge inside the Turkish bath but also extends into environment, as Mrs. Tarleton is embarrassed to discover that her punchbowl is deemed tacky since "the shopman [told her] it was in the best taste."[25] Similarly, in *Candida*, the furniture of Morell House, "in its ornamental aspect, betrays the style of the advertised 'drawing-room suite' of the pushing suburban furniture dealer."[26] Based upon this grouping of the word's appearances, advertising poses a particular danger to the critical autonomy of the individual.

For Shaw, the term grew to become shorthand for publicity for any dishonest enterprise in the service of unrepentant commercialism. He wrote to William Faversham in 1917 that he "always steadily set [his] face against the particular form of advertisement – for it is nothing else – which poses as philanthropy."[27] When Adolphus Cusins reveals in *Major Barbara* that Undershaft gave his Salvation Army donation anonymously, Charles Lomax is surprised and impressed that he wouldn't want the credit since "most chaps would have wanted the advertisement."[28] In the same way, while he disapproves of his father's "public work" because it "takes his mind off the main chance," Johnny Tarleton admits in *Misalliance* "it has its value as an advertisement [that] makes useful acquaintances and leads to valuable business connections."[29] Julius Sagamore, in *The Millionairess*, hastily rebuffs Epifania's characterization of him as "the worthless nephew of the late solicitor Pontifex Sagamore," retorting that, in taking over his uncle's practice, he does not "advertise himself as worthless."[30] Even Stegna, the pianist in "The Music-Cure," is thrilled at the prospective publicity when the distraught Reginald threatens to commit suicide in her studio, saying "Do! What an advertisement! It will be really kind of you."[31] In the marketplace, those who don't excel at advertising perish by it. In the preface to *Pygmalion*, for instance, Shaw bemoans that a failure to effectively market dooms Henry Sweet's superior system of Shorthand: "the triumph of [the popular Pitman system] was a triumph of business organization," and Sweet "could not organize his market in that fashion [with] his four and six-penny manual, mostly in his lithographed handwriting, that was never vulgarly advertised."[32]

The word also comes up frequently when Shaw writes about what he refers to as "propagandists of the Cross," including those convinced the Christian apocalypse is at hand who produced "warning pamphlets … in constant circulation" and "advertisements … in the papers."[33] When discussing the staging practices of the Salvation Army in the preface to *Major Barbara*, Shaw advises that, "when you advertise a converted burglar or reclaimed drunkard as one of the attractions at an experience meeting, your burglar can hardly have been too burglarious or your drunkard too drunken."[34] Similarly, in the preface to *Androcles and the Lion*, he contrasts the altruistic miracles of Jesus with those vindictively and judgmentally wielded by the apostles, animated in his view by a "spirit of pure display and advertisement."[35] He goes on to critique the absurd "notion that [Christ] was shedding his blood in order that every petty cheat and adulterator and libertine might wallow in it and come out whiter than snow: 'I come as an infallible patent medicine for bad consciences' is not one of the sayings in the gospels."[36] The language of marketing enables Shaw to articulate how the commodification of the religion's organizing figure is a self-serving misrepresentation.

For Shaw, the term gradually accrued an association with dishonesty, and advertising was just part of a larger system rife with hypocrisy and deception, an outrage to which he would return countless times throughout his career. For instance, in an 1889 lecture, he condemns commercial demagoguery as another by-product of capitalism:

> In the matter of advertizing, [Private Enterprise] is exempt from all moral obligations: the most respectable newspapers give up the greater part of their space every day to statements which every well-instructed person knows to be false, and dangerously false, since they lead people to trust to imaginary cures in serious illnesses, and to ride bicycles through greasy mud in heavy traffic on tires advertized as "non-slipping": in short, to purchase all sorts of articles and invest in all sorts of enterprises on the strength of shameless lies.[37]

Similarly, *The Revolutionist's Handbook* (1903) notes that "straightforward public lying has reached gigantic developments, there being nothing to choose in this respect between the pickpocket at the police station and the minister on the treasury bench, the editor in the newspaper office, the city magnate advertising bicycle tires that do not side-slip, the clergyman subscribing the 39 articles, and the vivisector who pledges his knightly honor that no animal operated on in the physiological laboratory suffers the slightest pain."[38]

In *Everybody's Political What's What* (1944), Shaw charges that "advertising enjoys impunity also for lying on matters of fact, with the object of obtaining money on false pretenses. This, the most obviously outrageous of such claims, is the one that is completely conceded; for though prosecutions for seditious, blasphemous, and obscene libel occur often enough to keep their possibility alive and dreaded, prosecutions for obtaining money by lying advertisements are unheard of today."[39]

Of course, advertising is not only a deceitful business in and of itself but is insinuated into the larger system of capitalist exploitation. The playwright was quite right that the practice was deeply rooted within the economy. In Britain, "estimates of expenditure in the interwar years vary considerably, but the lowest figure, for direct advertising in a single year, is £85,000,000 and the highest £200,000,000. Newspapers derived half their income from advertising, and almost every industry and service, outside the old professions, advertised extensively."[40] For Raymond Williams, advertising is "the official art of modern capitalist society."[41] Corporate entities routinely unleash a marketing tidal wave against the gullible consumer, an act which for Shaw connects to his vision of how capitalism poisons the collective. In an extended example from *The Intelligent Woman's Guide to Socialism and Capitalism* (1928), Shaw discusses the final phase of a distillery established by private capitalists:

> They will spend enormous sums of money in advertisements to persuade the public that their whiskey is better and healthier and older and more famous than the whiskey made in other distilleries, and that everybody ought to drink whiskey every day as a matter of course. As none of these statements is true, the printing of them is, from the point of view of the nation, a waste of wealth, a perversion of labor, and a propaganda of pernicious humbug.[42]

In the postscript to *How He Lied to Her Husband*, Shaw reports with some glee that "a leading New York newspaper, which was among the most abusively clamorous for the suppression of Mrs Warren's Profession, has just been fined heavily for deriving part of its revenue from advertisements of Mrs Warren's houses," illustrating for him the tentacles of the prostitution industry:

the profits of Mrs Warren's profession are shared not only by Mrs Warren and Sir George Crofts but by the landlords of their houses, the newspapers which advertise them ... in short all the trades to which they are good customers, not to mention the public officials and representatives whom they silence by complicity, corruption, or blackmail.[43]

Shaw expands his vision to conceptualize everyone living under capitalism as forced into prostitution, with advertising indicted as part of its mechanics; in *The Intelligent Woman's Guide*, Shaw provides a "few examples of the male prostitutions ... which are daily imposed on men by Capitalism":

the writer and publisher of lying advertisements which pretend to prove the worse the better article, the shopman who sells it by assuring the customer that it is the best, the agents of drugging and drink, the clerk making out dishonest accounts, the adulterator and giver of short weight, the journalist writing for Socialist papers when he is a convinced Liberal, or for Tory papers when he is an Anarchist, the professional politician working for his party right or wrong, the doctor paying useless visits and prescribing bogus medicines to hypochondriacs[,] ... the solicitor using the law as an instrument for the oppression of the poor by the rich, the mercenary soldier fighting for a country which he regards as the worst enemy of his own, and the citizens of all classes who have to be obsequious to the rich and insolent to the poor.[44]

In similar terms, Shaw pitched his battle with the censor over *Mrs. Warren's Profession* as one between "the author, the managers, and the performers, who depend for their livelihood on their personal reputations" and the "prohibitionists" who live on "rents, advertisements, or dividends."[45] He refused to make his play "a standing advertisement of the attractive side of Mrs. Warren's business," bowing to pressure from the "White Slave traffickers" that "are in complete control of our picture theatres [and] reserve them for advertisements of their own trade."[46]

Nowhere was the insidiousness and dangerous collusion of marketing and industry more pronounced for Shaw than in the field of proprietary medicine. He repeatedly lamented that one tragic effect of income inequality is that "beauty and health become the dreams of artists and the advertisements of quacks instead of the normal conditions of life,"[47] and there is no shortage of material by Shaw about this particular mode of advertising within his writings on the patent cure phenomenon. Medical practitioners in *The Doctor's Dilemma* (1906), for instance, bemoan the profusion of product promotion. Blenkinsop wonders, "what are [the medical papers] after all but trade papers, full of advertisements?" while B. B. exclaims, "Look at the papers! full of scandalous advertisements of patent medicines!"[48] Perhaps reminiscent of Tarleton's underwear promotion in *Misalliance*, Knox the shopkeeper, in *Fanny's First Play* (1911), disapproves of "those hygienic corset advertisements that Vines & Jackson want us to put in the window" because they "werent decent and we couldnt shew them in our shop."[49]

In 1932, Shaw wrote that "the [obtrusive and ubiquitous] advertisements of quacks and their remedies, and of proprietary medicines, are flaunting everywhere, and must achieve a considerable amount of manslaughter every year: indeed, some public restraint on these is probably inevitable in the near future."[50] Fifteen years later, his views still had not changed or conditions improved so, in the preface to *Farfetched Fables*, he advocates the creation of a Ministry of Statistics, to correct the "statistical pretensions [of] lying advertisements of panaceas, prophylactics, elixirs, immunizers, vaccines, antitoxins, vitamins, and professedly hygienic foods."[51] He had sounded the alarm four decades earlier in the preface to *The Doctor's Dilemma* against this practice in which

> even trained statisticians often fail to appreciate the extent to which statistics are vitiated by the unrecorded assumptions of their interpreters. Their attention is too much occupied with the cruder tricks of those who make a corrupt use of statistics for advertising purposes.[52]

The Ministry, according to Shaw, would need to be

> lavishly financed ... as there is an enormous trade in such wares at present [because] popular demand for miracles and deities has been transferred to "marvels of science" and doctors, by dupes who think they are emancipating themselves from what in their abysmal ignorance they call medieval barbarism when they are in fact exalting every laboratory vivisector and quack immunizer.

He calls for this "public department [to be] manned not be chemists analyzing the advertised wares and determining their therapeutical value, but by mathematicians."

His most sustained overview of the industry appears in *Everybody's Political What's What*:

> In dealing with public health as with diplomacy the statesman must never forget that, as Ferdinand Lassalle declared, "the lie is a European power." In sanitary matters it is a world power. Lying is privileged in commercial advertisements because commerce is rich and powerful, just as it was privileged for princes, as Machiavelli pointed out. Vaccination produced a lucrative trade in vaccines. Later on, the word vaccine was applied to prophylactics that had nothing to do with cowpox; and now we have a whole industry producing vaccines, pseudo-vaccines, therapeutic serums, gland extracts called hormones, antigens, antitoxins, in addition to the old-fashioned pills, purges, tonics, electric belts, and the like, all professing to avert or cure every known or imagined sort of illness, and some of them promising to rejuvenate their purchasers and prolong life by fifty years or so. Scraps of Greek or Latin, with "ose" or "in" or "on" or "ax" tacked on to them, replace the old names or provide new ones, impressing the public just as the big word Mesopotamia is said to impress simple people as religious. We read the advertisements of these products, buy them, use them, cure ourselves by our *vis medicatrix naturæ*, and, attributing the cure to medicine, send the manufacturers glowing testimonials which are duly published and sometimes duly paid for. A lady of my acquaintance received £800 for a letter ascribing the beauty of her complexion, which was entirely and thickly artificial, to a well advertized face cream. I have myself been offered a considerable sum to attribute my mental powers to an equally well advertized educational correspondence course. No doubt the cures are sometimes genuine, the testimonials disinterested, and the advertisers sincere enough to take their own medicines; but the residue of downright impudent venal lying is enormous.[53]

Considering the playwright's antipathy towards the field of professional advertising, how then can we explain his direct participation in various commercial campaigns for clients such as Harrods and Pan-American Airways and on behalf of products such as Formamint and Simmons mattresses? In the preface to *Farfetched Fables*, Shaw, calling himself an "old journalist and agitator," complained that, in England,

> platform and press are gagged by such an irresponsible tyranny of partisan newspaper proprietors and shamelessly mendacious advertizers, and by the law against seditious and blasphemous libel, that my speeches were never reported, and my letters and articles inserted only when I could combine what I believed and wanted to say with something that the paper wanted to have said.[54]

His motive and method for his contributions to product advertising seem to be identical, suggesting that advertising is for him not an irrevocably unilateral enterprise. Rather, as it does for Lina in *Misalliance*, it extends an opportunity to negotiate the relationship between the individual and overreaching authority, even becoming a space of resistance. For example, in the preface to *On the Rocks*, Shaw refers to a recent court sentence of flogging and penal servitude in which "the victim escaped his punishment and gave a sensational advertisement to its savagery by committing suicide."[55] In the same way, in *Pygmalion*, a "defiantly non-resistant" Liza threatens to use her newfound knowledge and inherent skill to ruin Higgins. To counter his "bullying and big talk," she intends to "advertise it in the papers that your duchess is only a flower girl that you taught, and that she'll teach anybody to be a duchess just the same in six months for a thousand guineas": "Oh, when I think of myself crawling under your feet and being trampled on and called names, when all the time I had only to lift up my finger to be as good as you, I could just kick myself."[56] The latent power in advertising can be wielded against systems of "bullying and big talk," especially by superhuman individuals.

If Shaw critiques the spin engineered by the disciples to promote the early church, Jesus is for him a figure who brilliantly *self*-advertises, an example of how essential marketing is to the playwright's lauded world-betterers. Accordingly, "Caesar's victories" are for Shaw "advertisements for an eminence that would never have become popular without them."[57] For true supermen, advertising is a key tool to employ towards realizing and maintaining a healthy collective. Confucius in *Back to Methuselah* outlines the process of evolution starting with the gathering of the long-lived:

> Each of them believes that he or she is the only one to whom the miracle has happened. But the Archbishop knows better now. He will advertise in terms which only the longlived people will understand. He will bring them together and organize them. They will hasten from all parts of the earth. They will become a great Power.[58]

Again, there is no better illustration of this principle than Shaw himself with his creation of "G.B.S." He discovered early on that assiduous promotion was the engine of enduring revered eminence:

In England as elsewhere the spontaneous recognition of really original work begins with a mere handful of people, and propagates itself so slowly that it has become a commonplace to say that genius, demanding bread, is given a stone after its possessor's death. The remedy for this is sedulous advertisement.[59]

He applies the cure liberally, writing in 1907 that "the English are only too anxious to recognize a man of genius if somebody will kindly point him out to them [and I have] pointed myself out in this manner with some success."[60] Later, he declares, "I have advertised myself so well that I find myself, whilst still in middle life, almost as legendary a person as the Flying Dutchman."[61]

In the Preface to *Major Barbara*, Shaw characterizes himself as a "comparatively insignificant Irish journalist ... leading them by the nose into an advertisement of me which has made my own life a burden."[62] One of the playwright's biographers wrote in 1969,

> To say that George Bernard Shaw had two quite distinct personalities is not to suggest that he was in any way schizophrenic. He was fully aware of the difference and always able at will to make the transition. ... The public image, he confessed, "I manufactured myself."[63]

Like Oscar Wilde, Shaw with intention "emblazoned [himself] in the public imagination for combinations of [his] distinct public [personality] and wardrobe, as much as [his] literary prowess."[64]

In public discourse and especially in relation to trendy issues of health, politics, and the arts, the playwright mined opportunities for self-advancement with mercenary vivaciousness, and his early biographers often felt they had to defend the playwright's propensity for publicity against charges of crude self-aggrandizement. Establishing a distance between the public and private Shaw was always the first step, as drama critic John Palmer shows in a 1915 essay for the *London Saturday Review* when he espouses the "fallacies" associated with Shaw:

> It is not true that Bernard Shaw is an immensely public person. Or perhaps I should put it this way: Bernard Shaw whom the public knows is not an authentic revelation of the extremely private gentleman who lives in Adelphi Terrace. The Bernard Shaw whom the public knows might more accurately be described as a screen.[65]

The next step was to provide an apologia for the dogged campaigning. The actor Maurice Colbourne, for example, justified Shaw's zealous initiative by arguing that,

> having no money to advertise his wares, he could only capitalize himself. Accordingly, in cold business blood, the man Bernard Shaw engaged the wit Bernard Shaw to advertise Bernard Shaw the philosopher and preacher. [His] success as a salesman [was that] he could charm publicity out of an egg-shell. His beard, his diet, catching cold, moving house, the tailoring of his coat, nothing is too trivial to be grist to his mill.[66]

In 1910, G. K. Chesterton addressed accusations of "vulgar self- advertisement," calling Shaw "a great cheap-jack, with plenty of patter and I dare say plenty of nonsense, but with this also (which is not wholly unimportant), with goods to sell. ... At least the cheap-jack does advertise his wares, whereas the don or dear-jack advertises nothing except himself."[67]

Augustus Hamon characterized the playwright in 1916 as a perpetual huckster:

> Never did there live a greater advertiser than Shaw. Wherever he could, and in every possible way, he proclaimed that he was a genius, and that the wares he had on offer were the best in the world, better than those of Shakespeare. He was his own Barnum; he puffed himself, and he continues to do so. Don't waste your breath by calling him a charlatan, for he will glory in the name.[68]

That being said, Hamon went on,

> It is certain that this unbridled advertisement, this deliberate and ceaseless blowing of his own trumpet, have notably contributed to Shaw's worldwide renown. It is perhaps thanks to his methods of advertisement that it took him ten years to arrive. Now that he is famous he does not cease advertising himself, for he enjoys the practice all the more in proportion as it shocks public opinion. "Stop advertising myself!" he said the other day. "On the contrary, I must do it more than ever. Look at Pears' Soap. There is a solid house if you like, but every wall is still plastered with their advertisements. If I were to give up advertising, my business would immediately begin to fall off. You blame me for having declared myself to be the most remarkable man of my time. But the claim is an arguable one. Why should I not say it when I believe that it is true?"[69]

Robert Lynd, writing in 1919, also stood up for the playwright: "His critics often accuse him in regard to the invention of the Shaw myth, of having designed a poster rather than painted a portrait. And Mr. Shaw always hastens to agree with those who declare he is an advertiser in an age of advertisement."[70] Even Bertolt Brecht, in 1926, approvingly stated that Shaw "knows that the tools of an honest man must always include boisterous self-advertising."[71]

Later scholars and biographers felt Shaw's self-promotion less problematic. Michael Holroyd, for instance, suggests that "G.B.S. was not only a vegetarian but a living advertisement for vegetarianism,"[72] while Sally Peters envisions the playwright as "an immaculate walking mannequin, an elaborate advertisement for the hygienic way of life."[73] For Fintan O'Toole, the G.B.S. campaign is not only a virtue but the preeminent quality of his genius and "one of the great achievements of the history of advertising":

> [Shaw] was one of the great masters of self-invention [who intuitively seemed] to grasp the possibilities of mass media and the age of mechanical reproduction for the creation of a different kind of power in the world [and was among] the first to understand that in this mass media age, performance is not just what happens on the stage, it is everywhere.[74]

What he was marketing of course was not simply himself but a Shavian intellectual and physical way of life, consistent with his political aims. Just as patent medicine copy sells the dream of perfect health, the rhetoric of Shaw's publicity was animated by a utopic social vision. In general, Fabians "deplored what they saw as the wasteful proliferation of retailers, wholesalers, and middlemen under the capitalist system, attacked advertising as creating further waste by deceiving consumers, and believed that the sovereignty of the private consumer in a market economy was characterised by anarchic irresponsibility."[75] Yet Shaw did not advocate banning advertisement. In fact, in the preface to *Heartbreak House*, the symptoms of "war delirium" through which the "ordinary war-conscious citizen went mad [with] the conviction that the whole order of nature had been reversed" included that "no advertisements must be sent to the newspapers."[76] Instead, as Shaw would later advocate in the preface to *Farfetched Fables*, advertising needed to be purified of its toxicity and directed towards more salubrious ends.

# 1   INTRODUCTION: "PRESS AS CORRECTED, G.B.S."

In a utopian vein of a 1914 tract, Shaw's fellow Fabian Sidney Webb integrated purified advertising into his vision for a healthy collective; he maintains that "the elimination from [advertising] of all motives of personal self-interest and private gain, and the bringing of it under Democratic public control," will transform it into "public gramophones," prophesizing that

> the advertising of the future will ... not be decided on by irresponsible individuals, intent only on their own pecuniary profit, and not even pretending that their statements are either true or for the common good. The advertising of the future ... will aim, in all cases, in so far as Collectivist organization prevails, at what is believed to be some advantage to the community as a whole; it will not be swayed by any considerations of individual gain; it will be directed by persons acting only as the servants of the particular branches of public administration concerned; and it will be controlled not by private capitalists but by the representatives of the community.[77]

An earlier Fabian tract put it more succinctly: "The modern municipality can no more dispense with advertising than can the soap man."[78] For the superman, then, self-promotion is an imperative.

If Shaw was eager to perform the role of self-advertiser, he sometimes discussed his dramaturgy in similar terms, as he does in the preface to *Man and Superman*, when offering a rationale for the inclusion of the dream sequence:

> I have resorted to the trick of the strolling theatrical manager who advertises the pantomime of Sinbad the Sailor with a stock of second-hand picture posters designed for Ali Baba. He simply thrusts a few oil jars into the valley of diamonds, and so fulfills the promise held out by the hoardings to the public eye.[79]

Shaw claims, in his "easy device," that the "valley of diamonds" is his "perfectly modern play" and the "oil jar" is the extraneous third act. Frank Duba rejects Shaw's claim, calling "the bait and switch of the theatrical manager" a "particularly inapt analogy" since, while both *Arabian Nights* stories "differ in subject not in kind," the Dream sequence is unlike anything else in the play or various versions of the myth.[80] Shaw's explanation though does provide insight about how he conceptualizes the ways in which his plays work in marketing terms, in relation to their promotional tactics and the "G.B.S." branding. In the preface to *Three Plays for Puritans*, Shaw presents himself as "a very old-fashioned playwright" and attributes his success on the modern stage to critics who "find originality and brilliancy in [his] most hackneyed claptraps."[81] The source of this novelty derives partly from their infusion with "the advanced thought of [his] day," but he postulates their success as a marketing coup, a direct result of what he terms his "trumpet and cartwheel declamation":

> The trumpet is an instrument that grows on one; and sometimes my blasts have been so strident that even those who are most annoyed by them have mistaken the novelty of my shamelessness for novelty in my plays and opinions. ... The critics were the victims of the long course of hypnotic suggestion by which G.B.S. the journalist manufactured an unconventional reputation for Bernard Shaw the author.[82]

Of course, one of the fundamental dictates of the copywriter's art is to strive for total self-effacement. *Advertising Copy*, a 1924 American manual, makes clear that "the personality of the copywriter ordinarily does not enter the equation at all".

The less he thinks about self-expression and the more he strives for self-effacement, the better chance he has for making the desired impression. He is not supposed to be selling himself or his copy, and the less obtrusive his personality is, the more distinctly the merits of the subject appear. He does not want his readers to say "That's a good ad," but rather "That must be a good article."[83]

The two exceptions to the copywriter anonymity rule, according to *Advertising Copy*, are (1) if the copywriter "is the proprietor of his business and its success has been built about his personality" and (2) "if he is an author of some repute who has been engaged to write a series of advertisements [with] the added weight of his signature and his characteristic style."[84] Both cases of course apply to Shaw, a formerly nameless scribe who escaped anonymity by honing marketing tactics to become not only a copywriter who did sign his name to his work but one whose signature was vigorously sought after for product endorsement purposes. In another sense, though, Shaw's understanding of his work did retain a certain element of the copywriter's position. That everything in advertising is creatively subordinate to a single overarching purpose, which transcends the specific names of the copywriters, agencies, and manufacturers involved, might well be an articulation of Shaw's artistic credo. John Bertolini claims the playwright's self-referential moment in *The Doctor's Dilemma* that "appears to vaunt himself only to erase himself" perfectly epitomizes Shaw's ambivalence about the artist's identity: "the artist is at once everything and nothing. ... The paradox by which self-advertisement becomes self-effacement conforms perfectly to Shaw's sense of the artist's working in the service of the Life Force and not for himself or herself."[85] Shaw has, as Stephen Spender put it, "faith [that he] will direct the powers of the surrounding world from evil into better courses through the exercise of the superior social or cultural intelligence of the creative genius, the writer prophet."[86] For him, the product to market was Creative Evolution, and he was its copywriter as well as its living copy.

His initial experiment with product endorsement began in June of 1885 when he purchased his first Jaeger woolen suit and affirmed what would become a lifelong brand loyalty. Shaw's commodity performance of Jaegar's woolen system became integral to his G.B.S. persona and the lifestyle it envisioned; as G. K. Chesterton observed in 1909, "his costume has become a part of his personality; one has come to think of the reddish brown Jaegar suit as if it were a sort of reddish brown fur, and, were, like the hair and eyebrows, a part of the animal."[87] This self-transformation into embodied copy served Shaw's purposes but also gave an enormous boost to the Jaeger brand which had opened its first London outlet only the year before. Company chairman H. R. Tomalin claimed, after Shaw's death, that "the growth and success of the Jaeger Company throughout the world is very largely due to the support given to the Jaeger Movement in the 1880's by Bernard Shaw and certain other prominent people."[88] A 1937 *Commercial Art* essay that focused on the evolution of Jaeger from the "Health Gospel of 1884" into the "Fashion Movement of 1937" included a picture of a young, en-woolened Shaw ("pioneer of the Jaeger cult") underneath a photograph of one of Jaeger's "new art" shops. The article's author, Malcolm McKenzie, focuses largely on the company's changes in its marketing of the "house of Jaeger" over the course of a half century, noting that, while Oscar Wilde "conducted parties of ladies to the premises," it was Shaw who "proceeded on his way up Oxford Street ... thus attired [in his] remarkable suit made for him in brown knitted wool ... complete from sleeves to ankles in one piece."[89] Besides portraits of three generations of Tomalins (the company's founder and successive managing directors), Shaw is the only human being pictured in the article among photographs of shops and display windows as well as numerous facsimiles of periodical adverts and brochure designs. A living mannequin indeed.

A half-century after his merger with Jaeger, a more grotesque synthesis of G.B.S. and product apparatus is extolled by L. Fritz Gruber in a 1938 feature for *Gebrauchsgraphik: International Advertising Art* entitled "English Shop Windows". In it, he highlights a London display demonstrating "the pleasant effects of softened water" on behalf of the Permutit Company that inscribes the product's distinction and value by literally merging it with another well-known brand. Standing at the display's center is "Bernard Shaw's head, larger than life-size in brass" and insistently cylindrical to resemble the central container of a water treatment apparatus. "In his hand," Gruber describes, "is a card on which Shaw has expressed his satisfaction with Permutit."[90] The Shaws had installed a Permutit purification/softener at Ayot,[91] and the card contains the playwright's signature and handwritten address underneath an endorsement in typescript.

This kind of radical hybridizing of personality and product became a trend in marketing, beginning in the 1920s, when, according to Jackson Lears, "more professionalized advertising aimed to animate the inanimate commodity with the appearance of life, and sometimes explicitly with magical powers."[92] If testimonial endorsement sought to *associate* the product with a well-known celebrity, the goal of this more animistic tactic was to endow the product itself with personality, "taking up instead the discourse of simple objects, foods or places, described subjectively and through language intentionally framed to provide new perspectives."[93] Shaw's high-profile success at personality branding made him a figure of considerable interest within the industry, and references to him in trade papers and the field's own self-promotion abound. For instance, in an early 1930s advert in a trade magazine, W.S. Crawford Ltd., a mid-sized British agency that flourished in the 1920s, used Shaw to demonstrate how "British Trade Can Win Through – by Constructive Advertising":

> As the public responds to a vigorous and masterly personality in a statesman or actor or author, so it responds to a vigorous and masterly advertising campaign. But Bernard Shaw must remain Bernard Shaw. ... And that is why, when Crawfords have created out of the cold facts of a product a vivid advertising personality, they concentrate every word and every line of every advertisement, every piece of sales literature, every penny of expenditure, on keeping that personality warm and alive in the public mind.[94]

If the manufacturer provides the commodity, the function of the modern advertising agency is to provide the personality. That Shaw is a chosen illustration of "masterful" celebrity underscores how much that "vigor" and "mastery" is a part of the "G.B.S." brand. (A 1926 *Commercial Art* feature on "Motor-Car Posters" characterizes French manufacturer Ettore Bugatti as "the Bernard Shaw among motor-car designers" in that "all his models show the finger-marks of a strong personality."[95]) Sounding very Shavian indeed, Crawford in the copy faults other agencies for their "lack of this concentration on a single purpose," namely to "[drive] a single sharp wedge into public opinion."[96] In the ad, a large black dagger inscribed with the Crawford name and its London, Paris, and Berlin addresses dominates the page, and the copy boldly asserts its founder's concise summary of their marketing ethos: "three words – concentration, domination, repetition."[97] The agency itself is thus figured as a dominant personality, and the Fascist undertones of the advertisement text are hard to ignore.

J. Walter Thompson's president, Stanley Resor, felt that celebrity testimonials work because "people are eternally searching for authority": "Democracy, even in name, is new. Royalty, aristocracy, feudalism dominated the world for scores of centuries, instilling in the masses a sense of inferiority and an instinctive veneration for 'their betters'."[98] Of course, Shaw too had great faith in the authority of individuals of will, what he called "world-betterers," and he admired leaders like Stalin and Mussolini as "provisional supermen ... who by their ruthless action could compel order and efficiency, mold an unruly and recalcitrant population into a disciplined social body, and therefore clear the ground for the true supermen who would evolve biologically in the distant future."[99] Crawford criticizes its agency competitors for dissipating their "energy along too many channels" and "through trying to get everywhere – [they are] apt to get nowhere."[100] If Shaw's creation of "G.B.S." was a deliberate branding that capitalized upon the commodity culture he frequently chided, the profession also followed his lead in self-consciously and profitably merging personality with product.

Biographers and scholars have mapped the skirmishes with presses Shaw had over the ways his published work was marketed; while not as radical as John Ruskin, who "opposed the 'evil trade' of advertising, even to the point of refusing to allow his own works to be advertised,"[101] the playwright was frequently exasperated. Less consideration has been given to his participation in professional marketing campaigns. Besides mimicking the pitchmaking rhetoric of advertising copy for "G.B.S.," Shaw crafted what one field professional would call "near testimonials"—endorsements for various products that served celebrity endorser, agency, and client without compromise. *Bernard Shaw and Modern Advertising: Prophet Motives* takes as its focus specific campaigns in which "G.B.S." was prominently featured (for Formamint tablets, Harrods department store, Simmons mattresses, and Pan-American air travel) to explore the ways in which both Shaw and the agency/client used advertisement as an occasion for self-promotion. Throughout this study, along with material drawn from newspapers, medical journals, and mass cultural periodicals, trade publications belonging to the then burgeoning field of professional advertising will also be used as sources because they were primary contexts in which these trends and tactics were observed and discussed. As Roland Marchand has argued,

> given the unevenness of archival sources and the scarcity of good memoirs, the fullest sources on the advertising profession and advertising strategies of the 1920s and 1930s remain the trade journals – especially *Advertising Age*, *Advertising and Selling*, *Judicious Advertising*, *Printers' Ink*, *Printer's Ink Monthly*, and *Tide*. Many of the trade journals articles were written by advertising managers and agency leaders and were often self-serving and uncritical. But because they were written for other professionals rather than the general public, they often expose with striking frankness the internal debates within the trade.[102]

Recognizing similar caveats about their agendas, internal agency publications produced by the J. Walter Thompson agency for its own employees will also be a part of this book's critical context.

Anchoring its discussion with an interpretive analysis of *Misalliance* through the lens of the portable Turkish Bath, Chapter 2 charts Shaw's relationship to the proprietary medicine industry and its marketing practices, suggesting that he was profoundly indebted for his professional success to the techniques through which these ersatz remedies were promoted (techniques he frequently criticized), making his relationship with the industry symbiotic rather than simply antagonistic. Juxtaposing the playwright's seemingly involuntary appearance in a 1912 advertisement for Formamint formaldehyde lozenges with a reading of his 1916 play "O'Flaherty, V.C." as a critique of recruitment techniques, Chapter 3 looks at the development of the testimonial endorsement and the specific relationship between theater and advertising that surely informed Shaw's approach to his own brand marketing.

As recent scholarship has mapped productively the branding machinations of High Modernist authorship, Chapter 4 seeks to texture further this "collaboration" by providing insight into how executives and writers in the advertising industry worked to render profitable mergings of literary personality with commodities. For their part, High Modernists were eager to efface rather than embrace any symbiotic affinity between the worlds of literature and commerce. On the advertising side, executives wrangled to harness the potency of personality but avoid certain stigmas of testimonial endorsement when employing literary authors, including questions of compensation and authority that potentially undermined market effectiveness. Illustrating what is at stake in the proximity between the two fields, the chapter lays out two campaigns from the late 1920s. A Harrods campaign that featured Shaw garnered considerable transatlantic fanfare for crafting "near-testimonials" from literary authors as a way to ward off the specter of impropriety and maintain the integrity of stakeholders, each pursuing their respective aims. The influence of the series featuring Shaw, H. G. Wells, and Arnold Bennett is unusually far-reaching within the evolution of modern advertising and the fashioning of literary modernism. Taken as a case study, it shows how the advertising industry and Shaw are using "collaboration" to further articulate professional identities and produce innovative formal strategies for the promotion of personality and product.

Around the same time, facing increasing public skepticism towards and government scrutiny of the celebrity testimonial over questions about solicitation and compensation practices, the J. Walter Thompson company, the American agency most committed to personality marketing, devised a Simmons campaign that took the "near testimonial" in a new direction and situated Shaw at the center of a controversy over the efficacy of a tried and true marketing technique. In the series, he and other famous personalities provided thoughts about the importance of sleep but did not explicitly mention the product or endorse the company in an attempt to restore the loss of consumer faith. Despite the taint, the continued turn towards "personality marketing" provoked innovation in form, the professionalizing of writers within the industry, and the delineation of *modern* advertising. For Shaw, the ad space presented another opportunity to act on the prophet motive, marketing the Shavian lifestyle.

Chapter 5 focuses on Shaw's participation in a 1948 campaign for Pan-American air service to Ireland. In order to continue to repair the public image of the celebrity testimonial against charges of insincerity and fraud, the campaign decided to foreground Shaw's role in the copywriting process, nearly obscuring the actual product. Revising descriptions of Ireland and inducements to travel there, the playwright struggles against the imperialist undertones inherent in advertising discourse trying to appeal to American tourists. Nonetheless, his "near testimonial" once more illustrates the synergistic relationship between Shaw and modern advertising. All of the marketing campaigns in which Shaw participated become key crucibles within which agency and personality could renegotiate their relationship to one another and to the consuming public, and this study underscores how Shaw's brilliantly calculated "near-testimonials" presage the iconoclastic style of contemporary "public personality" and techniques of celebrity marketing.

## Notes

1. John Palmer. "George Bernard Shaw: Harlequin or Patriot?" *The Century Magazine* 89 (November 1914–April 1915): 768–82. 770.
2. "Pride." *The New Yorker* (18 November 1950): 42.
3. Raymond Williams. "Advertising: The Magic System." In *The Cultural Studies Reader*, 2nd edition. Ed. Simon During. London: Routledge, 1999. 320–36. 329.
4. Roy Church. "Advertising Consumer Goods in Nineteenth-Century Britain: Reinterpretations." *The Economic History Review* 53.4 (November 2000): 621–45. 641, 627.
5. T. R. Nevett. *Advertising in Britain: A History*. London: The History of Advertising Trust, 1982. 79, 84.
6. Gerry Beegan. *The Mass Image: A Social History of Photomechanical Reproduction in Victorian London*. New York: Palgrave Macmillan, 2008. 10.
7. Winston Fletcher. *Powers of Persuasion: The Inside Story of British Advertising: 1951–2000*. Oxford: Oxford University Press, 2008. 18.
8. John Strachan and Claire Nally. *Advertising, Literature and Print Culture in Ireland, 1891–1922*. New York: Palgrave Macmillan, 2012. 36.
9. Bernard Shaw. *Shaw's Music*, vol. 1. Ed. Dan H. Laurence. *The Bodley Head Bernard Shaw*. London: The Bodley Head, 1981. 67.
10. Brad Kent. "Bernard Shaw, the British Censorship of Plays, and Modern Celebrity." *English Literature in Transition, 1880–1920* 57.2 (2014): 231–53. 231.

11. Letter to Otto Kyllman (9 September 1903). In *Bernard Shaw: Collected Letters*, vol. 2 (1898–1910). Ed. Dan H. Laurence. New York: Viking, 1985. 367–8.
12. Alice McEwan. "Commodities, Consumption, and Connoisseurship: Shaw's Critique of Authenticity in Modernity." *SHAW: The Journal of Bernard Shaw Studies* 35.1 (November 2015): 46–85. 76.
13. Bernard Shaw. *Misalliance*. In *The Bodley Head Bernard Shaw: Collected Plays with Their Prefaces*, vol. 4. London: The Bodley Head, 1971. 143–253. 204.
14. Ibid., 208.
15. E. S. Turner. *Taking the Cure*. London: Michael Joseph, 1967. 232.
16. Matthew Yde. *Bernard Shaw and Totalitarianism: Longing for Utopia*. New York: Palgrave Macmillan, 2013. 9.
17. Bernard Shaw. *The Intelligent Woman's Guide to Socialism and Capitalism*. New York: Wm. H. Wise & Company, 1931. 347.
18. Bernard Shaw. *Widowers' Houses*. In *The Bodley Head Bernard Shaw: Collected Plays with Their Prefaces*, vol. 1. London: The Bodley Head, 1971. 33–121. 112.
19. Bernard Shaw. *Getting Married*. In *The Bodley Head Bernard Shaw: Collected Plays with Their Prefaces*, vol. 3. London: The Bodley Head, 1971. 547–662. 624.
20. Bernard Shaw. *You Never Can Tell*. In *The Bodley Head Bernard Shaw: Collected Plays with Their Prefaces*, vol. 1. London: The Bodley Head, 1971. 667–794. 669.
21. Bernard Shaw. *The Devil's Disciple*. In *The Bodley Head Bernard Shaw: Collected Plays with Their Prefaces*, vol. 2. London: The Bodley Head, 1971. 51–141. 131.
22. Bernard Shaw. *Mrs. Warren's Profession*. In *The Bodley Head Bernard Shaw: Collected Plays with Their Prefaces*, vol. 1. London: The Bodley Head, 1971. 272–356. 352.
23. Bernard Shaw. *Man and Superman*. In *The Bodley Head Bernard Shaw: Collected Plays with Their Prefaces*, vol. 2. London: The Bodley Head, 1971. 533–733. 697.
24. Bernard Shaw. *Dramatic Opinions and Essays with an Apology from Bernard Shaw*, vol. 2. New York: Brentano's, 1928. 189.
25. Shaw, *Misalliance*, 156.
26. Bernard Shaw. *Candida*. In *The Bodley Head Bernard Shaw: Collected Plays with Their Prefaces*, vol. 1. London: The Bodley Head, 1971. 513–94. 517.
27. Bernard Shaw. *Collected Letters, 1911–1925*. Ed. Dan H. Laurence. New York: Viking, 1985. 496.

28. Bernard Shaw. *Major Barbara*. In *The Bodley Head Bernard Shaw: Collected Plays with Their Prefaces*, vol. 3. London: The Bodley Head, 1971. 67–185. 143.
29. Shaw, *Misalliance*, 153.
30. Bernard Shaw. *The Millionairess*. In *The Bodley Head Bernard Shaw: Collected Plays with Their Prefaces*, vol. 6. London: The Bodley Head, 1971. 882–969. 883. While it may seem a stretch to class Sagamore with Undershaft and Tarleton, the associations with the names Shaw chooses aren't subtle. While "sagamore" denotes an Algonquin chief, a "pontifex" was a member of the council of priests in Ancient Rome, considerably enhancing the resonance of "Julius". In a play that is about the necessity of productive labor and capital put to productive use, Sagamore claims he is striving to "succeed to as much of his business as I can persuade his clients to trust me with." Fittingly, the play's original title was "His Tragic Clients."
31. Bernard Shaw. "The Music-Cure." In *The Bodley Head Bernard Shaw: Collected Plays with Their Prefaces*, vol. 4. London: The Bodley Head, 1971. 877–94. 888.
32. Bernard Shaw. "Preface" to *Pygmalion*. In *The Bodley Head Bernard Shaw: Collected Plays with Their Prefaces*, vol. 4. London: The Bodley Head, 1971. 659–64. 661-2.
33. Bernard Shaw. "Preface" to *Major Barbara*. In *The Bodley Head Bernard Shaw: Collected Plays with Their Prefaces*, vol. 3. London: The Bodley Head, 1971. 15–63. 43.
34. Ibid., 42.
35. Bernard Shaw. "Preface" to *Androcles and the Lion*. In *The Bodley Head Bernard Shaw: Collected Plays with Their Prefaces*, vol. 4. London: The Bodley Head, 1971. 455–579. 545.
36. Ibid., 551-2.
37. Bernard Shaw. *Essays in Fabian Socialism: Major Critical Essays* 30. New York: Wm. H. Wise & Company, 1932.
38. Bernard Shaw. "The Revolutionist's Handbook." In *The Bodley Head Bernard Shaw: Collected Plays with Their Prefaces*, vol. 2. London: The Bodley Head, 1971. 739–80. 768-9.
39. Bernard Shaw. *Everybody's Political What's What*. London: Constable and Company, 1944. 150.
40. Williams, 331-2.
41. Ibid., 334.
42. Shaw, *The Intelligent Woman's*, 151.
43. Bernard Shaw. "Postscript" to the "Preface" of *How He Lied to Her Husband. John Bull's Other Island and Major Barbara: Also How He*

*Lied to Her Husband*. London: Archibald Constable & Co. Ltd., 1907. 119–24. 122.
44. Shaw, *Intelligent Woman's*, 226–7.
45. Shaw, "Postscript," 124.
46. Bernard Shaw. "Preface" to *Mrs. Warren's Profession*. In *The Bodley Head Bernard Shaw: Collected Plays with Their Prefaces*, vol. 1. London: The Bodley Head, 1971. 231–66. 238, 266.
47. Shaw, "Preface" to *Androcles*, 528.
48. Bernard Shaw. *The Doctor's Dilemma*. In *The Bodley Head Bernard Shaw: Collected Plays with Their Prefaces*, vol. 3. London: The Bodley Head, 1971. 321–436. 344, 346.
49. Bernard Shaw. *Fanny's First Play*. In *The Bodley Head Bernard Shaw: Collected Plays with Their Prefaces*, vol. 4. London: The Bodley Head, 1971. 347–441. 416.
50. Bernard Shaw. *Doctors' Delusions*. In *The Collected Works of Bernard Shaw*, vol. 22. New York: Wm. H. Wise & Company, 1932. 1–170. 56.
51. Bernard Shaw. "Preface" to *Farfetched Fables*. In *The Bodley Head Bernard Shaw: Collected Plays with Their Prefaces*, vol. 7. London: The Bodley Head, 1971. 381–428. 417.
52. Bernard Shaw. "Preface" to *The Doctor's Dilemma*. In *The Bodley Head Bernard Shaw: Collected Plays with Their Prefaces*, vol. 3. London: The Bodley Head, 1971. 225–320. 289.
53. Shaw, *Everybody's*, 294–5.
54. Shaw, "Preface" to *Farfetched Fables*, 402.
55. Bernard Shaw. "Preface" to *On the Rocks*. In *The Bodley Head Bernard Shaw: Collected Plays with Their Prefaces*, vol. 6. London: The Bodley Head, 1971. 573–628. 586.
56. Bernard Shaw. *Pygmalion*. In *The Bodley Head Bernard Shaw: Collected Plays with Their Prefaces*, vol. 4. London: The Bodley Head, 1971. 669–819. 780–1.
57. Bernard Shaw. "Notes to *Caesar and Cleopatra*." In *The Bodley Head Bernard Shaw: Collected Plays with Their Prefaces*, vol. 2. London: The Bodley Head, 1971. 293–305. 302.
58. Bernard Shaw. *Back to Methuselah*. In *The Bodley Head Bernard Shaw: Collected Plays with Their Prefaces*, vol. 5. London: The Bodley Head, 1971. 340–684. 487.
59. Bernard Shaw. "Preface" to *Three Plays for Puritans*. In *The Bodley Head Bernard Shaw: Collected Plays with Their Prefaces*, vol. 2. London: The Bodley Head, 1971. 11–48. 32.

60. Bernard Shaw. "Preface" to *Major Barbara*. In *The Bodley Head Bernard Shaw: Collected Plays with Their Prefaces*, vol. 3. London: The Bodley Head, 1971. 15–63. 32.
61. Shaw, "Preface" to *Three Plays for Puritans*, 32.
62. Shaw, "Preface" to *Major Barbara*, 32.
63. R. J. Minney. *The Bogus Image of Bernard Shaw*. London: Leslie Frewin, 1969. 9.
64. Shaw, *Intelligent Woman's*, 232.
65. Palmer, 769.
66. Maurice Colbourne. *The Real Bernard Shaw*. New York: Dodd, Mead & Company, 1940. 102, 103.
67. G. K. Chesterton. *George Bernard Shaw*. London: John Lane, 1910. 233, 245–6.
68. Augustus Hamon. *Bernard Shaw: The Twentieth Century Molière*. Trans. Eden and Cedar Paul. New York: Frederick A. Stokes Company Publishers, 1916. 107.
69. Ibid., 107–8.
70. Robert Lynd. *Old and New Masters*. New York: Charles Scribner's Sons, 1919. 143.
71. Bertolt Brecht. "Ovation for Shaw." Trans. Gerhard H. W. Zuther. *Modern Drama* 2.2 (Summer 1959): 184–7. 184.
72. Michael Holroyd. *Bernard Shaw, Volume One: 1856–1898, The Search for Love*. New York: Vintage Books, 1988. 86.
73. Sally Peters. "Shaw's Life: A Feminist in Spite of Himself." In *The Cambridge Companion to George Bernard Shaw*. Ed. Christopher Innes. Cambridge: Cambridge University Press, 1998. 3–24. 12.
74. Fintan O'Toole. *Judging Shaw: The Radicalism of GBS*. Dublin: Prism, 2017. 4, 22.
75. Richard Toye. *The Labour Party and the Planned Economy, 1931–1951*. Woodbridge: Royal Historical Society, Boydell Press, 2003. 16.
76. Bernard Shaw. "Preface" to *Heartbreak House*. In *The Bodley Head Bernard Shaw: Collected Plays with Their Prefaces*, vol. 5. London: The Bodley Head, 1971. 11–58. 23.
77. Sidney Webb. "Introduction." In *Advertising: A Study of a Modern Business Power*. G. W. Goodall. London: Constable & Co., 1914. ix–xvii. xvi–xvii.
78. "The London Education Act 1903: How to Make the Best of It." Fabian Tract No. 117. London: The Fabian Society, February 1904. 17.
79. Bernard Shaw. "Preface" to *Man and Superman*. In *The Bodley Head Bernard Shaw: Collected Plays with Their Prefaces*, vol. 2. London: The Bodley Head, 1971. 493–532. 503.

80. Frank Duba. "'The Genuine Pulpit Article': The Preface to *Man and Superman*." *SHAW: The Annual of Bernard Shaw Studies* 25 (2005): 221–40. 235.
81. Shaw, "Preface" to *Three Plays for Puritans*, 31, 32.
82. Ibid., 30, 32. As such, he predicts a short shelf life for the plays, that, as thinking evolves, they will "lose [their] gloss" and be "exposed" as "threadbare popular melodrama."
83. George Burton Hotchkiss. *Advertising Copy*. New York: Harper & Brothers Publishers, 1924. 20.
84. Ibid., 20.
85. John A. Bertolini. *The Playwrighting Self of Bernard Shaw*. Carbondale: Southern Illinois University Press, 1991. 92.
86. Stephen Spender. *The Struggle of the Modern*. Oakland: University of California Press, 1963. 72.
87. Chesterton, *George Bernard Shaw*, 93.
88. Allan Chappelow, ed. *Shaw the Villager and Human Being: A Biographical Symposium*. London: Charles Skilton Ltd., 1961. 238.
89. Malcolm Mckenzie. "Jaeger: Health Gospel of 1884, Fashion Movement of 1937." *Commercial Art* 23.134 (1 August 1937): 42–57. 45.
90. L. Fritz Gruber. "Englische Schaufenster (English Shop Windows)." *Gebrauchsgraphik: International Advertising Art* 15.11 (1 November 1938): 57–63. 63.
91. See note 81 of Alice McEwan's "The 'Plumber-Philosopher': Shaw's Discourse on Domestic Sanitation." *SHAW* 34 (2014): 75–107. 105.
92. Jackson Lears. "Uneasy Courtship: Modern Art and Modern Advertising." *American Quarterly* 39.1 (Spring 1987): 133–54. 136.
93. Rod Rosenquist. "Copywriting Gertrude Stein: Advertising, Anonymity, Autobiography." *Modernist Cultures* 11.3 (2016): 331–50. 336.
94. "British Trade Can Win Through—By Constructive Advertising." *Commercial Art* 9.54 (1 December 1930): 8 and 10.56 (1 February 1931): 8.
95. "Motor-Car Posters: Selections from Different Nations." *Commercial Art*, vol. 1. London: The Studio Limited, 1926. 208–13. 213.
96. "British Trade Can Win Through—By Constructive Advertising," 8.
97. Ibid., 8.
98. Stanley Resor. "Personalities and the Public: Some Aspects of Testimonial Advertising." *New Bulletin* 138 (April 1929): 1. J. Walter Thompson Information Center Records, Box 4, Testimonial Advertising, 1928–1977. John W. Hartman Center for Sales, Advertising, and Marketing History, Rare Book, Manuscript and Special Collections Library, Duke University. 1.

99. Yde, 6. Unfortunately, Shaw's success with "G.B.S." and his impatience for social change would lead to his offensive support in the 1930s and 1940s of totalitarian figures, an egregious error for which Fintan O'Toole attributes some culpability to the brand itself: "Shaw, who had done much to invent modern literary celebrity, was also one of its more obvious victims. The isolating effects of extreme celebrity worked against both the humility and the connectedness that Shaw would have needed" (291).
100. "British Trade Can Win Through—By Constructive Advertising," 8.
101. Toye, 16.
102. Roland Marchand. *Advertising the American Dream: Making Way for Modernity, 1920–1940.* Berkley: University of California Press, 1985. 421.

CHAPTER 2

# Prescription and Petrifaction: Proprietary Medicine, Health Marketing, and *Misalliance*

It comes as no surprise that, when Elbert Hubbard rewrote one of Shaw's articles and published it as a Roycroft book, the seething playwright knew exactly the precise insult to hurl back, characterizing its prose style as "feeble patent-medicine-advertisement English."[1] The playwright often inveighed against the infusion of an entrepreneurial ethos into health care and expounded at length about the detrimental effects of the profit motive in medicine. His lifelong indictment of a flawed system of medical research and practice is well documented, particularly in *The Doctor's Dilemma* (1906), its preface, and *Doctors' Delusions* (1932), and has been much discussed by both scholars and biographers. Less attention has been given to Shaw's annoyance with the proprietary-cure industry and its advertising practices; according to "The Revolutionist's Handbook," "witchcraft, in the modern form of patent medicines and prophylactic inoculations, is rampant."[2] He produced a "history of quack medicine" in the 1880s (now regrettably lost, according to Dan Laurence)[3] and was sharply critical of the mass marketing phenomenon's complicity in economic subjugation. It is a bit of a surprise then that, during his early London attempts at making a living as a freelance writer, Shaw supposedly received his greatest sum by producing copy for a patent medicine advertisement, although details about this stint are elusive.

Biographers Hesketh Pearson, B. C. Rosset, Stephen Winsten, and Archibald Henderson (among others) all note that Shaw made £5 for such a writing when accounting for his earnings during his early years in

London. This claim subsequently got recycled now and again in advertising trade journals. For instance, a 1911 *Printers' Ink* piece about the advent of signed advertisements refers to Henderson's biography *George Bernard Shaw: His Life and Works*:

> In a recently issued "authorized" biography of George Bernard Shaw, the writer declares that from 1876 to 1885 Shaw's adventures in literature netted him the princely sum of exactly six pounds. Although he composed during these nine years half a dozen novels and a passion play in blank verse his biographer tells us he received his biggest fee – five pounds – for a patent medicine advertisement. Unfortunately, we are not given any further particulars about this stroke of luck, but if the manufacturers of that patent medicine are still selling their remedy, I believe it would prove a profitable piece of business on their part to reissue the advertisements under the full signature of the now celebrated creator of the "Superman."[4]

Similarly, E. McKenna begins a 1920 *Printers' Ink* article on the narrative continuity between drama and advertisements by positing that

> it is perhaps not generally known that George Bernard Shaw earned his first money by writing patent medicine advertisements. These compositions are probably not to be found now, but if they could be, it is possible that it could be shown that young Mr. Shaw dramatized his appeal and did it successfully.[5]

Yet, when Shaw recounts the assignment in *Sixteen Self-Sketches*, he describes it as a "job ... not from a publisher or editor, but from a friendly lawyer who wanted a medical essay, evidently for use in an agitation concerning patent medicines."[6] This would suggest that the piece of writing may be closer to what Dan Laurence talks about as that lost "history of patent medicines" solicited by George Radford, for which Shaw was paid but which may never have been ultimately published.[7] Shaw's word choice—"agitation"—is potentially apt either to describe material for a lawsuit or a public appeal against a manufacturer *or* ad copy content intended to provoke consumer spending. Regardless, Shaw was profoundly indebted to the techniques through which these ersatz remedies were promoted, making his relationship with the industry symbiotic rather than antagonistic.

Shaw's marketing of the "G.B.S." persona, according to Alice McEwan, was "more than simply advocating a certain taste or a different kind of shopping [but] about promoting the image of a Shavian individual 'lifestyle'."[8] In this sense, the playwright emulated the marketing tactics of the wellness industry and in particular proprietary health remedies and devices that promised access to robust mental and physical health. Sounding like the copy of such advertisements, Shaw often railed against the toxicity of his environment, its draining effect and engendering of deleterious habits. Along with manufacturers and purveyors of health commodities, he also endowed *his* product with an imagined state of extreme fitness and productivity, a quintessence of vitality. In the preface to *The Doctor's Dilemma*, Shaw writes that "to advertise any remedy or operation, you have only to pick out all the most reassuring advances made by civilization, and boldly present the two in the relation of cause and effect; the public will swallow the fallacy without a wry face."[9] In marketing the Shavian "rational social programme" and "secular religion,"[10] the playwright clearly followed the field's lead through traditional and emergent media. In fact, the influence of the promotional practices of the much-maligned industry has been far-reaching. As T. R. Nevett maintains, "sordid though this form of enterprise unquestionably was, the medicine vendors may well be regarded as the pioneers of modern marketing, branding their products, advertising them widely, and distributing them over large areas of the country."[11] Raymond Williams is more direct, noting,

> an obvious continuity between the methods used to sell pills and washballs in the eighteenth century ... and the methods used in the twentieth century to sell anything from a drink to a political party. In this sense, it is true to say that all commerce has followed the quack.[12]

According to historian Jackson Lears, "patent medicines represented the most profitable investment opportunity among all consumer goods: costs of production were low and an efficient distribution system in place; all that was needed was a lavish expenditure on advertising."[13] In the last decades of the nineteenth century, coextensive with the explosion of over-the-counter cures and devices, "an estimated two million pounds in Britain annually ... was spent on inserting advertisements for patent medicines in newspapers and periodicals and on pushing promotional pamphlets, diaries, and almanacs under people's front doors."[14]

Besides significant shifts in how adverts reached target demographics, modern patent medicine promotion, which accounted for more than a quarter of all advertisements, moved away from more traditional unadorned and terse column blurbs towards layout styles replete with lavish fonts, pictorial enhancement, and copy that promised direct access to a state of increased potency and well-being. Starting in the 1880s, the British Medical Association (BMA) launched a counter-offensive against this foray by what they characterized as "palpable quacks and vendors of either dangerous or insidious wares."[15] Orthodox medical journals such as *The Lancet* were filled with articles that attacked these products as both ineffectual and potentially virulent, their purveyors as roguish charlatans and bounders in the field. As James Gregory maintains,

> labeling [them all] as "quackeries," "heresies," or "fads" [was] part of the wider efforts to reform medicine by removing questionable practices, [but also] stemmed from the competing claims for customers in the health market, and the assertion of status and authority by a nascent profession which could not yet claim to be more successful than alternatives.[16]

In 1909, the BMA collected pieces that had appeared previously in its journal into *Secret Remedies: What They Cost and What They Contain*, a meticulous record of both the chemical formulae for and the therapeutic claims made by various patent medicines. Concerned that the BMA's activities might gain legislative traction, drug corporation representatives produced a rejoinder entitled *A Sequel to "Secret Remedies"* in 1910. It charged the BMA with self-serving gatekeeping and hypocrisy, denouncing government intervention in the pharmaceutical market by claiming *Secret Remedies* to be rife with factual inaccuracies about formulae and charging that trained doctors and chemists were behind most patent medicines. Seizing upon the doctors' pretense of acting in the public interest, the opposition waged a media war through newspapers and further booklets, arguing that free market capitalism was the only way to ensure consumer satisfaction, protection, and innovation.

Nonetheless, the original *Secret Remedies* sold so well (despite the major newspapers' refusal to advertise or print any mention of it) that a BMA follow-up, *More Secret Remedies*, appeared three years later. That same year, in the spring of 1912, a committee of inquiry was convened in the House of Commons to investigate patent medicines; the press extensively covered the two years of hearings that culminated in a thousand-page report exposing unethical deception on the part of patent drug companies. As Thomas Richards points out, the investigation became itself a media spectacle:

> The Select Committee held thirty-three public sittings and directed 14,000 questions at forty-two witnesses[, all of which] came close to arousing the kind of ongoing public interest the French displayed for the Dreyfus trials and the Americans for the trial of President McKinley's anarchist assassin, Czolgosz.[17]

Unfortunately, by the time it was published on August 4, 1914, the summary was obscured by more pressing current events, and legislation to protect the public from fraudulent cures would have to wait a couple of more decades.[18]

The committee report's characterization of the network of patent medicines as a "system of quackery" is an unconscious echo not only of the phrasing of Shaw's frequent characterization of the medical-industrial complex but also of his character B.B.'s indictment in the 1906 play *The Doctor's Dilemma* of the "huge commercial system of quackery and poison."[19] For Shaw, the booming late Victorian and Edwardian fitness industry was a particularly irksome capitalist entity, its wares relentlessly marketed with virtually no oversight or regulation. Created on the heels of the appearance of *Secret Remedies*, his comedy *Misalliance* dovetails its critique of middle-class pretension with an assault against the commodification of health. Critics and scholars have tended mainly to follow its preface's lead in pinpointing *Misalliance*'s thematic interests, analyzing it in terms of familial relationships, gender roles and marriage, and theories of evolution and education. However, the play's investment in marketing and commodity transaction is undeniable, particularly its characterization of patriarch John Tarleton. Tarleton is modeled, according to scholar Margery Morgan, on Gordon Selfridge, the self-made American entrepreneur known not only for lavish expenditures on mammoth retailing campaigns but also for his aggressive promotional style.[20] Elizabeth Outka identifies a major shift in department store advertisement practices occurring in the spring of 1909, right before the grand opening of Selfridge's and the celebration of Harrods Diamond Jubilee,[21] and, supposedly, Selfridge "spent £36,000 on promoting his Oxford Street shop even before it had opened."[22] *Misalliance* was written in the autumn of 1909, six months after Selfridge's initial publicity blitzkrieg produced immediate counter-campaigns among his competitors (including Harrods), and periodicals were saturated with hyperbolic ad copy and ostentatious fashion show notices. In the play, Shaw clearly wishes to address this frenzy of merchandising, particularly as it connects to the Edwardian anxiety over national fitness.

Cure advertising, via periodical and pamphlet in particular, used to its retail advantage the country's perceived health crisis. The 1904 report issued by the Inter-Departmental Committee on Physical Deterioration in England intensified concern over a specifically national decline and spurred public debate over the deterioration of the national body, leading to welfare reform and the formation of societies, organizations, and monthlies dedicated to physical and moral fitness. The physical culture movement had begun in the 1890s, "part of a wider international health and life reform movement which advocated not only exercise but also dietary reform such as vegetarianism, sun- and air-bathing, dress reform, personal cleanliness and temperance."[23] Urban, working-class men had long been at the center of discussions of degeneration, but the sedentary lifestyles of men from other classes were equally targeted. The Health and Strength League was established in late 1906 and counted 30,000 members by the start of the war while the circulation of its weekly journal reached 75,000 in 1909, mirroring the upsurge in "physical culture clubs, institutes, and gyms."[24] At the time, the larger implications of and solutions to this perceived loss of English vitality were fiercely discussed in the media by "national efficiency" proponents and eugenics advocates on both sides of the political spectrum.

By all accounts, at the time *Misalliance* was written, "London [was] a city flooded with remedies, where the threat of incurable disease hung over everyone and cure-alls promised the only relief possible."[25] Shaw situates at the visual center of his set design one of the most notorious of such panaceas, a portable Turkish bath, that original audiences would have immediately associated with the crazed mass-marketing of home remedies as well as issues of personal and public hygiene. In critical commentary on *Misalliance*, the unit is often mentioned but almost always in terms of its plot utility during a bit of comic business, when Gunner eavesdrops on Hypatia Tarleton as she aggressively woos Joey Percival. For the few scholars who have approached the play through the lens of economics, however, the Turkish bath becomes symbolically crucial. J. Ellen Gainor feels the set piece's prominent stage position acts as a conspicuous index to the imperial content of all Shaw's plays, a topic she feels urgently requires further analysis.²⁶ Margery Morgan posits a dense web of connective tissue between Shaw's play and Harley Granville Barker's *The Madras House* (1910), the Turkish bath in the former taking up "the oriental theme" of the latter.²⁷ If both Morgan and Gainor emphasize the item's "Turkishness" in their commentaries, this analysis seeks to explore how the object functions as a cynosure for matters of commercialized health in the play. Because Shaw is so specific that the bath unit is only "recently unpacked, with its crate beside it, and on the crate the drawn nails and the hammer used in unpacking,"²⁸ the quirky item's thematic import also seems tied to its packaging and, by extension, its commercial image.

Yoking together the obsessive pursuit of wellness and the advent of mass marketing, the history of the Turkish bath in England is dramatic, beginning with "too good to be true" curative promises and ending with sordid impropriety. Introduced in the middle of the century, such establishments were appearing everywhere by the 1860s; according to Peter Kandela, English "Turkish Bath mania" was engendered not by aggressive entrepreneurism or even "vague Victorian interest in matters oriental" but rather by "the poor state of health and hygiene of the urban masses."²⁹ The public baths purported to remedy the poor health and non-existent hygiene among the urban poor. Despite a lack of evidence for such a sweeping claim, public and private baths were opened in a number of factory towns around England, in addition to major cities, ostensibly to boost the productivity of the working men. Early advocates had a democratic vision that provided access to the baths for those lacking adequate health care as well as for the rich, and baths were additionally constructed in hospitals as well as mental institutions. By the 1880s, though, the popularity of the baths was abating rapidly, due to increased skepticism towards its cure-all claims, ongoing hostility from the medical community, their unflattering "reputation as a restorative for the debauched and as a cover for perversion,"³⁰ and the development of mass-produced *portable* units for the home.

Advertisements for home Turkish baths were ubiquitous in British magazines for decades. While Kandela claims that home baths "were consigned to the attic or the cellar by the start of the 20th century,"³¹ the surge of periodical advertisement for them persists through the early 1900s. For instance, a short piece entitled "Turkish Baths at Home" that appeared in *The Pall Mall Magazine* in April of 1909 still trumpets the "wonderful cleansing and invigorating action of this form of bathing" and targets those who "cannot tolerate breathing the heated air inseparable from public baths" and who wish instead to bathe "in perfect safety and comfort in the seclusion of the home."[32] One of the most prominent Turkish bath manufacturers in the first decade of the twentieth century was the Century Thermal Bath Cabinet Company who advertised their portable bath units in, among other periodicals, *The Windsor Magazine*, *Pearson's Magazine*, *The Pall Mall Magazine*, *The Strand Magazine*, *The Railway News*, and *The Bystander*. Within the medical community, the Century Thermal Bath Company was notorious for shady practices, and, beginning in the fall of 1899, *The British Medical Journal* received specific complaints about its improper marketing practices. In a two-pronged effort to both market directly to the public and to secure retailers, the American company attempted to broaden their territory and allegedly offered secret commissions to British doctors who sold their bath units as well as product discounts to those who agreed to recommend them to their patients. In 1901, the Company was again admonished by the *Journal* for allegedly using the names of British doctors in their advertising without first securing permission to do so. The BMA was not the only professional group who tracked the Century Company on its radar. The January 1902 "Trade Notes" section of *Chemist and Druggist* questions the retailer's tactics in offering multiple chemists and ironmongers in Wisbech "entire control of sales in [the] district": "Perhaps the company will explain the matter, especially [since] the circular invites every one to whom it is addressed to remit money for a cabinet of double the value. If all respond there will be no exclusiveness about the matter."[33] Most pointedly, in its March 21, 1903 *Journal*, the BMA expressed their support for the Prevention of Corruption Bill, then moving from the House of Lords to the House of Commons, and specifically cited the tactics of the Century Thermal Bath Company as an egregious example of what the legislation intended to curb. The fate of the Century Thermal Bath Company is in microcosm that of the patent medicine industry as a whole.

The Century Thermal campaign with which late Victorian and Edwardian consumers would have surely been familiar (if for no other reason than the fact that it employed familiar techniques used to market a wide variety of products) offered readers a "highly valuable and beautiful illustrated book" free of charge, provided one wrote and inquired. In the booklet, entitled "The Power of Heat: Turkish Baths at Home," the portable Bath unit is presented as a modern technological wonder that makes available a practice rooted in the wisdom of Greece and Rome as well as American Indian culture but without the "unwholesome atmosphere" of the public bathhouse and its lack of adequate drainage.[34] Reproducing an 1880 excerpt from *The Lancet*, the pamphlet decries "the air of a public Turkish Bath [as] laden with germs of disease thrown off from the lungs and body of a fever or consumptive patient [and lacking] currents to carry the particles away" (9–10). Resembling a moral tract, the booklet rails against the use of alcohol, tobacco, meat, and drugs, all viewed as poisons that unnaturally sap physical and mental vitality. The copy advocates for its product as an "incomparable artificial preservative" of hygiene that counters the "manifold evils" that "arise from exhausting mental labour" and "perseverance in sedentary habits" and can take "the place of out-door exercise" in such a way that "[n]o home is complete without one" (8, 14). Wildly formatted, using capitalization and boldface for emphasis, the pamphlet seeks to stoke its audience's anxieties over social status as well as health, proclaiming that "the wealthy have embraced [vapor cures] by visiting Baden-Baden, Weis-Baden, Carlsbad, and other places; but our Cabinet brings it within the reach of ... Business Men and Working Men [who] cannot afford to be ill" (35, 44).

What immediately reverberates from Century Thermal's booklet in relation to *Misalliance* is its rhetorical style. Employing a range of state-of-the-art sales tactics, the Century pamphlet features a chorus of disparate voices (customer and professional testimonials, celebrity and authority endorsements, literary quotations and trite clichés, medical and social theory), all centered (like the stage picture of *Misalliance*) on the portable thermal bath cabinet. Acting upon the consumer's fears and often class prejudice, the wide-ranging lists of ailments, symptoms, and conditions are supported by overblown claims of certainty and unanimity among researchers. The parade of scientific experts, their credibility buoyed by their acronymed institutional affiliations, is quickly followed by detailed testimonials from practitioners, customers, and even celebrities. (Lily Langtry famously endorsed Turkish bathing for the complexion.) Most interesting is the seemingly random use of quotation marks to give statements the impression of authority without the annoyance of attribution. However, as Richards describes, "far and away the favorite form of authority among quacks was the faceless authority of literary convention," and "the quack columns teem with literary quotations taken out of context," possessing "all the weighty pretentiousness of authority without the inconvenience of an actual author."[35] The desired effect of such source material, ersatz and otherwise, was "a form of literary aspiration where advertising, a cultural form fairly low down the ladder of artistic esteem, elevates itself by utilizing poetry, a highly prestigious art form."[36]

In the Century booklet, highbrow literary quotations sit side by side on the page with clichéd homespun aphorism (e.g. "an ounce of prevention is worth a pound of cure") and the occasional stray unattributed quoted statement (e.g. "Man is dragged into the world and drugged out of it") (11, 14).

For all of its insistence upon independent thought and authenticity, Century marketing was quite committed to recycling copy. For instance, the booklet follows an excerpted statement from pioneer hydropathist James Manby Gully with a quote from Goethe:

> Thus with our hellish drugs, death's ceaseless fountains
> In these bright vales, or these green mountains,
> Worse than the very plague we raged.
> I have myself to thousands poison given,
> And hear their murderer praised as blest by Heaven,
> Because with nature's strife he waged.

By the early 1900s, this particular passage from *Faust* is an old chestnut within the discourse. Among other places, the quotation appears in *Hydropathy; or the Cold Water Cure* (1842), *Homoeopathy and Its Principles Explained* (1801), *Hydropathy For the People: With Plain Observations on Drugs, Diet, Water, Air, and Exercise* (1855), *Caloric: Its Mechanical, Chemical and Vital Agencies in the Phenomena of Nature* (1859), and on the title page of *Yellow Fever: Its Origins, Improper Treatment, Prevention and Cure* (1860). The literary thus becomes commodity, and this appropriation reaches absurdity when the source is corrupted, as when the Century Company buttresses their claim by quoting from Alexander Pope's translation of Homer's *The Odyssey*: "reviving sweats repair the mind's decay, and take the painful sense of toil away" (11). Pope is misquoted ("sweets" becomes "sweats"), and, intentional or not, the error itself had an extended shelf life, appearing frequently in other periodicals and even books.[37] As Jennifer Wicke points out, "ads rendered literary work into fragments of raw material, trading on an author or a character's auratic prestige, sometimes without evoking any of the surrounding text,"[38] and the Century Thermal booklet is itself, like its many counterparts, a deliberate pastiche.

*Misalliance*'s style of course is similar. In assessing its postmodern elements, Tony Stafford argues that "the sheer bulk of quotations, appropriations, and allusions [constitute] the fabric of the work" such that the "very composition of *Misalliance* is pastiche."[39] This quality is largely the result of Tarleton himself who seems to take a cue from his own pamphlet, his manner of speech frequently sounding like ad copy: "Why should a woman allow Nature to put a false mask of age on her when she knows that she's as young as ever? Why should she look in the glass and see a wrinkled lie when a touch of fine art will shew her a glorious truth?"[40] Even the Charles Swain poem he unexpectedly recites late in the play—"Theres magic in the night / When the heart is young"[41]—was frequently reproduced in periodical advertising. What is most noteworthy about Tarleton is his encyclopedic retrieval of literary allusion. Indeed, he is a charmingly prototypical Wikicharacter, a "computerized Digest of Western Literature, delivering up the desired data on demand, every item uniformly encapsulated in preformed syntactical structures."[42] What J. L. Wisenthal deems a "foolish ... display of undigested reading"[43] resonates within Shaw's savvy exposure of the intersection between culture and consumerism, of the strategy of literary citation to provide a moral and philosophical foundation for consumer spending. Tarleton's reason, for example, to read Shakespeare is for its use-value, because "he has a word for every occasion" (210). As John Mills observes, Tarleton performs on one level what Shaw accused doctors of doing, "needlessly [chattering] away, automatically repeating and administering their own or a colleague's favorite nostrums, with never a thought about the degree of their applicability to the phenomena at hand."[44] In essence, the character is an automaton of empty talk, trading in literature and language itself as commodity. Tarleton's distinctive verbosity operates for Shaw as a class critique, one that anticipates that of Eugène Ionesco who described the bourgeois individual as "the personification of accepted ideas and slogans, the ubiquitous conformist" given away by "his automatic use of language ... composed of ready-made expressions and the most tired clichés."[45]

Nonetheless, Tarleton's adeptness in creating copy is key to his success as a commercial underwear distributor; as he says, "Anybody can make underwear. Anybody can sell underwear. Tarleton's Ideas: thats whats done it" (167). The title page copy of his own advertising pamphlet—"The Romance of Business, or The Story of Tarleton's Underwear. Please Take One!" (148)—takes up the language of melodrama, and its content undoubtedly spins Tarleton's self-made social ascension and entrepreneurial prosperity into an opportunity for direct marketing.[46] The degree to which Tarleton's consciousness has been saturated thoroughly by consumerism is also evident by his spending choices. When Mrs. Tarleton reveals that "Turkish baths are [Tarleton's] latest" (174), original audiences might have deemed Tarleton's *new* interest in what was by 1910 a dated gadget an indication of his lack of sophistication in relation to consumer trends, akin to his wife's purchase of unstylish pottery and a betrayal of their humbler origins and bounding pretensions. More importantly, it suggests that Tarleton has bought into the claims of mass marketing directed towards men of all classes that emphasized the connection between commodity acquisition and lifestyles of "success, ease and leisure, as well as the chance to escape the confines of home, workplace and the urban environment."[47] Tarleton's faith in marketing discourse is also shared by his wife and informs their choices with regard to their country home in which *Misalliance* is set.

When the curtain rises, the bath unit is just one object within a larger stage picture rife with commodities, since from the start the Tarleton home is figured as a site of indulgent leisure and mass cultural consumption. Lacking any "solid furniture" (109), with the exception of a fully furnished sideboard, the set is conspicuously dominated by the accouterments of drinking, smoking, and garden sport, and it of course frames, at the play's start, the somnambulant Johnny consuming a cheap paperback. As Shaw describes it, the décor of the Tarleton house betrays the fact that "the proprietor's notion of domestic luxury is founded on the lounges of week-end hotels" (143). In 1901, architect Edward S. Prior railed against suburban house-building practices that preferred "the cheap substitute in place of the genuine article":

> We have to take not only what does not suit us, but what is not the real thing at all – fatty compounds for butter, glucose for sugar, chemicals for beer: and just as certainly the sham house for the real building, its style a counterfeit, its construction a salable make-believe, ... everything charmingly commercial and charmingly cheap.[48]

Indeed, the style of the Tarleton house is awash in mass-produced homogeneity and style dictated by marketing. Helen C. Long notes that "contemporary photographs show middle-class houses far more cluttered with objects and furniture than wealthy homes or their mid-nineteenth-century equivalents."[49] The idealized English house was itself a commodity sought after by aspirant and rising middle-class families, their furnishings deliberately staged. Newly available periodicals, pamphlets, and books on home furnishing provided essential guidance for newly upper middle-class families like the Tarletons: "If their recommendations were followed, a tasteful home was guaranteed; such assurance was crucial to those without previous experience in matters of taste but for whom nuances of class were all-important."[50]

Epitomizing the numbingly uniform style of pottery that decorates the Tarleton house, the eventually shattered punchbowl is denigrated as tacky by Bentley much to the shock of Mrs. Tarleton who says she was told by "the shopman … it was in the best taste" (156). Typifying how the rising middle class cultivated style by imitating what they read and saw in shop windows, she is mortified that the vendor has apparently misled her and at the ramifications of the breach in taste. Shaw's original audiences would surely have perceived more at stake at this moment than simply the perception of style since "books linking ideas of nation and domesticity became something of a craze during the Edwardian period," and "circulated through the machinery of consumer culture, Edwardian representations of the English house symbolized desires of national inclusion for many upwardly mobile middle-class consumers."[51]

Margery Morgan, although correct in deeming Tarleton's portable bath unit quite "incongruous in the hall of a mansion at Hindhead" (191), doesn't mention that the biggest incongruity proceeds from the playwright's specification of *visible* hot-water pipes in the stage picture, implying the presence in the house of at least one bathroom. Possessing both a presumed bathroom and the portable unit pointedly reveals something about the Tarletons' consuming habits. As historian David J. Eveleigh notes, "by the early 1900s, acquiring a bathroom became an important social indicator for the upwardly mobile artisan classes. Owning a bath demonstrated that the family cared about their cleanliness and in turn this was a statement of their respectability."[52]

Contemporary design manuals recognized the emerging popularity of a room solely devoted to the fixed bath. In *Our Homes and How to Beautify Them* (1902), for instance, H. R. Jennings remarks that "there is a room that no self-respecting householder can do without and that is the bathroom."[53] The probability of a bathroom in the Tarleton house makes the appearance of a new portable bath unit that much more intriguing, especially considering such units were marketed explicitly to (usually urban) residents in houses *without* bathrooms. The visible pipes and the portable unit reveal that the owners are especially anxious over class position, moral decorum, and hygiene, once more approaching the staging of their homes and their commodity consumption as opportunities for performing status.

Shaw's scenic direction in the play mirrors an Edwardian construction of the English house as, according to Jon Hegglund, "an organizing structure of national ideology [in which] the health of individual bodies and the collective health of the nation are intimately connected" and duly threatened with contamination by "mass-culture" and "bodily deterioration."[54] From the start, the playwright depicts the atmosphere of the Tarleton country house as toxic, contaminated not only by mass cultural consumption but also by idleness and physical degeneration. The English characters in *Misalliance* suffer from a pronounced abatement of stamina, from the senescent infirmity of Tarleton and Summerhays to the physical and mental lethargy of Johnny, Hypatia, and Bentley. Bentley pesters Johnny at the beginning of the play to "argue about something intellectual" because "after a week in that filthy office [his] brain is simply blue-mouldy" (145). He is also physically out of shape; in response to a command to "skip about," Bentley explains that he "tried exercises with an indiarubber expander; but I wasnt strong enough: instead of my expanding it, it crumpled me up" (175). Bentley's issues, for American health advocate J. H. Kellogg, would belong to a "class of deformities which may be recognized ... among the so-called 'upper' classes [marked by] such congenital defects as flat or narrow chest, weakness of the heart, feeble digestive powers, a neurotic temperament, and various idiosyncrasies of mind and body."[55] *Misalliance* enacts what Wisenthal calls the "exhaustion of two English ruling classes, the capitalist middle class and the aristocracy."[56] It recognizes two serious threats to health: the industrialized class system and a state of leisure and commodity consumption.

In the preface to *Misalliance*, Shaw warns that the lack of meaningful work will produce "a new sort of laziness [that] will become the bugbear of society: the laziness that refuses to face the mental toil and adventure of making work by inventing new ideas or extending the domain of knowledge, and insists on a ready-made routine."[57] Such inertia has overcome Tarleton, who laments, "I'm getting sick of that old shop. Thirty-five years I've had of it: same blessed old stairs to go up and down every day: same old lot: same old game: sorry I ever started it now. I'll chuck it and try something else: something that will give a scope to all my faculties" (167). At the other end of the play's social hierarchy, Gunner describes his professional routine in similarly debilitating terms:

> I spend my days from nine to six – nine hours of daylight and fresh air – in a stuffy little den counting another man's money. Ive an intellect: a mind and a brain and a soul. ... Of all the damnable waste of human life that was ever invented, clerking is the very worst. ... How can a man tied to a desk from nine to six be anything – be even a man? (214–15)

The character is a member of the class Kellogg described as "confined in counting-rooms, stores, factories" and "already many hundred thousand strong": "a deformed creature which might be termed "the sedentary man" who is known by his round shoulders, his flat, hollow, feeble chest, his weak heart, his sunken stomach, his lax and puny muscles, his sallow, sunken, and lusterless eye."[58] Especially for clerks, life away from work was equally enervating; as Hegglund points out, the leisure industry in cities bombarded consumers with empty-calorie temptations including mass culture entertainments and junk food.[59] Nonetheless, Shaw's unusually specific setting of the play—May 31, 1909—means that Johnny, Bentley, Tarleton, Gunner, and even Percival are errant from the workplace on a Monday (although "Friday to Monday" represented a standard weekend in the country for those who could take them), indicating that the crisis of health and idleness that so many patent medicine adverts alarmingly proclaimed and that aroused so many public advocates crossed class lines.

Even the country house itself seems unable to purge internal toxins; quite immediate to Mrs. Tarleton's concerns in the play are the lethal threats in established households posed by poor sanitation. Alice McEwan has written extensively about Shaw's views on proper plumbing and how they dovetail with the Edwardian middle-class obsession with domestic drainage in which "sewage operates as part of a language of pollution, disturbing and disrupting, posing a threat to the health of the nation" and even became "something of a literary trope,"[60] one which Shaw in *Misalliance* satirically takes up, perhaps because of plumbing issues he and Charlotte were currently experiencing at their house in Ayot. In the play, one of the Tarletons' children has died as a result of faulty drainage, and Mrs. Tarleton expresses her shock that the local aristocracy so frankly discusses their systems. Encountering a duchess who "began talking about what sour milk did in her inside and how she expected to live to be over a hundred if she took it regularly," Mrs. Tarleton's dyspeptic response is to flee, "never [having] dared to think that a duchess could have anything so common as an inside" (159). Middle-class moral pretensions dangerously silenced frank talk of matters of personal and structural drainage.

In his book, *The Commodity Culture of Victorian England*, Richards makes clear that advertising copy for patent medicines in Edwardian periodicals

> avoided any implication that any existing social structure was to blame for disease in the first place. In other words, they neatly separated the effects from the causes of disease ... Nowhere in patent medicine advertising does one find the remotest suggestion that society at large is to blame for the social reality of sickness. Illness in England is neither endemic to the capitalist system nor historically determined.[61]

Surprisingly, in its own crusade against "effete matter" that "[poisons] the entire system" (13), the Century pamphlet goes both ways. On the one hand, it figures these ailments as ubiquitous across time and cultures, the cure a blend of wisdom derived from Native American, East Asian, classical, and contemporary technological innovation. On the other, the bath is marketed specifically to the professional class whose work necessitates large amounts of time spent inside crowded city offices performing non-physical tasks. Implicitly, then, the pamphlet lodges a critique that is systemic, against a lethargic, robotic middle class made up of "ministers, doctors, lawyers, bankers, editors, teachers, and stenographers, and all those who follow a vocation which allows but little active exercise" (11). A testimonial included in the Century pamphlet, reputedly from a fellow of the Royal College of Surgeons of Canada, directs attention to environmental sources of corruption: "circumstanced as we are in cities, [deprived of] the effect of bracing air and the sun's rays ... [existing] in an artificial state of life, with clothes that exclude the air, enervated with excesses, late hours, and unwholesome food, ... we require something that will help the skin to act" (14). The Pamphlet acknowledges the health costs of a rapidly industrializing and urbanizing society and speaks directly "to those of sedentary habits, who do not take exercise sufficient to throw off impurities of the skin and blood by perspiration," to the "thousands of people [who] exist in a lifeless sort of way, year after year, dragging themselves about with a skin the colour of a lemon, and a body loaded with poisons" (11, 13). Yet, in the end, its prescription doesn't directly offer remedy to that miasmatic environment but tallies with the industry's rhetoric of self-improvement; the Century booklet exhorts its readers to "HAVE A MIND OF YOUR OWN! Too many people can't think and act for themselves, they wait and watch to let others lead. Be a Leader Yourself!" (2). Purchasing a mass-produced commodity becomes an expression of individual thought and free will, illness ultimately a personal failing rather than a cultural one. Shaw too represents the decline as the result of both individual infirmity and the caste system and similarly packages his diagnosis with a prescription.

Arriving from a world far away from the Hindhead house, Gunner initially seems the most likely choice for cultural renewal and (not coincidentally) is the only character who inhabits the Turkish bath unit during the play. For McEwan, "Tarleton's portable cleansing contraption is contaminated by a working-class radical," epitomizing the playwright's "socialist critique of Edwardian middle-class anxieties about dirt and waste in terms of a fear of contagion."[62] Yet, Gunner's radicalism is merely a pose, its edge sapped by "slavery" to the economic system not only as a clerk but, oddly enough, as a consumer. Characterized by his son as "mad on reading," Tarleton has created a series of free libraries, an act that frustrates Johnny even though he sees "its value as an advertisement" (153). As his son shrewdly observes, Tarleton's libraries have a marketing agenda, inculcating a literacy that transforms the reader into a consumer, the great authors into copy. Tarleton is furious when he finds out that Gunner has been educating himself with books from the free library, recognizing that the young man's revenge posturing betrays a puerile sensibility proscribed by melodrama and armchair Marxism. Gunner musters no resistance to the lure of commodity within the Tarleton household either when, as Shaw writes "his attention is caught by the Turkish bath. He looks down the lunette, and opens the panels" (204). What is it that so entrances the young clerk? The unit's novelty, its class resonance, its copy-reputed rejuvenative properties? In any case, his fixation is interrupted by the arrival of Hypatia and Joey, and his refuge *into* the bath will further illustrate his immaturity by activating his own kneejerk middle-class morality. In contrast to Samuel Beckett's fascination with disembodied figures to illustrate existential fragmentation, the cyborg union of Gunner and the bath literalizes the process through which human beings become commodities, not only in

Gainor's political sense but according to the logic of late capitalism. This too is the endgame of patent medicine advertising, "not only directly to address the consumer's self but in a very real sense to transform it, in its entirety, into a spectacular commodity."[63] Unable to think outside the box, Gunner falls victim to the conspiracy of middle-class hegemony disseminated through mass-produced cultural forms: "I'm so full of your bourgeois morality that I let myself be shocked by the application of my own revolutionary principles" (221).

Gunner's experience in the bath enervates rather than invigorates him, reversing the expected process. Indeed, the transformative potential of the Turkish bath not only was a prominent feature of patent cure advertisement copy but points to the well-known literary and cultural trope of bathing. In *Misalliance*, Lord Summerhays's title—Knight Commander of the Bath—evokes the medieval confirmation process from which the name is derived that began with bathing in order to purify the candidate. Within a Christian framework, the practice generally has been figured as a first step towards purging sinfulness and symbolic rebirth. The trope also appears in *Pygmalion*, replete with a cheeky nod to Salvation Army practices, when Eliza's vigorous bath marks the first step in her transformation. In *Shaw's Daughters*, Gainor understands the *Misalliance* Turkish bath, replete with its Orientalist overtones, as a touchstone for Shaw's view that the "class distinction and cultural distance between [Gunner and the Tarletons] correspond to the kind of apartheid found in colonized areas."[64] Both Gunner and Eliza emerge from the bath transfigured, according to Gainor, "into an oppressed Other[, part of a] network of polarized social groups that all feel the force of imperial domination." In another sense, though, Gunner emerges from the unit with a degree of material power, armed with a pistol and secret knowledge about both Tarleton and Hypatia, threatening the integrity of the household. (After all, Turkish bath units also reputedly had the propensity to explode.) Gunner's potential though evaporates when he is easily disarmed, and the family unites to incapacitate and lethargize him. If Gunner emerges from the bath occupying a moral high ground and pregnant with revolutionary potential, the outraged outsider in this Hindhead culture is in the end corrupted by gin, humiliatingly abused, and ultimately silenced, unable to realize his initial desire to administer justice and escape so as not to "breathe this polluted atmosphere a moment longer" (219). The task of revitalization will thus fall to an even more alien intruder.

Polish acrobat Lina Szczepanowska intimidates and dominates for much of the play and is given by the playwright the climactic aria diagnosing the degenerative state of its English characters: "This is a stuffy house. ... It is disgusting. It is not healthy" (248). Shaw renders the foreigner a figure of health and vitality, a force for spiritual and sexual renewal; in a letter to Irene Vanbrugh, Shaw called Lina "the St Joan of Misalliance," her way of living "a hieratic act on her part."[65] Be that as it may, the character's genesis may partially have consumerist roots as well since, right before Shaw began writing *Misalliance* in 1909, Louis Bleriot's monoplane was displayed by Selfridges in its famous windows, capitalizing upon its notoriety. Plus, if Tarleton explicitly apes copy style, Lina is his counterpart in spectacle, replete with her own product to sell and an equally distinct way of speaking.

Closer perhaps to P. T. Barnum than Gordon Selfridge, Lina displaces the Turkish bath at the center of the play, retaining to a degree its foreign exoticism but modeling a different approach to health. Lina arrives in the play to break the stalemate the Tarleton household represents. When she asks for six oranges, Tarleton immediately assumes "she's doing an orange cure of some sort" (198), making clear not only his familiarity with that industry but also the limitations of his consumerist approach to cultural revitalization. Committed to physical challenge and perpetually engaged in self-conditioning, Lina successfully integrates physical, spiritual, and mental agility and resists commodification in the traffic in women, nimbly rebuffing sexual advances from Tarleton, Johnny, and Lord Summerhays. Her long speeches about her lifestyle, her various demonstrations of vigor, and her final speech denouncing the effete Tarleton household display her autonomy and strength, a stark contrast to the country house's other inhabitants. Her initial attempts to transform the withered English family members though are largely failures. After she whisks Tarleton off to the gymnasium for exercise to stop him from crying, he reappears "exhausted by severe and unaccustomed exercise" (208) and sapped by the exertion. Similarly, Bentley emerges from his session with Lina "as if he too had been exercised to the last pitch of fatigue" (247). After witnessing the brazen flirting between Hypatia and Joey, Gunner becomes self-righteously indignant, prematurely declaring, "I went into that Turkish bath a boy: I came out a man" (219). In response, Lina, after quickly disarming him, advises Gunner that he "doesn't need Turkish baths" but to "put on a little flesh" (219), a contrast drawn between cure-all product and individual action that underscores the play's critique of an Edwardian masculinity that aligns commodity consumption with hypocritical middle-class moral pretension. Frustrated, at the end of the play, Lina expresses her desire to "get out of this [stuffy house] into the air: right up into the blue" (247).

Lina is a version of the Shavian realist, the world-betterer, the superman—individuals animated solely by their own will who "by their ruthless action could compel order and efficiency, mold an unruly and recalcitrant population into a disciplined social body, and therefore clear the ground for the true supermen who would evolve biologically in the distant future [bolstered by] a dynamic ever-moving biological Life Force."[66] The Century Thermal pamphlet describes their bath unit as enabling the body's inherent ability to purge itself of toxins, in principle a kind of corporeal Fabianism; the bath performs nothing radical or revolutionary and merely accentuates the system's own drainage process to achieve verdure, vitality, and balance.[67] *Misalliance*'s abrupt recalibration, in which Lina displaces the Turkish bath at its center, may indicate a shift in Shaw's political thinking, away from therapeutic gradualism within parliamentary democracy and towards the dynamic individual of will weeding out the intractable, unproductive elements and rehabilitating those who can be swayed. In a letter written to Beatrice Webb in December 1910, Shaw described his strenuous effort at a recent Fabian speaking engagement: "in a hall crammed with a howling opposition, I spent an hour and a half shouting, bullying, chaffing, challenging, thundering and reparteeing until I was as one in a Turkish bath."[68] In contrast to marketing claims, Shaw envisions the patient in the bath as exhausted, worn out rather than rejuvenated, a sign perhaps of his frustration and impatience with the Fabian process and movement, the endless debates and slow progress. *Misalliance* provides an alternative in the form of *deus ex machina*, a kind of positive soft eugenics in which those with the potential to evolve are plucked from the jaws of commodity capitalism and conventional morality. At play's end, only Bentley expresses a renewed vigor and vision in his desire to embrace Lina's lifestyle and sensibility. The acrobat thus provides an antidote to the toxic ecology of the country house, one that produces strong bodies and adventurous souls who desire risk, and takes her place as one of the forerunners of later characters in Shaw's 1930s plays and on the world stage, for whom the notions of purity and hygiene are taken to terrifying extremes.

Glimpsed retrospectively through *Misalliance*, the first half of 1909 was a perfect storm in terms of thematic raw material about commercialization and health, and Shaw skillfully weaves his perspectives on everything from *Secret Remedies* to Selfridge into what would become a prototypical "play of ideas."[69] Yet, as much as he uses *Misalliance* to articulate his skepticism about foolish proprietary cures and endorse the proper way to apply physic to an invalid civilization, three of its characters complicate his position, as images of their creator. Shaw's statement in a letter to Matthew Edward McNulty that "Gunner is ME"[70] has invited comparisons between the character and the young playwright when he first arrived in London, frustrated by mundane clerking and murky parentage, practicing self-education, and engaged with socialism. The particular tableau of Gunner's head atop the portable bath unit though has implications with regard to Shaw's public persona ("G.B.S."), itself a hybrid creation of man and wellness advertisement.[71] In countless interviews, op-ed pieces, and reviews, "G.B.S." so presented himself and his lifestyle as triumphantly salubrious that he became copy incarnate.

Two characterizations of the playwright made by contemporary scholars already cited in this volume's first chapter bear repeating, Michael Holroyd's suggestion that "G.B.S. was not only a vegetarian but a living advertisement for vegetarianism"[72] and Sally Peters's vision:

> Carrying his woolen bedsheets with him when he traveled, pulling on gloves to keep his hands clean in the streets, wearing digital socks, garbed in the yellowish red suit, the scrupulously clean Shaw was an immaculate walking mannequin, an elaborate advertisement for the hygienic way of life.[73]

In this sense, Lina also functions as a stand-in for the playwright's public face, as she is consistently engaged in performing herself as the poster child of physical and spiritual health. Considering the playwright's own proclivity for mouthing maxims, Tarleton too is a version of "G.B.S."[74] As Gustavo Rodríguez Martín has argued, his plays "are filled with quotations from the most popular to the most obscure authors [that discursively] provide an authoritative argument, generally in a higher register than the vernacular."[75] In fact, all of Shaw's writing is shot through with the shrewd ideological deployment of what Martín calls "modified quotations," suggesting a substantial debt owed on the part of his media persona to the mode of patent medicine advertising the Century Thermal Bath Company deploys so well in their booklet. Clearly, the playwright's public persona is an amalgam of all three characters, a creation resulting from a determined trademarking campaign that profitably took cues from the health commodity culture he often denounced but always with an eye not simply for advertising himself but promoting a Shavian way of living. The portable Turkish bath unit and its packaging at the core of *Misalliance* is thus, for the playwright, both an object of critique and emulation. In a larger sense, its complex figuration in the play epitomizes Shaw's larger ambivalence towards commodity culture as often fraudulent, "desultory and possibly detrimental to society's progress; yet [also potentially] a means of achieving social change and autonomy."[76] As he writes in *The Revolutionist's Handbook*,

> The Anarchist, the Fabian, the Salvationist, the Vegetarian, the doctor, the lawyer, the parson, the professor of ethics, the gymnast, the soldier, the sportsman, the inventor, the political program-maker, all have some prescription for bettering us; and almost all of their remedies are physically possible and aimed at admitted evils.[77]

## Notes

1. Bernard Shaw. *Collected Letters 1898–1910*. Ed. Dan H. Laurence. New York: Viking, 1985. 130.
2. Bernard Shaw. "The Revolutionist's Handbook." In *The Bodley Head Bernard Shaw: Collected Plays with Their Prefaces*, vol. 2. London: The Bodley Head, 1971. 739–80. 768.
3. Dan H. Laurence. *Bernard Shaw: A Bibliography*, vol. 2. Oxford: Clarendon Press, 1983. 881–2.
4. James C. Moffett. "Should Advertisements Be 'Signed,' Like Articles." *Printers' Ink* 76.1 (6 July 1911): 58, 60–1. 60–1.
5. E. McKenna. "The Dramatization of Advertising Ideas." *Printers' Ink* 112.8 (19 August 1920): 93–6. 93.
6. Bernard Shaw. *Sixteen Self-Sketches*. New York: Dodd, Mead & Company, 1949. 66.
7. Dan H. Laurence. *Collected Letters*, vol. 1. New York: Dodd, Mead & Company, 1965. 97.
8. Alice McEwan. "Commodities, Consumption, and Connoisseurship: Shaw's Critique of Authenticity in Modernity." *SHAW: The Journal of Bernard Shaw Studies* 35.1 (November 2015): 46–85. 73, 63.

9. Bernard Shaw. "Preface" to *The Doctor's Dilemma*. In *The Bodley Head Bernard Shaw: Collected Plays with Their Prefaces*, vol. 3. London: The Bodley Head, 1971. 225–320. 294.
10. Fintan O'Toole. *Judging Shaw: The Radicalism of GBS*. Dublin: Prism, 2017. 250.
11. T. R. Nevett. *Advertising in Britain: A History*. London: The History of Advertising Trust, 1982. 24.
12. Raymond Williams. "Advertising: The Magic System." In *The Cultural Studies Reader*, 2nd edition. Ed. Simon During. London: Routledge, 1999. 320–36. 329.
13. Jackson Lears. *Fables of Abundance: A Cultural History of Advertising in America*. New York: Basic Books, 1994. 98.
14. Takahiro Ueyama. *Health in the Marketplace: Professionalism, Therapeutic Desires, and Medical Commodification in Late-Victorian London*. Palo Alto, CA: The Society for the Promotion of Science and Scholarship, 2010. 25.
15. "The Press, the Quacks, and the Public." *British Medical Journal* 1726 (17 January 1894): 208.
16. James Gregory. *Of Victorians and Vegetarians: The Vegetarian Movement in Nineteenth-Century Britain*. London: Tauris Academic Studies, 2007. 70.
17. Thomas Richards. *The Commodity Culture of Victorian England: Advertising and Spectacle 1851–1914*. Stanford: Stanford University Press, 1990. 173.
18. Efforts to put forth bills on advertising in both houses of Parliament were not successful until the mid-1930s and early 1940s.
19. Bernard Shaw. *The Doctor's Dilemma*. In *The Bodley Head Bernard Shaw: Collected Plays with Their Prefaces*, vol. 3. London: The Bodley Head, 1971. 321–436. 344, 346.
20. For biographer St. John Ervine, Tarleton also evokes two other "mercantile men" notorious for their virtuosic marketing, Andrew Carnegie and William Whiteley (428): Carnegie, the self-educated Scottish industrialist who, in addition to establishing a system of free libraries in the United States, compulsively integrated Shakespearean quotations throughout his late nineteenth-century essays on public policy, especially economic matters; Whiteley, the self-proclaimed "Universal Provider," a prosperous department store entrepreneur and philanderer, shot dead by his illegitimate son in 1907. Shaw clearly drew upon both for plot and characterization in *Misalliance*. See St. John Ervine. *Bernard Shaw: His Life, Work and Friends*. New York: William Morrow and Company, 1956.
21. Elizabeth Outka. *Consuming Traditions: Modernity, Modernism, and the Commodified Authentic*. Oxford: Oxford University Press, 2009. 123.
22. Nevett, 74.

23. Ina Zweiniger-Bargielowska. "Building a British Superman: Physical Culture in Interwar Britain." *Journal of Contemporary History* 41.4 (October 2006): 595–610. 598.
24. Ibid., 601.
25. Richards, 173.
26. J. Ellen Gainor. "Bernard Shaw and the Drama of Imperialism." In *The Performance of Power: Theatrical Discourse and Politics.* Ed. Sue-Ellen Case and Janelle G. Reinelt. Iowa City: University of Iowa Press, 1991. 56–74. 57. Tracy Davis, also connects the play (albeit more broadly) to imperial discourse in "Shaw's Interstices of Empire: Decolonizing at Home and Abroad." In *The Cambridge Companion to Bernard Shaw.* Ed. Christopher Innes. Cambridge: Cambridge University Press, 1998. 218–39.
27. Margery M. Morgan. *A Drama of Political Man: A Study in the Plays of Harley Granville Barker.* London: Sidgwick and Jackson, 1961. 191.
28. Bernard Shaw. *Misalliance.* In *The Bodley Head Bernard Shaw: Collected Plays with Their Prefaces,* vol. 4. London: The Bodley Head, 1971. 143–253. 143.
29. Peter Kandela. "The Rise and Fall of the Turkish Bath in Victorian England." *Journal of Dermatology* 39 (2000): 70–4. 72.
30. E. S. Turner. *Taking the Cure.* London: Michael Joseph, 1967. 231.
31. Kandela, 74.
32. "Turkish Baths at Home." Supplement to *Pall Mall Magazine* 43.192 (April 1909): 14.
33. "Trade Notes." *The Chemist and Druggist* 60.2 (11 January 1902): 45.
34. "The Power of Heat: Turkish Baths at Home." Century Thermal Bath Cabinet Company Booklet, @1901. Special Collections, Cambridge University Library.
35. Richards, 193.
36. John Strachan and Claire Nally. *Advertising, Literature and Print Culture in Ireland, 1891–1922.* New York: Palgrave Macmillan, 2012. 31–2.
37. For example, the error turns up in an ad for the Quaker Hot Air and Vapor Bath Cabinet on page two of the *St. John Daily Sun* for 23 February 1897 and again on page 36 of the periodical *Good Health* 2.2 (July 1903) in a blurb entitled "Antiquity of the Bath" that charts Homer's allusions to the baths. The spurious quotation is used, too, in less conspicuously promotional writing, such as Durham Dunlop's *The Philosophy of the Bath* (1868) and an essay entitled "Baths and Bathing, in Their Historical and Hygienic Aspects" in *Self Culture: A Magazine of Knowledge* 6.2 (November 1897).

38. Jennifer Wicke. *Advertising Fictions: Literature, Advertisement, and Social Reading*. New York: Columbia University Press, 1988. 81.
39. Tony Stafford. "Postmodern Elements in Shaw's *Misalliance*." *SHAW: The Annual of Bernard Shaw Studies* 29 (2009): 176–88. 184.
40. Shaw, *Misalliance*, 165.
41. Ibid., 197.
42. John A. Mills. *Language and Laughter: Comic Diction in the Plays of Bernard Shaw*. Tucson: University of Arizona Press, 1969. 130.
43. J. L. Wisenthal. *The Marriage of Contraries: Bernard Shaw's Middle Plays*. Cambridge, MA: Harvard University Press, 1974. 131.
44. Mills, 130.
45. Eugène Ionesco and Jack Undank. "The Tragedy of Language: How an English Primer Became My First Play." *The Tulane Drama Review* 4.3 (March 1960): 10–13. 13.
46. The title of Tarleton's pamphlet "The Romance of Business" certainly invites comparison with Selfridge's notorious book *The Romance of Commerce*, in which he articulates his philosophy and legitimates his work as valuable. Although Selfridge claimed he had written it before the war, *Commerce* was not published until 1918, almost a decade after *Misalliance* premiered. As such, the tantalizing possibility exists that Selfridge drew inspiration from a fictional character based partially on himself.
47. Laura Ugolini. "Men, Masculinities, and Menswear Advertising, c.1890–1914." In *A Nation of Shopkeepers: Five Centuries of British Retailing*. Ed. John Benson and Laura Ugolini. London: I.B. Tauris, 2003. 80–104. 96.
48. Edward S. Prior. "Upon House-Building in the Twentieth Century." In *Modern British Domestic Architecture and Decoration*. Ed. Charles Holme. London: Offices of the Studio, 1901. 9–14. 11–12.
49. Helen C. Long. *The Edwardian House: The Middle-Class Home in Britain 1880–1914*. Manchester: Manchester University Press, 1993. 18.
50. Ibid., 26.
51. Jon Hegglund. "Defending the Realm: Domestic Space and Mass Cultural Contamination in *Howards End* and *An Englishman's Home*." *English Literature in Transition 1880–1920* 40.4 (1997): 398–423. 399.
52. David J. Eveleigh. *Bogs, Baths, and Basins: The Story of Domestic Sanitation*. Thrupp: Sutton Publishing, 2002. 87.
53. H. R. Jennings. *Our Homes and How to Beautify Them*. London: Harrison & Sons, 1902. 236.
54. Hegglund, 399.
55. J. H. Kellogg. "Are We a Dying Race?" *Good Health: A Journal of Hygiene* 33.1 (January 1898): 1–4. 2.

56. Wisenthal, 134.
57. Bernard Shaw. "Preface" to *Misalliance*. In *The Bodley Head Bernard Shaw: Collected Plays with Their Prefaces*, vol. 4. London: The Bodley Head, 1971. 13–142. 58.
58. Kellogg, 2.
59. Hegglund, 410.
60. Alice McEwan. "'The 'Plumber-Philosopher': Shaw's Discourse on Domestic Sanitation." *SHAW: The Annual of Bernard Shaw Studies* 34 (2014): 75–107. 93, 91.
61. Richards, 188–9.
62. McEwan, "Plumber-Philosopher," 93.
63. Richards, 195.
64. Gainor, 68.
65. Irene Vanbrugh. *To Tell My Story*. London: Hutchinson, 1950. 205–6.
66. Matthew Yde. *Bernard Shaw and Totalitarianism: Longing for Utopia*. New York: Palgrave Macmillan, 2013. 6, 9.
67. Coincidentally, Shaw's neighbor and friend Arthur Conan Doyle made the Turkish bath an ongoing element in his Sherlock Holmes stories as the detective and Watson frequent public baths, and "The Illustrious Client" (1924) even begins with the pair "drying out" after a steam. Appearing in *The Strand* in December of 1911 (the year following the premiere of *Misalliance*), "The Disappearance of Lady Frances Carfax" begins with an exchange about the treatment's benefits. Holmes queries why Watson prefers "the relaxing and expensive Turkish rather than the invigorating home-made article." The doctor replies that he has been "feeling rheumatic and old" and that "a Turkish bath is what we call an alterative in medicine—a fresh starting-point, a cleanser of the system." *The Final Adventures of Sherlock Holmes*. New York: Heritage Press, 1957. 1330.
68. Alex C. Michalos and Deborah C. Poff, eds. *Bernard Shaw and the Webbs*. Toronto: University of Toronto Press, 2002. 104.
69. Of course, still another recent event surely in the mix for Shaw was the appearance of H. G. Wells's latest work, itself prominently concerned with the art and profession of advertising. First serialized in the *English Review* between December 1908 and March 1909 and appearing in book form in February 1909, *Tono-Bungay* was "the first major English novel to place promotion at its center" (Ross 32). Michael L. Ross. *Designing Fictions: Literature Confronts Advertising*. Montreal: McGill-Queen's University Press, 2015.

70. *Collected Letters*, 233.
71. It may be worth remembering that Shaw, in *The Quintessence of Ibsenism*, describes Shakespeare's portrait as a "laundry advertisement of a huge starched collar with his head sticking out of it" (283). Bernard Shaw. *The Quintessence of Ibsenism*. In *Selected Non-dramatic Writings of Bernard Shaw*. Ed. Dan H. Laurence. Boston: Houghton Mifflin Company, 1965. 205–306.
72. Michael Holroyd. *Bernard Shaw, Volume One: 1856–1898: The Search for Love*. New York: Vintage Books, 1988. 86.
73. Sally Peters. "Shaw's Life: A Feminist in Spite of Himself." In *The Cambridge Companion to George Bernard Shaw*. Ed. Christopher Innes. Cambridge: Cambridge University Press, 1998. 3–24. 12. For additional information on the psychological underpinnings of Shaw's health regimens, vegetarians, and clothing idiosyncrasies, see Peters's *Bernard Shaw: The Ascent of the Superman*. New Haven: Yale University Press, 1996.
74. Margery Morgan nicely summarizes the way in which Tarleton and so many elements of the play he inhabits are parts of Shaw himself (179–83).
75. Gustavo A. Rodríguez Martín. "'I Often Quote Myself' (and Others): Modified Quotations in the Play of Bernard Shaw." *SHAW: The Annual of Bernard Shaw Studies* 31 (2011): 192–206. 194–5.
76. McEwan, "Commodities," 77.
77. Shaw, "The Revolutionist's Handbook," 758.

CHAPTER 3

# "The Shadow of Disrepute": G.B.S. and Testimonial Marketing

A 1910 piece that appeared the week before the premiere of *Misalliance* in *The Editor and Publisher* boldly announced that "theatrical managers … have discovered that the stage of a theatre is too pitifully limited and impotent to present 'questions of the day' in a play lasting two and a half hours. Of course, the public discovered this before the managers, and thinking people who seek truth, and are unblinded by the spectacular, saw it long ago."[1] Shaw in this article is singled out as the

> "cleverest" of the socio-economico-politico dramatists [that] in the last decade … [have] suddenly assumed the authority of philosophers and statesman with little or no training in the intellectual processes of philosophy and statesmanship [and] have turned out batches of plays dealing with "questions of the day."

Referencing the playwright's struggles against the censor and his advocacy of the theater as an essential institution of societal critique, the piece claims that "the public of England and America does not take Mr. Shaw seriously" and offers the following rationale:

> There are about eighty-five theatres in New York. Perhaps ten of them are given over, at present, to plays that "preach" a "sermon." A high total average attendance nightly at those ten theatres would be about 12,000.

© The Author(s) 2018
C. Wixson, *Bernard Shaw and Modern Advertising*,
Bernard Shaw and His Contemporaries,
https://doi.org/10.1007/978-3-319-78628-5_3

> Every evening in New York 3,000,000 people read sermons in the newspapers. Indeed, there is a vast deal of nonsense in the talk of the theatre contingent.

Of course, Shaw had already for decades been preaching across media, never limiting himself to a single generic platform and endeavoring to reach as wide an audience as possible. He balanced a steady program of public speaking and pamphlet writing with forays into print periodicals via letters to editors, becoming a critic and a playwright, ensuring his continued presence in the review section.[2] Shaw's self-marketing campaign ingeniously refused to be confined to a single medium.

Initially relegated only to back covers or classified sections, commercial advertising also eventually insinuated itself beyond its designated spaces within print publications. At first,

> advertisements were placed on the outside of newspapers and periodicals, segregated from editorial matter, and most newspapers would not admit advertising with bold "display" type or illustrations. ... By the 1890s, however, the presses were opening up their editorial pages to illustrated advertisements [so that] the editorial and advertising content of the illustrated periodical now formed an interlocking whole [and] it was impossible to draw a line between editorial matter and ads. ... Culture and commerce mingled intimately in the structure of the magazine.[3]

In illustrated magazines starting in the 1840s, "advertisements had been incorporated among their articles and images," and, a half century later, "advertisers were increasingly successful in their attempts to insert their material into the journalistic sections of the magazine, either as editorial plugs, advertisements disguised as editorial features, or overt advertisements."[4] Particularly after the dailies followed suit, the result, as Gerry Beegan writes, was a print media in the 1890s that "created, traced, and maintained a culture of the mass-produced commodity" in which "both commercial and editorial material reinforced each other, each of them reflecting and shaping the reader's concerns" and "mobilizing mass consumption."[5]

What Shaw surely saw in that culture was another public stage, in which ideas are commodities and editorial writing mixes with product marketing, affording the creation of connective tissue between, say, a testimonial appearance in an advert and a letter to the editor or a critical review. These forums bleed into one another as opportunities to reach and shape readers, each one a context for the advancement of ideas, the promotion of a sensibility, the work of the Life Force. The elasticity of the periodical page enables Shaw to look at every section as a chance to promote, and he takes advantage of porous borders between sections to diversify outlets for G.B.S. and build what Jonathan Goldman calls "self-fashioned iconicity."[6]

As Michael Holroyd writes, Shaw realized early on that public interest often dwelled within other periodical sections besides those specifically dedicated to the discussion of current events and the performing arts; thus, he, for instance, "spread his political views through the sports pages as he would the music and art columns," and one way of understanding his participation in commercial marketing campaigns is as another attempt to reach a different segment of readership.[7] While we may struggle with the notion of a professed socialist signing on with consumer commodity culture, we can recall other examples that seem just as puzzling, such as how "his long affair with boxing [would] worry some of his admirers [who wondered why] this ascetic, humanitarian, anti-vivisectionist champion of the vegetable world [would] involve himself in brute pugilism." In that case, as Holroyd writes, "he saw at once the great publicity in pugilism and used it to draw attention to himself, not just personally, but as a vehicle for his developing ideas [as newspapers] were indispensable as creators of public opinion."[8] In that context, his eventual application of the kind of viral G.B.S. marketing he had already performed in periodicals and newspapers to specific product advertisements makes sense. When Shaw was interviewed in 1908 by a French journalist, the question of his promotional activity arose:

> "Why," asked the Frenchman severely, "do you carry on such a campaign of self-advertisement? Is it necessary for you to declare yourself superior in many ways to Shakespeare and to proclaim yourself the most remarkable man of your epoch; This sort of thing might easily be explained while you were a young, unknown man desirous of notoriety; but now that you are renowned throughout Europe, do you not think that it is high time to throw overboard that G.B.S. whom you have endowed with a quasi-legendary personality?"

To which, the playwright responded,

> "What? Stop advertising myself?" cried Shaw. "No! I must advertise more than ever. Look at Pears' Soap. If there is one business house that is solid it is the house of Pears. Do they cease for that reason to cover walls with their posters? If I should give up advertising myself I should ruin my business."[9]

His analogy is revealing, and, just as patent medicine had provided a broad stylistic framework for his development of G.B.S., the continued honing of the testimonial technique in commercial advertising would prove anything but a misalliance with his own rhetorical prowess.

The style of mid-nineteenth-century ads was dominated by what one executive characterized as "copy that threw the book at the reader":

> There was the hit-'em-over-the-head school which consisted of hardworking advertisements that yelled, shouted, screamed, and hollered. They said everything kind about the product it was possible to say and they started out with headlines that read "Science proves ..." ... The thesis was that you dragged them in with your sideshow-barker treatment in the headline and then gave them the hard sell once you got them inside the tent, and this was the body copy. The text was just *loaded* with copy points.[10]

The conceit undoubtedly contributed to commercial advertising's "reputation for deceit and fraud which undermined credibility":

> At least by the 1850s, ... advertising by the print trade ... and by vendors of patent medicines was associated in the minds of middle-class readers with fraudulent and false claims. Practitioners frequently presented medications of doubtful efficacy for dubious purposes in language which combined ambiguity, innuendo, or even sensationalism, testing the credulity of the public and attracting to advertising generally an attitude which regarded the practice as dishonorable, this at a time when respectability was becoming a widespread aspiration in society.[11]

While newspapers sought ways to deter such advertisements casting shade on their periodicals, manufacturers

> chose to distance themselves and their products from the excesses of such advertising [and tackle] the problem of overcoming public skepticism of hostility to their products [by adopting] a minimalist approach

[that] announced the products coupled with the name of the supplier and sometimes a message of no more than two or three words, [opting for] a more restrained approach ... which assisted the gradual penetration by the advertisers of staple products into the pages of respectable newspapers and magazines.[12]

The advent of "new journalism" in the late 1880s made ripples in the copy world as well, that further made space for the testimonial:

> The long descriptive passages, verbatim reports of speeches, and detailed political analysis that had been the norm in the established press were now being replaced by short, varied paragraphs of gossip and opinion [cast in] a lighter, more conversational tone, with an overall emphasis on personality and human interest [geared towards] a broad middle-class audience.[13]

In the 1870s, technological innovation in lithography made it possible for "advertisers [to dispense] with the presentation of products illustrating a message directly related to them and [to substitute] instead an arresting picture or design ... to which the brand name could be attached"; this moment marks a turn in which "associational images began to take precedence over informational content on utility, price, and quality."[14] In a 1919 piece in *Advertising & Selling*, Felix Orman goes to Shaw as a way to illustrate the contrast between advertising styles:

> I don't know whether you like the plays of Bernard Shaw. I do. They are full of pith and point. They are remarkable advertisements of *ideas*. Perhaps you have seen or read "Man and Superman." Here the Shavian wit struck a high note. John Tanner, the opinionated and very controversial and iconoclastic hero of the play, has been submerging the charming Ann under an ocean of words. He feels that she has been duly impressed, converted to his theories. Then Ann, with the airy condescension of a pretty woman addressing a spoiled child, bids John just to go on talking.[15]

In juxtaposition to the play, Orman evokes a second "fictional incident" from a "standard puppy-love story ... wherein an enraptured youth exclaims in an impassioned voice to the haughty object of his adoration, 'Oh, just let me look at you!'" In the analogy, the "Eastern standardized" technique "keeps on talking," emphasizing substantive copy text, while the "Minnesota-style" consists mainly of large color images for the reader to "look at." As to which is more effective, he concedes that understanding one's audience is key, that "there are a lot of people who like words, regardless of what they mean or whether they agree with them," just as "there are also a good many people who like to look at something pretty, even though its meaning and quality are much inferior to the surface attraction." Nonetheless, he ultimately affirms the primacy of words, the style embodied by Shaw's plays, deeming the "pretty pictures" of so-called flash advertising an "ephemeral" form.

Testimonial endorsement often successfully synthesized both approaches, anchoring the layout with a photograph or drawing of the "personality" in tandem with his or her words, together appealing "to the viewer on the basis of emotion, aspiration, and fantasy."[16] For much of the nineteenth century, commercial promotion, largely on behalf of patent medicine, refashioned an old concept into a marketing technique:

> The term "testimonial" was used as early as the sixteenth century as a personal introduction, reference, or commendation, often in the context of the search for employment. ... Over time, such personal testimonials shifted from the private realms of correspondence between two parties to small-scale, often local advertisements. In mass-circulated testimonial advertising, the commendation is transferred from an individual to a firm or corporation, or even more abstractly, to the consumer goods and services.[17]

In practice, the testimonial was employed as a way to legitimize products and services via statements from professionals, researchers, and ordinary citizens with firsthand experience. As such,

> testimonial advertisements [inserted] into the negotiation between buyer and seller the words of a third party, presented as disinterested in the commercial transaction but in some way knowledgeable about the product at hand and willing to share that knowledge. ... Though the writer or speaker of the testimony is not involved in the actual commercial exchange, his or her words are packaged and publicized by the producer, retailer, or service provider as part of a marketing campaign.[18]

The success of the testimonial proceeds largely from its timing within the larger process of industrialization and the onset of the

## 3 "THE SHADOW OF DISREPUTE": G.B.S. AND TESTIMONIAL MARKETING 65

alienating forces of modernity – brought about by a host of factors including rapid urbanization; mass immigration; the rationalization of manufacturing processes and the deskilling of labor; the expansion of corporate entities and the increase in white collar, middle management; and the swift movement of goods, people, and ideas across national and international borders – [so] the person-to-person communication that testimonial advertising invited was understandably appealing.[19]

Rapidly, as William M. Freeman observed in 1957, "the testimonial [became] the heart of modern advertising."[20]

In Britain and Ireland, advertising often traded upon names drawn from royalty and the aristocracy with claims of their patronage, while patent medicine manufacturers sought medical and scientific professionals to legitimate their wares. In the second half of the nineteenth century, famous personalities from mass culture increasingly became prominent endorsers. This shift, according to Jonathan Goldman, from "state- or society-authorised hierarchies of achievement" to "figures from cultures of mass entertainment" is accomplished through

> new technologies of mass reproduction, which enable instant recognition and a sense of simultaneous ubiquity and inimitability. Due to the mechanical reproduction of photographs, print images, and text, a celebrity can be everywhere at once, repeatedly, and recognised widely, if not literally universally.[21]

Against a backdrop of "growing fears of lost individuality and fractured community," personality testimonials urged readers "to equate consumption with a coherent sustainable identity and membership within an established, recognizable community."[22] If such appeals encouraged the consumer to join a community via "emulation" and furthered the mechanisms of individual and collective identity formation, Shaw realized that his participation in this process would not only keep "G.B.S." in the public eye but move readers towards what he believed was a healthier and more ethical state of being and facilitate the creation of a community of consumers animated by a shared vision.

In a 1911 *Printers' Ink* series on the testimonial, James W. Egbert itemized the qualities of successful endorsements:

> The source of a good testimonial must be a person whose judgment is respected.
> 
> The source of a testimonial must know something about the goods; and not only must he know, but people must know that he knows.
> 
> A good testimonial is not a paid advertisement.
> 
> A testimonial may be either an advertisement for the writer of it, or the goods. It is seldom both.
> 
> The valuable testimonial is known to be hard to get. The best testimonials give facts in detail backed up with figures and dates.[23]

Tenet number 4 is strange, considering that one component of the technique's attractiveness derives from its mutual benefit for advertiser and endorser alike; whether or not financial compensation is involved, the latter experiences expansion and enhancement of their renown and the reach of their name even as the former benefits from their notoriety and product affirmation. In essence, testimonials, as Shaw well understood, "both derive from and confer the prestige and authority of those who testify to the worthiness of a brand-name product, service, or experience."[24]

Doubtless an inspiration for Shaw's distinctive mode of brand marketing was his keen observation when he got to London of the nexus between commerce and theater. In their study *Theatre and Fashion: Oscar Wilde to the Suffragettes*, Joel H. Kaplan and Sheila Stowell chart "the commercial interplay of stage and stalls [in which] playhouses became second showrooms, with London's leading ladies serving as living mannequins," that marks a "convergence in the early 1890s of an aggressive fashion press, innovative merchandising by a new breed of independent dress makers, and the transformation of a select group of West End theatres into an essential part of the London season."[25] A *Printers' Ink* retrospective, appearing in 1938, pointed out that, in America, "in the early eighties, a change took place in theater programs. Single sheer playbills became pamphlets that carried advertising. Theater managers even in those days were advertising minded to a high degree – were, in fact, proportionately the most active advertisers in any given community."[26] Within this network, the theater relied upon the press for publicity, and the press depended on the theater for content and advertising. ... Theaters placed advertisements in magazines, which in turn publicized their stars, while these same stars appeared in the advertisements in the magazines. ... The success of the star system was built on the public visibility of actors and actresses in the press, and so they were not only fixtures on the stage, but appeared in the editorial pages and advertising sections of magazines. The theater, as well as being one of the major leaders in visual advertising, also lent its stars to the selling of mass-produced goods; the promotion of products by professional beauties and actresses became an important tool for advertisers from the 1880s onwards.[27]

Although Shaw critiqued the commercialization of the stage, famously referring to conspicuous product placement in shows as "a tailor's advertisement making sentimental remarks to a milliner's advertisement in the middle of an upholsterer's and decorator's advertisement,"[28] he surely noticed the explosion of product endorsements by performers in periodicals and newspapers by the early 1890s as well as "the press's ability to rapidly circulate the appearance, personal details, and opinions of personalities on a huge scale."[29]

However, almost as soon as the technique of incorporating the names of well-known figures into advertisements was deemed effective, starting in the early nineteenth century and flourishing well into the twentieth, its success was marred by both overusage and improper attribution without consent, engendering an atmosphere of public mistrust. Indeed, stage actresses'

> indiscriminate endorsement of anything and everything ultimately undermined the value of the testimonial by raising questions in consumers' minds about the truthfulness of their claims. ... By the late 1890s, a series of scandals involving the use of fake or "tainted" testimonials by patent medicine companies further tarnished the testimonial's reputation [so that] by 1900 testimonial advertising was largely discredited, and actresses all but disappeared from the advertising pages for almost a decade.[30]

A historical retrospective that appeared in *Printers' Ink* in 1938 described the stumble of the testimonial at the turn of the century:

Ultimately, the whole thing became a competition of names and ran the cycle of abuse which has since become familiar in testimonial advertising.

So great waxed the demand for big-name testimonials that the securing of them became an organized business. ... [In the end,] the testimonial craze caused public ridicule. Theatrical travesties in advertising were received with uproarious applause by audiences everywhere.[31]

In addition to the proliferation of endorsements in advertising of all kinds, there was a zealous backlash emerged, intent on exposing "the worthlessness of patent medicines and their exaggerated claims," which counted among its collateral damage the "credibility and viability" of the testimonial technique.[32] In an effort to put the taint of patent medicine behind it, the field tried to re-brand itself:

> The testimonial scandal cast a pall over the advertising industry, [and,] in an effort to restore dignity to the profession and refute lingering charges of charlatanism, advertising agents abandoned their Barnumesque techniques and began to reinvent themselves as professional business men.[33]

Nonetheless, in the early twentieth century, attempts by advertising agencies to attract consumers through various media included a return to the celebrity testimonial technique but with a difference. Rather than simply indiscriminately associating a famous name with products, campaigns in the 1910s sought to capitalize the particular authority of the spokesperson to deepen the persuasiveness of the appeal.

Stage actresses were sought to endorse products directly related to their profession, especially in the areas of fashion and beauty, and the testimonial staged a comeback. They indirectly follow Shaw's model of professional branding via ventures into advertising that were, as Marlis Schweitzer has shown, "an extension of the actress's other promotional activities, including writing articles and delivering lectures on beauty and fashion":

> Acting independently or through an agent, these women who made arrangements with advertisers allowed them to profit from their own success, enhance their public profile, and promote themselves as fashion experts. For performers whose careers were often circumscribed by male producers, managers, and directors, testimonial advertising also presented an opportunity to take responsibility for at least one aspect of their professional lives.[34]

Yet, as Schweitzer goes on to argue, there was also a particular danger with the testimonial to the actress's professional autonomy:

> Whereas fashion articles and onstage fashion endorsements allowed performers to monitor and shape their self-commodification, testimonial advertisements limited their ability to control the meanings associated with their names and images.[35]

Unfortunately, promotional agents would run unauthorized and uncompensated endorsements, a trend actresses were powerless to stop, and agencies often tried contractually to forbid spokeswomen from participating in advertising for other products, forcing them to turn over exclusive control of their name for a certain period of time.[36] Legally, "viewed as public property – and therefore public commodities – celebrity performers found it increasingly difficult to control and shape their public personae."[37] An added effect on the industry, especially when actresses refused to comply with directives to limit their commercial exposure, was that endorsement was again beginning to saturate advertising, re-challenging in the 1920s the effectiveness of the technique by re-igniting public skepticism. Advertising posed for actresses the same risks that Shaw envisioned, making the control of one's brand a most urgent imperative. Indeed, the playwright's early ventures into testimonial advertising illustrate how predatory the market could be in poaching successful brands.

Despite his negative outlook on patent medicine as an industry and revulsion at the industry's deceitful marketing practices, Shaw nonetheless purchased and used many proprietary products. A glance at the various postcards and letters from Shaw kept by his Welwyn pharmacists reveals that, even into the late 1940s, Shaw was well-versed in proprietary brand names and the health commodity market. Starting his professional relationship with Shaw in 1908, chemist E. P. Downing admitted that these requests for products give the impression that "Shaw was a bit of a hypochondriac" but that his requests for "medicines or other goods we sold [occurred] much less than most customers" and are just the result of an "ever-inquiring mind [that] led him to an interest in vitamins."[38] However, appearing in such proximity to his market critiques in *Doctor's Dilemma* and *Misalliance*, it still is startling at first to encounter Shaw's 1912 endorsement of Formamint.

Developed in Germany, Formamint was a lozenge made of lactose and formaldehyde and promoted as a throat antiseptic agent. Analyzed and approved by the *British Medical Journal* as an alternative to gargles in February of 1908 and put to wide use by the Red Cross, hospitals, and the British army, Formamint tablets were marketed as both therapeutic and preventative. Even surgeons took them as part of the process of preparing for a procedure. In its March 1908 issue, the *Dublin Journal of Medical Science* provided an overview of international research on Formamint conducted between 1905 and 1907, indicating it had no irritative effects and was "proved to have very well-indicated uses in all cases of asepsis of the oro-pharyngeal regions" even extending into "all infective throat conditions" like scarlet fever and diphtheria (240).[39] The ad copy adopted a "scientific approach" and detailed a purifying process to clear out toxic bacteria (not unlike that of the Turkish bath), this time via a "candy-like tablet" that dissolves in the mouth and "frees the germicide." The product was widely advertised in medical journals as well as popular newspapers and periodicals, always deploying a testimonial-based approach, often citing the journal articles as well as citing names of prominent users, both medical practitioners and famous figures such as Enrico Caruso and Jack London.

The product did face some challenges right from the start. Seven months after its affirmation of the tablet, on September 12, 1908, the *British Medical Journal* reported on a documented case the previous June of poisoning by Formamint as well as additional evidence contained in the testimony of a civil lawsuit, concluding that the "tablets cannot be regarded as completely harmless."[40] The piece was reprinted subsequently in *The British Dental Journal*. That its developer Wulfing & Co. kept up with medical journals is clear from the swift rebuttal that appeared a month later in the "Letters, Notes, etc." section, claiming it "only fair to state" that in *Medizinsche Klinik* (July 12) a company representative says that the unpleasant side-effects were "due to idiosyncrasy" and identifies supporting witnesses to certify it "impossible" (including in cases of accidental overdoses in children), "even after the most searching examination, to discover any ill effect."[41]

A much more dramatic and sustained pushback occurred when Formamint was introduced in the USA in 1911, typical of the struggles new commercial remedies faced for legitimacy, especially among medical practitioners. The April 10, 1913 issue of *Printers' Ink* used Formamint as a case study to illustrate how the "protection of dealer's profit on [the] first of [a] family of products makes it far easier to secure distribution for the second."⁴² According to the article, less than a year after its introduction in America in 1911, "10,000 dealers" of Formamint were secured by leveraging the company's success in preventing its other product Sanatogen from price cutting. In unusual detail, the piece provides a window into the steps of the marketing process taken for Formamint, from an initial phase of "circularized" physicians and dentists, moving to advertisement in trade papers for both industries, and culminating in letters to druggists across the country. What *Printers' Ink* valorized as an effective roll out was greeted with suspicion and scorn by the American Medical Association (AMA). Interestingly, their objection seemed to be not so much with the product (one of countless arriving every year) but with the marketing, done "by that cheapest of all methods of advertising 'patent medicines,' through the medical profession":

> Doubtless it will be only a matter of time when the required number of testimonials from American physicians are forthcoming when we may expect to find the newspapers of this country heralding through their advertising pages the fact that Formamint is "recommended by thousands of American physicians."⁴³

The piece goes on to identify *by name* the journals carrying the first wave of Formamint advertisements and concludes,

> How much longer will the medical profession permit itself to be used as an unwitting agency for the exploitation of "patent medicines"? ... That it should still be considered workable is complimentary neither to the standard of advertising ethics of medical journals that accept the Formamint advertisements nor to the intelligence of the members of the medical profession who will "fall for it."

For the AMA, "the game has been worked so often that it has become transparently thin [but] evidently not worn out, however, or shrewd nostrum promoters would not waste their time or money on it."

The 1913 *Printers' Ink* piece also revealed that the introduction of the product to the American public via salesmen and newspaper notices didn't gain much traction, due (according to the company) to a poor choice of seasonal timing for the launch. What is striking is that, among the incredible detail it presents about publicity and strategies—from counter signs and window displays to the use of testimonials and "microscopic slides" in the copy—no mention is made of Shaw who had (inadvertently, it seems) by that time become the celebrity anchor of new Formamint advertisements. The playwright mentions the product by name in two published personal letters to Charlotte. In one, dated May 2, 1912, he relays that he has bought Formamint for an ailing friend, and that it was "rather successful" against her cold.[44] In the other, dated August 22, 1912, he complains, almost sounding like the tablet's ad copy, "I left my bottle of formamint behind and cant get any here: a serious matter, as I am constantly picking up germs that develop into diphtheria in ten minutes if not promptly poisoned."[45] He seems to have continued to use the product in subsequent decades. In August of 1945, Shaw sent a postcard to E. P. Downing, his chemist in Welwyn, that had taped to it a print advertisement for Redoxon (the first synthetic vitamin to be mass-marketed). In addition to asking for two bottles, he inquires whether Formamint is available and, if so, whether he might have "a couple of units" sent.[46] But it was his mention of Formamint in a July 1912 piece for *Christian Commonwealth* that would trigger a change of direction for the tablet's advertisements, starting in August 1912.

In a letter to the editor, Shaw took issue with a sermon delivered by Reginald John Campbell, the minister of the City Temple, that figured the Life Force as "blind, senseless, and void of intelligence."[47] The playwright critiqued the "capital danger in popular Christianity" of "detaching God from Man" and the "capital difficulty of the apparent incompatibility of the existence of malignant creatures with benevolence in their creator": "It is no use putting all the failures into one parcel, labeled 'Life Force: care of Bernard Shaw,' and all the successes into another, labeled 'The Father: care of R.J. Campbell, City Temple.' They both come through the same post office." One must, he went on, admit that "the failures and mistakes of Man are the failures and mistakes of the Life Force":

> The cry of God to men, as I hear it, is "Pity me; help me; stop flattering me; above all, stop talking damned nonsense in your superstitious terror of me; for I am also beset with error and burdened with unimaginable labours; and I have created you to be my helpers and servers, not my sycophants and apologists."

Far from an endorsement, Shaw mentions the tablet brand in a throwaway example to illustrate his point: "When a man breaks a cobra's neck or puts a Formamint lozenge into his mouth to kill a few thousand bacilli he is trying to wipe out the consequences of old mistakes of creation."

The following month, Formamint's print advertisements were trumpeting the reference, seemingly without the explicit consent of the playwright. The decision marked a moving away from the "scientific" and practitioner testimonial techniques that had so drawn the ire of the AMA. Alice McEwan mentions Shaw's appearance for Formamint as an example of Shaw's use of his celebrity "to authenticate and promote health-related products"; yet, while she quotes his statement about the tablets' ability to eradicate germs, she doesn't comment on the unusual form of the endorsement (see Fig. 3.1).[48] Just underneath a line sketch of the playwright's head directly engaging the reader, the copy was structured as a single column, mimicking the style of an article, and entitled in bold "Mr. Bernard Shaw on Formamint." It begins: "Many famous persons have voluntarily given us testimonials to Formamint. But Mr. Bernard Shaw has paid us the still higher compliment of publicly treating Formamint as a 'household word.'"[49] The indirect endorsement is expressed as a quotation from his letter to the editor:

> Writing in the Christian Commonwealth (July 3rd, 1912), he casually refers to Formamint as a thing universally known and used – which indeed it is – for killing bacteria in the mouth, and so preventing the diseases they cause. Mr. Shaw says – and we quote this "Shavian" utterance with all due apologies: "When a man ... puts a Formamint lozenge in his mouth to kill a few thousand bacilli he is trying to wipe out the consequences of old mistakes of creation."

Clearly, the intent behind this emphasis upon Shaw's "casual" and unsolicited mention of the product in the marketplace of ideas is to side-step the ethical and credibility drawbacks personality advertising (especially in patent medicine) presented at the time. The rest of the copy recycles the earlier description of the tablets and the claims about their healing properties. The new advertisement ran widely for the next three years in a variety of periodicals, including *The Sketch, Collier's, the Illustrated London News, The Graphic, The Bystander, the New York Times, the London Times,* and *Punch's Almanack*. A revision of the original "scientific" advertisement but newly containing Shaw's quote (with attribution) arrives in late 1914 and 1915 in, among other places, *McClure's, The New Outlook,* and *Scientific American*. The eagerness and excitement with which Shaw's image and words were circulated on behalf of

**Fig. 3.1** Formamint advertisement, from *Collier's Magazine* (5 December 1914), p. 26

Formamint confirm that, as Alice McEwan points out, "the construction and cultivation of the 'GBS' figure as a marketable commodity in the modern global marketplace was well advanced by the close of the Edwardian era" (Fig. 3.2).[50]

The identification of Shaw with Formamint was prominent enough to produce a few cheeky allusions elsewhere. A comic piece written in June 1913 for *The New Age* entitled "Health for Intellectuals" mocked the association of playwright with product:

> Some time ago I suffered from a virulent Shaw rash. Everything I wrote was diluted Shaw. A man who is easy to imitate is not exactly a good model, though I was not to know that until some time after. However, not being a fool even in the period of eruptive adulation, I soon wearied of the parrot life. Knowing the close relation between food and output, I determined on a drastic remedy. I cut my meals down to one a day.

**Fig. 3.2** Formamint advertisement, digital collections at the New York Public Library

In a very short time this left me with little or no desire to write, but I profited by my abstinence in having more time and a clear head for study. The Shaw rash is now quite gone, and with it all interest in the Formamint specialist.[51]

A decade later, in a 1922 playlet by Pierre Loving, published in *The Drama*, an aging matinee idol exclaims, "I'm no longer fit to play the young lover or ... Marchbanks," rhapsodizing that

> even Shaw wrote to me once in London, adding, contrary to custom, only a single short postscript in which he said I interpreted the part very much as if I had written youthful lyrics for Formamint in my time, instead of trying to ape Henry Irving's conception of a poet, which seemed to be the vogue.[52]

In any case, as the new ads continued to roll out, the delegitimizing of Formamint by the AMA went on. In August of 1915, in *The Propaganda for Reform in Proprietary Medicines*, a report dedicated to analyzing the promotional claims of products and the research used to support them, the organization concludes that the claims made for Formamint are "grossly unwarranted," "very extravagant and misleading," that "the use of these tablets may be, in some cases, fraught with danger and are a menace, not only to the health of the individual, but also to the safety of the community," and that "dependence on Formamint for the prevention of infection and for curing disease is not only unwise but dangerous."[53] In 1919, another *Journal* article again cited this report, horrified that formaldehyde tablets such as Formamint were advertised "during the recent epidemic of influenza" and are "still being advertised."[54] The piece reminded physicians that "an inefficient antiseptic is more than merely useless; it is a menace to public safety in that it tends to lead to the neglect of rational and effective protective measures."

Through a couple changes of agency, Formamint continued to be aggressively marketed into the mid-1920s, although the future of the German-based brand was threatened at the onset of the First World War by the Patents, Designs, and Trade Marks Act (1914). Within two months of its passage, according to a 1914 piece in *Scientific American*, "about one hundred applications were received from British businessmen asking for permission to make products protected by English patents granted to Germans, and about the same number of applications for the right to use German trade-marks which have been widely advertised in England."[55] In the February 20, 1915 issue, *The British Medical Journal* articulated its position in relation to the "special legislation, passed shortly after the commencement of the war," empowering the "Board of Trade to make drastic alterations in regard to the continuance of patent rights and trade-mark rights in this country held by alien enemies" (339). No action is taken until an application is made to suspend proprietary rights and license manufacture of a product "for the public interest and not merely for the private interest of the applicant." Reviewing such cases, the *Journal* concludes that "the Board has been guided solely by a consideration of the importance, from the public point of view, of keeping in existence the production of certain articles, and has never avoided or suspended the rights of patentees or the owners of registered trade-marks merely on the ground that they were alien enemies."

The article notes that an application was made to suspend the trade-mark Formamint but was denied.[56] Yet, in its December 16, 1916 issue of the *Journal*, the AMA reported that

> the English assets of Wulfing, including all stocks of santogen, formamint, albulactin, and cytospurin, have been, like other German-owned undertakings in this country, sold by order of the government. They have been purchased by Lord Rhondda, a business magnate, in conjunction with others. In the future, therefore, the business will be entirely British and free from enemy capital or influence.[57]

The new proprietors announced their intention, "with the encouragement of the medical profession, to offer ample funds and facilities for experimental research work in synthetic chemistry, in the hope that English investigators may devise new products of no less value"—they hope to win back physicians who had "only abandoned on patriotic grounds" prescribing the products, particularly as they had heard from "many physicians" how disappointed they were by the inferiority of their "numerous imitations."

In the meantime, like Formamint, Shaw's trademark persona seemed to be at a moment of crisis. An editorial that appeared in *The Nation* in October 1909 declared that the time has come ... when the insolent Shavian advertising no longer fills us with astonishment or discovery or disables our judgment from a cool inspection of the wares advertised. The youthful Athenians who darted most impetuously after his novelties are already hankering after some new thing. The deep young souls who looked to him as an evangelist are beginning to see through him and despair.[58]

In his 1916 biography of Shaw, Augustus Hamon suggested that "G.B.S." was at a critical juncture, analogical perhaps to the one increasingly faced by testimonial advertising in general, over questions of truthfulness:

It is this outrageous system of advertisement, in conjunction with the humorous fashion in which he presents his most serious ideas, which have prevented, and continue to prevent, people from taking him seriously. "He is a very clever man, his plays are extremely amusing, but he is neither serious nor sincere," say of him most of his countrymen. Others, somewhat less dogmatically, are content to ask themselves, "Is he in earnest?"[59]

However, it was his *Common Sense about the War*, appearing in the *New Statesman* in November of 1914, that dealt Shaw's reputation the most serious blow and turned him into what A. M. Gibbs describes as an "extraordinarily isolated and reviled figure in England."[60] Running counter to the atmosphere of fierce nationalism, his essay was intensely critical of British leadership, and the playwright ascribed culpability to both sides for the conflict. Shaw's "reasoning was impeccable; his offence emotional," and the outcry was immediate and severe.[61] As Dan H. Laurence recounts,

*Common Sense about the War* shook the nation to its underpinnings, generating a fury of outrage and splenetic derogation from the press. He was denounced as a traitor, an enemy "within our walls." Former friends cut him dead at committee meetings and in the streets. Booksellers and librarians removed his works from their shelves.[62]

The newspapers that had so eagerly published anything by and about him now "instructed their readers to boycott his plays,"[63] and "Shaw was effectively expelled from the Dramatists' Club and forced out of his positions on committees of the Society of Authors."[64] Among the personal losses for Shaw was his long friendship with playwright Henry Arthur Jones; in 1915, Jones wrote to his daughter, "There is no use talking or thinking about the war. It's awful, and Shaw is only anxious to get an advertisement out of it."[65] He was prophetic, in a sense. When, in 1915, the British Army anxiously turned to Shaw to get a war advertisement out of him, the playwright responded with a one-act meditation on the celebrity testimonial.

\*\*\*

> A nation is forced to advertise its needs in order to win recruits, just as a manufacturer is forced to advertise his promises in order to gain purchasers.[66]

Throughout the war, advertising revenue sharply decreased, and "by the end of 1915 it became clear that newspapers had also suffered a large drop in the volume of advertising they carried ... not so much the result of cutbacks by advertisers as of a shortage of newsprint, which was forcing them to run smaller issues, with the column inches available for advertising correspondingly reduced."[67] At the same time, government advertising in various media surged to disseminate national propaganda and imitated professional marketing techniques in recruitment notices. For instance,

> [On October 30, 1915] the entire front page of the *Freeman's Journal* was dedicated to a recruitment advertisement that declared, "Irishmen! You cannot permit your Regiments to be kept up to strength by other than Ireland's sons! It would be a deep disgrace to Ireland, if all her regiments were not Irish to a man." The advertisement summoned "50,000 Irishmen to join their brave comrades in Irish regiments." (A detachable form that men could complete in order to enlist was even included at the bottom of the page.)[68]

In turn, commercial advertising put the war to work on its own behalf. Accounts of battlefield heroism and soldier life and appeals to home front morale and support "became grist to the copywriters' mill, and manufacturers ... often boasted of their popularity with the troops up the line."[69] Copy that made reference to the war and layout crafted to mimic the form of official journalism could catch the attention of readers with enlisted loved ones desperate for any information as advertisers sought to "tap into nationalist sentiment and align their brands with the values often associated with wartime service: courage, sacrifice, heroism."[70]

The industry had for decades often mimicked the journalistic article in form and headline as a strategy. In *Advertising, Literature and Print Culture in Ireland, 1891–1922*, John Strachan and Claire Nally survey the ways in which advertising borrowed the likeness of official news by analyzing specific adverts:

> At first glance, before the realization that we are in the presence of a commercial advertisement dawns, this looks like part of the recruitment effort, with its banner evoking the recruitment banner so common elsewhere in the contemporary Irish press. ... Such semi-disguised advertisements, which gesture towards the spirit of the age around them, were especially popular in the turbulent period under discussion here, when readers were hungry for news of war, rebellion and the rebirth of a nation.[71]

These masked advertisements built upon a tradition of patent medicine marketing that aped the form of articles in medical journals and often deployed testimonials from war participants in a way similar to the legitimating endorsements from health-care practitioners in their predecessors. In America, for instance, images of "war casualties quickly popped up in advertisements for a range of commercial products, from Swan pens to Santanogen, a topical disinfectant, [and were] upbeat in tone, mirroring the stories of cheerfully wounded soldiers that filled wartime newspapers."[72] In Ireland, "testimonials from the front were also very common in First World War advertising copy, as members of the soldiery supposedly put pen to paper to commend manufacturers of cigarettes, porridge, nourishing hot drinks and the like, which had sustained them in their hour of darkness."[73] Testimonial performance also was a key facet of enlistment drives, and Shaw's 1915 playlet "O'Flaherty V.C." reveals a shrewd understanding of the interplay between the war industry and modern advertising.

During the summer and fall of 1915, the British army launched an intense enlistment campaign in Ireland, trying to improve recruit totals that were significantly lower than those from England and Scotland. In July, Michael John O'Leary had returned home after becoming the first Irish soldier to be awarded the Victoria Cross for his single-handed capture of two German barricades (including the killing of eight German soldiers) and became the effort's centerpiece, featured prominently in posters and leading parades. When asked by Sir Matthew Nathan, Under-Secretary for Ireland, to aid the sluggish drive, Shaw appropriated O'Leary's celebrity in both the English and Irish press and, as Michael Holroyd puts it, "Shavianized it for the stage."[74] Needless to say, the one act play was not the hoped for endorsement; in consultation with General Sir John French, Commander-in-Chief of Home Forces, Nathan "requested that Shaw postpone the 1916 Abbey Theatre production by the Irish players ... for fear of rioting in Ireland, and because it was felt that some passages of the play taken out of context might be used by the Central Powers for propaganda purposes."[75] "O'Flaherty V.C." would have to wait until February 1917 in Belgium for its first performance.

In their account of the sale of the Formamint brand name, *JAMA*, echoing widespread frustration with patent medicine among medical professionals, bemoans that "the gullibility of the public and unfortunately of many physicians with regard to these preparations appears to be inexhaustible." Similarly irked, Shaw, in so much of his writing about the war, targeted a public gulled by propaganda, and the beginning of "O'Flaherty V.C." seeks to awaken its audiences to the ways in which the war industry marketed patriotism. Building upon the play's subtitle ("A Recruiting Pamphlet"), Shaw begins the preface by again characterizing "O'Flaherty V.C." as a print advertisement: "It may surprise some people to learn that in 1915 this little play was a recruiting poster in disguise."[76] In doing so, he situates the play not only in relation to issues of the war and Irish nationalism but also to advertising, both national and commercial. During the war, such posters and pamphlets were of course ubiquitous and deployed many of the same marketing strategies as product advertising.

When the army began to specifically address Ireland in their recruitment materials,[77] O'Leary, upon whom Shaw bases Dennis O'Flaherty, had been used in 1915 posters in the ways endorsers appeared in patent medicine adverts (among others). Bold banners directly addressing the viewer: "AN IRISH HERO! **1** IRISHMAN DEFEATS 10 GERMANS" heads a likeness of O'Leary's face at the center of a medal "for valour" situated above his name: "SERGEANT MICHAEL O'LEARY, V.C." with "IRISH GUARDS" in green underneath. Consistent with his denials of "any direct correlation between his character and the real life O'Leary," Shaw's play acts in dialogue not with the man but with this advertisement representation. Nonetheless, as Lauren Arlington points out, "the seeming correlation between the fictional soldier and the real-life O'Leary would do little to endear his play to either the civil or the military authorities."[78] Shaw's O'Flaherty, replete with his own Victoria Cross and fresh off a sensational battlefield exploit, seems a similarly perfect testimonial provider. The play's subtitle sets up assumptions as to its ideological thrust only to have them, in typical Shavian fashion, upended in a turnaround that reveals as much about the playwright's understanding of promotional technique as it does his conviction of the "futility of nationalism."[79]

The play begins at the conclusion of a recruiting appearance at an Irish country house, against the aural backdrop of "God Save the King," "It's a Long Way to Tipperary," and cheering from the crowd. The title character emerges onstage "wearily" and "exhausted"[80] in his promotional role, claiming he "never knew what hard work was til [he] took to recruiting":

> What with the standing on my legs all day, and the shaking hands, and the making speeches, and – what's worse – the listening to them, and the calling for cheers for king and country, and the saluting the flag til I'm stiff with it[.]
>
> Already it's drove me to the pitch of tiredness of it that when a poor little innocent slip of a boy in the street the other night drew himself up and saluted and began whistling [Tipperary] at me, I clouted his head for him.[81]

Hardly a ringing affirmation from a celebrity spokesman. As Arlington notes, O'Flaherty is an "unenthusiastic participant in the recruitment campaign," and Shaw "takes a sharp jab at British recruiting propaganda" by evoking the conventional anthems of the war.[82] In contrast, General Sir Pearce Madigan arrives still spewing recruitment copy: "Though I am a general with forty years of service, that little Cross of yours gives you a higher rank in the roll of glory that I can pretend to" (988). Yet, even Madigan is familiar with the mythologizing tendencies of such events. After O'Flaherty's confession that he has lied to his mother and that he is a "ready liar" (992), the General responds by suggesting that, "in recruiting, a man gets carried away" (992) but nonetheless some prudent pruning of the soldier hero's copy might be in order:

## 3 "THE SHADOW OF DISREPUTE": G.B.S. AND TESTIMONIAL MARKETING   83

I stretch it a bit occasionally myself. After all, it's for king and country. But if you won't mind my saying it, O'Flaherty, I think that story about your fighting the Kaiser and the twelve giants of the Prussian guard singlehanded would be the better for a little toning down. I don't ask you to drop it, you know; for it's popular, undoubtedly, but still, the truth is the truth. Don't you think it would fetch in almost as many recruits if you reduced the number of guardsmen to six? (992)

Ignoring the copywriting advice, O'Flaherty swerves away from endorsement, undercutting the reputed heroism of his battlefield act as well as his motives for enlistment. He claims to have no idea what the war is about (994) and isn't sure "about its being a great war [although] it's a big war; but that's not the same thing" (995). In response, Sir Pearce is incredulous: "have you no knowledge of the causes of the war? Of the interests at stake? Of the importance—I may almost say—in fact I will say—the sacred rights for which we are fighting? Don't you read the papers?" (994). O'Flaherty's extended reply squarely takes on Dublin Castle's ideological cloaking:

> It's in the nature of governments to tell lies ... what use is all the lying, and pretending, and humbugging and letting on, when the day comes to you that your comrade is killed in the trench besides you, and you don't as much as look round at him until you trip over his poor body, and then all you say is to ask why the hell the stretcher-bearers don't take it out of the way. Why should I read the papers to be humbugged and lied to by them that had the cunning to stay at home and send me to fight for them? Don't talk to me or to any solider of the war being right. No war is right. (1005, 996)

As Terry Phillips suggests, "from almost the first words he speaks, O'Flaherty is transformed from the ignorant peasant he at first appears to a version of the Shakespearean Fool enunciating uncomfortable truths, anticipating Joan."[83] In marketing terms, the veteran is also transformed from the celebrity personality enlisted to endorse the product into one whose testimony leads in another direction.

For Shaw, O'Flaherty's "experience in the trenches has induced in him a terrible realism and an unbearable candor" that renders him unable to tow the promotional line.[84] As a result, Murray Biggs argues that this play is not the merely amusing trifle it at first seems to be but, rather, an uncomfortably pessimistic account of the way things are and for the foreseeable future will be. As the work's protagonist gloomily prophesies, one war or another will make "no great differ" to the state of the world as it fundamentally is.[85]

However, in the preface, Shaw writes that it may come as a "surprise" to the reader that the play is in fact a "recruiting poster in disguise"; if O'Flaherty's shreds the army's patriotic appeal derived from romanticized British nationalism, Shaw replaces it with a different marketing approach. For Terry Phillips,

> the word "surprise" suggests a tension between intention and effect, a tension that ... resides in the question of audience. The basis for regarding the play as a recruiting play is fairly sound, given the assumption that it was written, at least in the first instance, for an Irish audience.[86]

Writing his preface from a postwar perspective in 1919, Shaw claims that "Irish recruiting was badly bungled in 1915" because, while "it was quite easy to enlist them by approaching them from their own point of view[,] the War Office insisted on approaching them from the point of view of Dublin Castle." Hence, the "placards headed 'Remember Belgium' ... led Irishmen to remember Limerick and its broken treaty" while, in response to "a fresh appeal [of] 'Irishmen: Do You Wish to Have the Horrors of War Brought to Your Own Hearths and Homes?', Dublin laughed sourly" (986). In contrast, Shaw claims he, with his play, sought to "appeal to [the Irishman's] discontent, his deadly boredom, his thwarted curiosity and desire for change and adventure." In short, Irish recruitment will be successful when it seeks to capitalize on the fact that "an Irishman's hopes and ambitions turn on his opportunities of getting out of Ireland."[87]

Shaw's manifesto on recruitment is consistent with contemporary thinking about marketing in general. The J. Walter Thompson Agency revolutionized the practice before the war with a decision to "approach the reader from his own point of view, instead of the manufacturer's," a move that would accelerate the development of market research and focus group testing as well as significantly enhance the profile of the celebrity testimonial.[88] Unfortunately, as Shaw suggests, even though his "own [promotional] line was the more businesslike," his "play thus carefully adapted to its purpose was voted utterly inadmissible" (987). Overall, the play's deflation of recruitment rhetoric is consistent with "Shaw's wartime prose [which], like his 1890s theatre criticism, is an attempt to educate the public to be good, alert, demanding critics instead of sentimental dupes."[89]

In *Judging Shaw*, Fintan O'Toole argues that, on the one hand, "the Great War marks the natural death of GBS [because] it revealed, through the scale of its horror, all the hidden truths that GBS delighted in exposing; the shock of 'Common Sense About the War' ... finished GBS."[90] On the other, though, it was an opportunity to rebrand "G.B.S." from a critic who "[shows] liberal society the beasts in its cellars" to a "saint and prophet of a new religion," the Life Force:

> The killing off of the comic version of GBS had the odd effect of making GBS even more famous as a serious visionary. ... To have been reviled for standing out against the hysteria of war fever was, as the war became ever more cataclysmic, a sign that Shaw saw things other people did not. In the disillusioned post-war atmosphere, he became less of a devil and more of a saint, less of a provocateur and more of a prophet. ... He was popular before the war and even more so after it[, but] it was not the same *kind* of popularity. The dead version of GBS could not simply be resurrected – a different one took its place.[91]

In this light, Shaw's direct participation in the Harrods and Simmons campaigns in the late 1920s can be ascribed to a specific desire not so much to repair his popular reputation as to orchestrate a "brand reboot" and to affirm his ethos as a public advocate. Besides Formamint, every campaign in this study is marked by the playwright's volitional and conspicuous participation. With the viability of public personality and marketing tactics in question, Shaw and modern advertising would have to continue to hone the testimonial to recover from "old mistakes of promotion."[92]

That both are unmistakably on the same page is clear from "O'Flaherty V.C.". In its preface, Shaw discerns the British army's recruitment failure to be a marketing miscalculation with regard to its target audience, and his proposed correction, illustrated through "O'Flaherty V.C.," mirrors a significant, simultaneous shift in the world of commercial advertising to "approach the reader from his own point of view, instead of the manufacturer's," a move that rescues the testimonial technique from the patent medicine scrapheap.[93] The copy text in the recruiting poster that featured Michael John O'Leary was explicit in directly addressing its reader: "HAVE YOU NO WISH TO EMULATE THE SPLENDID BRAVERY OF YOUR FELLOW COUNTRYMAN? JOIN AN IRISH REGIMENT TO-DAY." It boldly articulates the subtext of so-called "personality advertising," what Stanley Resor of the J. Walter Thompson agency deemed the "spirit of emulation" in which consumers seek to imitate "those whom we deem superior to us in taste, knowledge or experience."[94] Before he turns to direct participation in product campaigns, Shaw's place in the earliest moments of the genealogy of the personality testimonial and thus the history of modern advertising is evident in how he brokered print appearances to market both that "G.B.S." was "a superior mind [who] therefore must be given the reader's attention" and that "this superiority was a kind of temporary state, that the reader too, in learning how to be skeptical, could rise to the same level."[95]

## Notes

1. "Comparative Values of Newspapers and Plays in Questions of the Day." *The Editor and Publisher* 9.34 (19 February 1910): 8.
2. He notoriously argued that critics "have no qualifications": We can say exactly what we like. Nobody will interfere with us at all. And we are irremovable. We are entirely irresponsible. ... Under those circumstances men always do their worst and they always will do their worst. There is no remedy whatever for it. Revealing again his approach to criticism as marketing, Shaw felt "consolation" that, although his plays were subject to their mistreatment, "every notice I get advertises me." Charles A. Selden. "Shaw Tells Critics They're Never Good." *New York Times* (12 October 1929): 7.
3. Gerry Beegan. *The Mass Image: A Social History of Photomechanical Reproduction in Victorian London.* New York: Palgrave Macmillan, 2008. 16, 126, 127.
4. Ibid., 16.
5. Ibid., 17, 16.
6. Jonathan Goldman. "Celebrity." In *George Bernard Shaw in Context.* Ed. Brad Kent. Cambridge: Cambridge University Press, 2015. 255–64. 263, 255.
7. Michael Holroyd. *Bernard Shaw, Volume One: 1856–1898: The Search for Love.* New York: Vintage Books, 1988. 105.
8. Ibid., 104.
9. "Mr. Charles Chassé Investigates Bernard Shaw's Philosophy." *New York Times* (13 December 1908): SM4.
10. William D. Tyler. "The Image, the Brand, and the Consumer." *Journal of Marketing* 22.2 (October 1957): 162–5. 162.

11. Roy Church. "Advertising Consumer Goods in Nineteenth-Century Britain: Reinterpretations." *The Economic History Review* 53.4 (November 2000): 621–45. 633.
12. Ibid., 633–4.
13. Beegan, 4–5.
14. Church, 636, 640.
15. Felix Orman. "Picture Advertising Is "Flash" Advertising." *Advertising & Selling* 28.28 (15 March 1919): 11.
16. Beegan, 16.
17. Marlis Schweitzer and Marina Moskowitz. "Introduction." In *Testimonial Advertising in the American Marketplace: Emulation, Identity, Community*. Eds. Marlis Schweitzer and Marina Moskowitz. New York: Palgrave Macmillan, 2009. 1–22. 5.
18. Ibid., 1.
19. Ibid., 7.
20. William M. Freeman. *The Big Name*. New York: Printers' Ink Books, 1957. 12.
21. Goldman, 256.
22. Schweitzer and Moskowitz, 7.
23. James W. Egbert. "What Makes a Good Testimonial." *Printers' Ink* 77.2 (12 October 1911): 44, 46.
24. Schweitzer and Moskowitz, 5.
25. Joel H. Kaplan and Sheila Stowell. *Theatre and Fashion: Oscar Wilde to the Suffragettes*. Cambridge: Cambridge University Press, 1994. 11, 10, 2.
26. "Fifty Years 1888–1938." *Printers' Ink* 184.4 (28 July 1938): Section Two, 49.
27. Beegan, 102.
28. Bernard Shaw. *Dramatic Opinions and Essays with an Apology from Bernard Shaw*, vol. 2. New York: Brentano's, 1928. 189.
29. Beegan, 5.
30. Marlis Schweitzer. "'The Mad Search for Beauty': Actresses' Testimonials, the Cosmetics Industry, and the 'Democratization of Beauty'." *The Journal of the Gilded Age and Progressive Era* 4.3 (July 2005): 255–92, 264. During his days as a critic, Shaw periodically wrote about renowned opera singer Adelina Patti. Her biographer writes that the playwright "admired the perfection of her voice [but] disapproved of her unambitious repertoire and her way of courting applause." Yvonne Rogers. *Adelina: A Biography of Opera Star Adelina Patti*. The Book Guild Ltd., 2017. Patti was an early and eager participant in product endorsement and contributed so many endorsements for myriad products that she garnered the sobriquet "Testimonial Patti."
31. 'Fifty Years 1888–1938,' 111, 118.

32. Kerry Segrave. *Endorsements in Advertising: A Social History.* Jefferson, NC: McFarland & Company, Inc., Publishers, 2005. 4.
33. Schweitzer, 264
34. Ibid., 273.
35. Ibid., 257.
36. T. R. Nevett. *Advertising in Britain: A History.* London: The History of Advertising Trust, 1982. 159–60.
37. Schweitzer, 274.
38. "E. P. Downing and C. Downing." In *Shaw the Villager and Human Being: A Biographical Symposium.* Ed. Allan Chappelow. London: Charles Skilton Ltd., 1961.
39. *Dublin Journal of Medical Science* 125 (January–June 1908). Dublin: Fannin & Company, Ltd., 1908. 239–40.
40. "An Epitome of Current Medical Literature." *The British Medical Journal* 2 (1908): 40.
41. "A Case of Poisoning by Formamint Tablets." *The British Medical Journal* 2.2494 (17 October 1908): 1224.
42. Charles W. Hurd. "How Price Maintenance of One Article Helps Another." *Printers' Ink* 83.2 (10 April 1913): 65–6, 69.
43. "Formamint: The So-Called Germ-Killing Throat Tablet." *Journal of the American Medical Association* 58.8 (24 February 1912): 572.
44. Bernard Shaw. *Collected Letters 1911–1925.* Ed. Dan H. Laurence. New York: Viking, 1985. 89.
45. Ibid., 112.
46. "E. P. Downing," 235. Curiously, Shaw asks for riboflavin if the Formamint is unavailable. Downing believes that him to be "a bit mixed up here" since the former is not "a substitute" for the latter. While the two products are "quite dissimilar in action," the chemist asserts that "both substances have in common some action on the taste-buds in the tongue."
47. Bernard Shaw. "The Life Force: Mr. Bernard Shaw's reply to Mr. Campbell." *The Christian Commonwealth* (3 July 1912): 655.
48. Alice McEwan. "George Bernard Shaw and his Writing Hut: Privacy and Publicity as Performance at Shaw's Corner." *Interiors* 2.3 (2011): 333–56. 344.
49. "Mr. Bernard Shaw on Formamint." *Collier's* 53 (5 December 1914): 26.
50. Alice McEwan. "Commodities, Consumption, and Connoisseurship: Shaw's Critique of Authenticity in Modernity." *SHAW: The Journal of Bernard Shaw Studies* 35.1 (November 2015): 46–85. 73.
51. Harold Lister. "Health for Intellectuals." *The New Age* 13.9 (26 June 1913): 228.
52. Pierre Loving. "Autumn." *The Drama* 13 (November 1922): 61–3. 61.

53. "Formamint." *Journal of the American Medical Association* 65.9 (28 August 1915): 816–9. 819.
54. "Formaldehyde Lozenges." *Journal of the American Medical Association* 73.14 (4 October 1919): 1077.
55. "German Patents and Trademarks in England." *Scientific American* 3.20 (14 November 1914): 402.
56. Formamint's patent had been annulled in November of 1913 in Berlin when the courts determined it was not, as claimed a "new" chemical compound.
57. "Purchase of the Santogen Company." *The Journal of the American Medical Association* 67.25 (16 December 1916): 1861–2. 1861.
58. "Chesterton on Shaw." *The Nation* (21 October 1909): 375. Quoted in Eric Bentley. *Bernard Shaw*. New York: Applause, 2002. 212.
59. Augustus Hamon. *Bernard Shaw: The Twentieth Century Molière*. Trans. Eden and Cedar Paul. New York: Frederick A. Stokes Company Publishers, 1916. 108.
60. A. M. Gibbs. *Bernard Shaw: A Life*. Gainesville: University Press of Florida, 2005. 349.
61. Michael Holroyd. *Bernard Shaw Volume Two: 1898–1918, The Pursuit of Power*. New York: Vintage Books, 1989. 356.
62. Bernard Shaw. *Collected Letters*, vol. 3. Ed. Dan H. Laurence. New York: Viking, 1985. 239–40.
63. Michael Holroyd. *Bernard Shaw: The One Volume Definitive Edition*. New York: Random House, 1997. 453, 452.
64. Fintan O'Toole. *Judging Shaw: The Radicalism of GBS*. Dublin: Prism, 2017. 245.
65. A. M. Gibbs, ed. *Shaw: Recollections and Interviews*. London: Macmillan, 1990. 231.
66. Lee Simonson. "Mobilizing the Billboards." *New Republic* 13 (10 November 1917), 41–43. 43.
67. Nevett, 139.
68. Terry Phillips. "Shaw, Ireland, and World War 1: 'O'Flaherty V.C.', An Unlikely Recruiting Play." *SHAW: The Annual of Bernard Shaw Studies* 30 (2010): 133–46. 89.
69. John Strachan and Claire Nally. *Advertising, Literature and Print Culture in Ireland, 1891–1922*. New York: Palgrave Macmillan, 2012. 226.
70. John Kinder. "Marketing Disabled Manhood: Veterans and Advertising since the Civil War." *Phallacies: Historical Intersections of Disability and Masculinity*. Eds. Kathleen M. Brian and James W. Trent, Jr. Oxford: Oxford University Press, 2017. 93–125. 103.
71. Strachan/Nally, 231–2.
72. Kinder, 103.

73. Strachan and Nally, 228.
74. Holroyd, *The One Volume Definitive Edition*, 466.
75. Bernard Shaw. *What Shaw Really Wrote About the War*. Eds. J. L. Wisenthal and Daniel O'Leary. Gainesville: University Press of Florida, 2006. xviii.
76. Bernard Shaw. "Preface" to "O'Flaherty V.C." In *The Bodley Head Bernard Shaw: Collected Plays with Their Prefaces*, vol. 4. London: The Bodley Head, 1971. 985–7, 985.
77. Terry Phillips refers to "one study of the recruiting posters collected in the Trinity College collection that concludes that 'in 1914 no poster referred to Ireland, while in 1916–17 Irish and unspecific posters were evenly balanced'" (135).
78. Lauren Arlington. "The Censorship of 'O'Flaherty V.C.'." *SHAW: The Annual of Bernard Shaw Studies* 28 (2008): 85–106. 90.
79. Phillips, 142.
80. Bernard Shaw. "O'Flaherty V.C." In *The Bodley Head Bernard Shaw: Collected Plays with Their Prefaces*, vol. 4. London: The Bodley Head, 1971. 983–1014, 988.
81. Ibid., 989–90.
82. Arlington, 91.
83. Phillips, 141.
84. Letter to Lady Gregory, quoted in *Shaw, Lady Gregory, and the Abbey*. Eds. Nicholas Grene and Dan. H. Laurence. Gerrards Cross: Colin Smythe, 1993. 95
85. Murray Biggs. "Shaw's Recruiting Pamphlet." *SHAW: The Annual of Bernard Shaw Studies* 28 (2008): 107–11. 110.
86. Phillips, 134.
87. Incidentally, "O'Flaherty V.C." again became a "recruiting poster in disguise" in another sense when Shaw, in 1924, read the play over the airwaves as part of British radio broadcasting's efforts to enlist the playwright "to lend his international reputation to its struggle for credibility." Robert G. Everding. "Shaw and the Popular Context." In *The Cambridge Companion to George Bernard Shaw*. Ed. Christopher Innes. Cambridge: Cambridge University Press, 1998. 309–33. 319.
88. "Mr. Resor Leads Discussion on 'Personality Advertising." *The J. Walter Thompson News Letter* 10.8 (13 April 1928): 137–50. 139.
89. J. L. Wisenthal and Daniel O'Leary. "Introduction." *What Shaw Really Wrote About the War*. Eds. J. L. Wisenthal and Daniel O'Leary. Gainesville: University Press of Florida, 2006. 12.

90. O'Toole, 240, 244.
91. Ibid., 290, 251, 248.
92. It would, of course, mark the start of one of Shaw's most creative and prolific periods as a playwright, a decade that would see the arrival of *Heartbreak House*, *Saint Joan*, *Back to Methuselah*, and a Nobel prize, buoyed by what Michael Holroyd deems a "recovery of interest" in his earlier plays through productions in Ireland, America, England, and across Europe (467).
93. "Mr. Resor Leads Discussion" 139. The innovative Stanley Resor took over as president and co-owner of the J. Walter Thompson agency in 1916.
94. Stanley Resor. "Personalities and the Public: Some Aspects of Testimonial Advertising." *New Bulletin* 138 (April 1929): 1. J. Walter Thompson Information Center Records, Box 4, Testimonial Advertising, 1928–1977. John W. Hartman Center for Sales, Advertising, and Marketing History, Rare Book, Manuscript and Special Collections Library, Duke University, 1.
95. O'Toole, 308.

CHAPTER 4

# "The Biggest Scoop in Advertising History": Personality Marketing, G.B.S., and the Near-Testimonial

In the fall of 1911, as the testimonial sought to put its association with patent medicine far behind it, James W. Egbert wrote a five-part series in *Printers' Ink* on the technique in the spirit of rehabilitation. He noted "a certain prejudice" against the testimonial "on the part of the general public," proceeding less from "a determination not to be influenced by them [than] a tendency to skip them – to regard them as rather dull and uninteresting affairs." His advice in one column is to endow them with "some attention-getting qualities,"[1] and agencies sought in the decade after the war ways to not only differentiate their testimonial marketing from that of their competitors but also distance it from its own checkered past. The "G.B.S." brand too had suffered a challenge to its efficacy after the publication of *Common Sense about the War* in 1914 but showed signs of recovery when Shaw was invited to tour the Front in 1917 and witnessed a resurgence of stagings of his plays in Britain, Ireland, Europe, and the United States.[2] Heading into the 1920s, advertising, the testimonial technique, and Shaw were on the rebound.

If his involuntary participation in the Formamint campaign demonstrates the ways in which his brand could be appropriated by others, he seems with "O'Flaherty V.C." to be turning the testimonial inside out, laying the groundwork for his "near-testimonial" contributions to product campaigns in the next decade. Shaw is vehement that his play is not satirical but a genuine recruitment pamphlet in which the central character refuses to endorse enlistment in terms dictated by the British army but lays bare motives for young Irishmen to sign up. In that sense, the play is not an "anti-testimonial" but perhaps more accurately characterized as a "near testimonial," the phrase used by an advertising executive to describe Shaw's contribution to a commercial campaign for Harrods in 1929 but one that just as aptly fits his participation in later campaigns for Simmons and Pan-American World Airways.

Characterized by T. R. Nevett as "the golden age of advertising,"[3] the interwar period saw enormous growth in the industry, fierce competition between newspapers, the advent of new media (most notably radio and cinema), and an increase in both professional and governmental regulation to enhance credibility. In addition,

> all facets of the endorsement industry grew strongly in the 1920s, including ads featuring testifiers who were ordinary citizens, and sometimes companies. However, the concept of the unsolicited testimonial letter arriving in the morning mail was mainly fiction. They were actively sought.[4]

If the theater had been integral to the phenomenon of testimonial endorsement in the late nineteenth century, it is the Hollywood "star system" in the 1920s that reanimated the testimonial industry but regrettably allowed its endorsers much less autonomy than stage actresses had enjoyed. Making "it a custom to prevent its stars from signing any letters of endorsement [without] permission,"[5] the studios often would receive a portion of the proceeds for loaning a performer out and eventually exploited such arrangements as part of the cycle of publicity for films. In *The Story of Advertising* (1958), James Playsted Wood retrospectively characterizes the advertising of the 1920s as "exaggerated, devious, [and] strident," and attributes the hyperbolic proliferation of endorsements more to mass culture than economics:

> With the eagerness of newly made converts at a prayer meeting, celebrities pressed to testify to their exclusive use of one brand of cigarettes to coffee, soap or automobile [for] the publicity and the fees.[6]

As a result, by the end of the decade, as it had at the turn of the century, the industry grew concerned that this critical mass of testimonials as well as the lingering stigma of scandal would not only torpedo an effective marketing strategy but call into question the whole business of advertising itself:

Alarmed, the advertising trade press inveighed against "tainted testimonials," as *Printers' Ink* called them. ... The Federal Trade Commission passed a ruling against the use of testimonials unless the advertisements containing them stated that a fee had been paid to the endorser whose name was used. The Better Business Bureau published a recommended code saying that testimonials should be honest, sincere, and reliable. None of this made much difference.[7]

In 1929, executive and one-time president of the American Association of Advertising Agencies, H. S. Gardner wrote,

> The advertising world has been bitten badly by the prostituted testimonial and the hue and cry which has been set up in protest is providing the publicity needed for the cure. The surest way to stop this business of commercializing matinee idols, heroes, debutantes, society leaders and royalty is to do more of what we are doing now – i.e., increase the agitation against the practice. If the searchlight of publicity is turned on full force it will soon become unpopular to practice the testimonial chicanery.[8]

Shaw's participation in two product campaigns in 1929, one for Harrods and one for Simmons mattresses, plants him in the middle of the industry controversy over what to do with the testimonial.

Throughout its journey from the mid-nineteenth century to early twentieth century, on behalf of proprietary health products, beauty supplies, and cosmetics, the narrative structure of the testimonial endured, drawing

> directly on patterns of evangelical culture [and] closely [resembling] the standard accounts of conversion experience: the cries of the converted testified to the soul's deliverance from suffering. In the patent medicine literature, soul-sickness took bodily form and required physical intervention.[9]

In typical Shavian fashion, Shaw's near-testimonials never followed such an arc, and their appeal for advertisers is not difficult to understand, as their uniqueness worked to erase any association with patent medicine marketing. Just as his early plays turned the conventions of melodrama inside-out, his copy flouted expectation, exploiting the opportunity not only to creatively evolve his personal brand but to do so on behalf of Creative Evolution itself. As Jonathan Goldman maintains, Shaw "became a totem of individuality, an icon whose self-production parallels that of the greatest celebrities and the most exemplary modernist writers of his time."[10] On the industry side, despite the taint, the continued turn towards "personality marketing" provoked innovation in form, the professionalizing of writers within the industry, and the delineation of *modern* advertising.

Always styling itself at the vanguard of groundbreaking industry practices, the J. Walter Thompson company originated the business model for the modern advertising agency, offering "clients a 'full service' based around the four pillars of creative work, research, media planning (print, radio, cinema and outdoor) and account managements, the bridge in the relationship between client and agency."[11] In a March 1929 address delivered to agency executives, JWT President Stanley Resor officially announced that a new cycle in advertising was underway:

> "People like to read about other people." That simple discovery has changed the complexion of every existing medium through which public opinion is formed. It has affected profoundly the editing of newspapers, magazines, books, lectures, movies, and the radio. It has raised up an army of publicity men, propagandists, "public relations counselors," and "ghost writers."[12]

Resor went on to assert that, since "advertising is in direct competition with editorial features for the reader's attention [and] when practically every publication of large circulation relies on personalities to secure and hold readers, it is obvious that the public will relish personalities when properly employed in advertising."[13]

A year before that address, the April 13, 1928 issue of *The J. Walter Thompson News Letter* provided an account of a "discussion" at a recent "production meeting" led by Resor, on the subject of what he called "personality advertising" in an era in which "the public imagination is captured by personalities."[14] During the presentation, previous JWT campaigns for "Ponds, Royal, Lux, Fleischmann, Simmons, Pennsylvania, Woodbury, Carter were called to the stand to bear witness to the power of personality in advertising" as department heads summarized the process of their creation, including the solicitation and compensation of celebrity endorsers.[15] The mandate was to create novel methods of commercially deploying "personalities" drawn from the theater, the movies, high society, and professional fields such as sports, science, industry, and occasionally even literature.[16]

Of course, the manufacture and marketing of personality were also consuming occupations of literary culture at the same time. Seeking to bridge the vexed relationship between High Modernism and mass culture via the emergent discourse of modern celebrity, a flurry of recent scholarship has charted a genealogy that usually credits Oscar Wilde with laying the conceptual groundwork for the branding techniques of James Joyce, Ezra Pound, and Gertrude Stein (among others) that reconceived the notion of authorship. Aaron Jaffe, for instance, posits an "unavoidable kinship between modernism's exaggerated forms of authorial immanence and the exaggerating work of publicity, promotion, and celebrity."[17] Similarly, Jonathan Goldman maintains that placing "modernism's view of the author alongside the production of popular celebrity [reveals] the relationship between these supposedly divergent spheres of culture as more of a collaboration than a parting of ways of cultural production."[18]

Goldman and Jaffe, among others, have compellingly illuminated the ways in which High Modernists appropriate promotional strategies from the marketplace to produce a discourse of elitist authorship that valorized the imprimatur in order to create distance between their work and mass culture.[19] This critical work attempts to ford the impasse created by the "long history of friction between champions of literature on the one hand and advertising on the other," each striving to impose a hierarchical and "radical incongruity" on their relationship.[20]

As scholars have mapped productively the branding machinations of High Modernist authorship, this chapter seeks to texture further this "collaboration" by providing insight into how executives and writers in the industry worked to render profitable mergings of literary personality with commodities. For their part, High Modernists were eager to efface rather than embrace any symbiotic affinity between the worlds of literature and commerce. On the advertising side, executives wrangled to harness the potency of personality but avoid certain stigmas of testimonial endorsement when employing literary authors, including questions of compensation and authority that potentially undermine its effectiveness. As *Advertiser's Weekly* put it in March of 1929, "while most of the authors, naturally enough, concern themselves with the possible menace of advertisement writing to literary standards, the advertising menace, also naturally enough, is apprehensive of the effect the practice would have on advertising standards."[21]

Illustrating what is at stake in the proximity between the two fields, two campaigns in the late 1920s garnered considerable transatlantic fanfare for crafting "near-testimonials" from literary authors as a way to ward off the specter of impropriety and maintain the integrity of stakeholders, each pursuing their respective aims. The influence of a Harrods campaign involving Bernard Shaw, H. G. Wells, and Arnold Bennett is unusually far-reaching within the evolution of modern advertising and the fashioning of literary modernism. JWT's Simmons campaign situates literary authors at the center of a controversy over the celebrity testimonial as a marketing technique. Taken together, both are case studies for how the advertising industry, like the High Modernists, emerges from their "collaboration" with new concepts in professional identity and strategies for the promotion of personality.

In his April 1927 speech at the opening of the British Industries Fair in Birmingham, the Prince of Wales directed "young business and professional men" to "adopt, adapt, improve" their methods; in particular, he urged them to investigate those American practices that had produced a "wave of industrial prosperity" and the degree to which they could be imported and implemented in England. His comments triggered an immediate reaction in the country's private sector and became an opportunity for professional self-assessment in many fields, including commercial promotion. As a way to "adapt and improve" methods of salesmanship, the marketing department at Harrods in May 1928 developed the idea of approaching England's most famous living writers because, according to one executive,

> we have long felt that advertising has not been keeping pace with the display of goods and the organization and art of business. Nor has the story of this firm and its romance ever been adequately presented by the written word as great writers are capable of presenting it. We went to the three leading writers of the world, hoping we might enlist their aid in improving the whole tone and the whole future of advertising. ... You cannot expect the man who makes the goods, and the man who sells them, to preach the gospel about them as these great writers could do. And that is why we approached them to give the benefit of their literary genius to the future of advertising.[22]

Arnold Bennett was the first author solicited because, according to Charles Wildes, director of Harrods, "he [had] long been an enthusiastic customer of the store."[23] The pitch was to be that, since "the stock of Harrods is 95 per cent British owned," creating a series of signed advertisements would enable Bennett "to repay the country for a lifetime of benefits received." After the author expressed concern that his book sales would suffer if he participated, Wildes claimed that Bennett then "was challenged to write an advertisement on the basis that he was unpatriotic and cowardly not to do so."[24] The author eventually agreed and, in a response entitled "I Will Not Flout Public Opinion," claimed that he was quite interested in accepting Harrods' offer but was forced to turn it down because of "public opinion in Britain," which was "not yet ripe to approve the employment of responsible imaginative writers to whom it has granted a reputation, in any scheme of publicity for a commercial concern."[25] While he disagreed with such a perception, Bennett was unwilling to "lose caste by attempting to create a precedent which could result, for [him], in nothing save a disadvantageous notoriety." Nevertheless, the first half of Bennett's rejection letter, in ostensibly reiterating Harrods' proposal for the reader, slyly provides ample suitable endorsements for the store:

> You remind me that, as is well known, your business is among the largest, most comprehensive, and most famous of its kind in the world. You say that it counts notably in the industrial and mercantile life of the community, that your regular staff comprises an immense and constantly increasing number of citizens of both sexes, and that you use every honest endeavor to be of commercial service to the community. You say further that you buy the best available materials and commodities that research can procure, and that you employ the best organisers, technicians, artists, designers, architects, and craftsmen of every sort that you can discover.

Over the next nine months, negotiations with H. G. Wells and Bernard Shaw took place, each invited by Harrods to write periodical publicity on any aspect of the store that inspired them. The store took a risk in not mandating complimentary pieces but made anything the writers produced the intellectual property of the store. Rather than simply refuse, both authors wrote letters of apologia as well.

Wells grounded his opposition in the idea that "in his heart [the writer] classes himself not with the artists but with the teachers and the priests and the prophets" and that his "only paymaster ought to be the reader."[26] Shaw's, the most elaborate, argues that his obligation to the common good prevented him from accepting the offer: "A writer who has been concentrated by Fame to the service of the public, and has thus become prophet as well as author, must take wages in no other service."[27] He begins with the assertion that "there is nothing new in what you call the linking of forces between the commercial and literary world," citing the examples of Callisthenes and the Fortnum and Mason catalogues as "two triumphs of commercial literature." They represent the perfect balance of posterity value in the future and consumer tantalizing in the present, "treasured by collectors and ... read by me with delight, and with just that watering of the mouth that they are intended to provoke." As Alice McEwan points out, Shaw's "satire ironically evokes Harrods's rival in elite consumption Fortnum and Mason, and simultaneously mocks the relationship of connoisseurs to this form of shopping (himself included)."[28] Original readers also would have immediately recognized "Callisthenes" as the author of numerous short "article-advertisements" opining on matters of commercial industry that appeared daily in newspapers for nearly thirty years. While some at the time suspected these pieces were written by Shaw, "Callisthenes" was actually the pen name used by another industry competitor, Gordon Selfridge, who supposedly "spent £60,000 pounds on this particular kind of advertising" that was adorned only with "the company's name, at top or bottom."[29] Selfridge's unique pieces, according to Elizabeth Outka, "achieved wide cultural capital; they were quoted in sermons, reprinted in periodicals such as the *Harvard Business Magazine*, and used as models of writing in schools."[30] This cheeky nod to two of Harrods' promotional antagonists sets the stage for Shaw's declinature.

Paralleling concerns expressed early on in his career over the ways in which commercialism was dangerously infusing theatrical practice, Shaw here recounts his discovery upon becoming a drama critic of a seamier underside to this relationship between trade and literature, what he calls "a secret alliance between the two forces" perpetrated by "unashamed and inveterate cadgers" in which publicity was obtained through an ersatz spoils system. Writers would leverage their media access to obtain perks (hotel rooms, meals, theater tickets, shop discounts, honoraria, etc.); in return, vendors, manufacturers, and producers received "puffs" (sly product placement and endorsement) in published journalism of various genres. For his part, Shaw claims he "could not bring [himself] to practice it or to regard it otherwise than as corrupt and personally dishonorable." By the end of the 1920s, he felt that this relationship has become legitimated: "Now that the art of selling has so much more importance than the routine of production, it is a matter of course for commercial firms to employ the best available artistic and literary talent to advertise their wares and services." Nothing wrong there, until the struggle for promotional supremacy devolves to a competition to bias the authorities rather than the consumer. He uses the analogy of a legal dispute between Harrods and Selfridges, for which each attempts to employ the most eloquent and persuasive attorney as opposed to each striving to curry favor with the judge and jury. Applied to theater, Shaw imagines a scenario in which he suggests to critics that, "in the event of their notices of [his] play being sufficiently flattering to be usefully quoted as advertisements," they would each receive £500 from the playwright for the copyright. For him, anyone who writes "in a judicial capacity" (which includes "all authors whose work is of sufficient weight and depth to have a formative effect on the public mind") is honor bound to remain aloof from the marketplace:

> To propose such a transaction to Mr. H. G. Wells is like offering the Archbishop of Canterbury a handsome cheque for dropping a recommendation of somebody's soap or shoes into his next sermon. For such an author to accept payment from a commercial enterprise for using his influence to induce the public to buy its wares would be to sin against the Holy Ghost.[31]

Despite their respective stances, Bennett, Wells, and Shaw, as Jackson Lears observes,

> were in fundamental sympathy with modernizing tendencies: the hegemony of technical expertise and bureaucratic organization, the mass production and marketing of consumer goods (though Shaw and Wells might have entered a few Fabian quibbles about ownership of the means of production or inequalities of distribution).[32]

All three had ambivalent views on commodity culture, well aware that it was often fraudulent, "desultory and possibly detrimental to society's progress; yet [at the same time potentially] a means of achieving social change and autonomy."[33] Among many of that generation, there existed too a progressive faith in advertisement, that it could be more than merely the "spark plug of the total industrial machine" that subjected citizens to Private Enterprise.[34] In 1914, for instance, Wells's and Shaw's fellow Fabian Sidney Webb argued for "the bringing of [advertising] under Democratic public control" and refashioned into an agent of the commonweal, animated by altruism, wholly engaged in public service rather than serving the ruthless appetite of capitalism.[35] Fulfilling its quid pro quo with Harrods, Shaw's refusal letter self-sculpts the author in similar terms, as having prophet rather than profit motives.

As Archibald Henderson put it,

> To those who understand Shaw, the popular conception of him as merely a super-clever journalist who could always make "the front page" is offensive and disgusting [because] he had the profoundest respect and jealousy for the sanctity of the written word, and regarded his function as writer as a high public responsibility [anathema to selling] his name, to [bartering] his influence for trade or commerce or propaganda.[36]

Ironically enough, though, Shaw's differentiation of artistic language and commercial copy in his Harrods response echoes the rationalizations of many stakeholders in the health industry; pharmaceutical companies, doctors, and proprietary medicine manufacturers also draped their marketplace maneuvers with the ideology of public interest and consumer protection in the early years of the twentieth century when their advertising techniques had come under heavy fire. The position was also one Shaw had surely seen before. In Ireland, throughout the second half of the nineteenth century,

> "advertising papers," gratis and paid for, both took advertisements and advertised themselves as vehicles for commercial messages. ... Advertising was vital to Irish newspapers long before the Free State and its champions ... claimed that it was spur to economic renewal. ... Advertisers, like philanthropic investors in home industries, claimed that their motivations went beyond mere money grubbing and, indeed, served a decidedly higher purpose in sponsoring the development of the nation.[37]

Ultimately, Harrods printed all three responses, "by permission and without comment" from the authors, in the March 3rd issue of the *Observer* to coincide with the annual British Industries Fair. The London *Times* printed only Wells's and Bennett's letters, refusing Shaw's because of the reference to the Holy Ghost. The letters also ran as a series of full-page *New York Times* ads in March of 1929, with Bennett's ad as the first on the 13th followed by Wells's on the 14th and Shaw's the last on the 15th.[38] The series made a considerable impression, not so much for the fact that noted authors contributed copy (which had been done before) but more for the unusual form the copy took (e.g. letters *refusing* to provide copy). For example, a contemporary *Advertiser's Weekly* cartoon by W. A. Mann envisions all three authors as school children (see Fig. 4.1). Wells and Bennett cling to the black skirts of the very Victorian-looking "Mother Public Opinion," the latter entranced by the coin held up by Sir Woodman Burbidge, managing director of Harrods. Standing behind him, Shaw puckishly prepares to pour a pitcher of water into Woodman's top hat. The caption reads, "Uncle Woodman finds Arnold, Herbert, and Bernard untippable, but Mother Public Opinion thinks he's such a kind gentleman, nevertheless."[39]

One of the unique footnotes to this series was the amount of paratextual apparatus it generated that blurred the lines between commerce and journalism since excerpts from the letters were printed again and again in feature pieces on the campaign that appeared in periodicals of various kinds. Trade journals from both sides of the Atlantic were quick to air their own perspectives while also making space in their pages for those of numerous professionals. On March 21, *Printers' Ink*, a New York-based weekly and the industry's leading trade publication, noted that "many publishers, advertising men, and, it is presumed, members of the general public, wondered and talked about the recent full-page advertisements of Harrods, London department store, in the New York *Times*."[40] Appearing in the same issue of the *New York Times* that ran Shaw's ad, an op-ed entitled "Ingenious Advertising" conveyed the saga of how the "suspiciously long letters of refusal … were seized upon by Harrods as making a really effective form of advertising":

> To be able to print pictures of eminent authors rejecting the proffered gold was almost better than to have secured their acceptance. It certainly is a clever idea which works as well backward as forward, and turns out a success whether its fundamental proposal is quietly complied with or indignantly spurned.[41]

The piece went on to recognize the invaluable publicity also generated for the authors but praised especially the "inescapable" Shaw who "in this lofty pose [of separating art and commerce] easily surpassed both Bennett and Wells": "It has been said that it is impossible to place [Shaw] in a position, no matter how apparently awkward, out of which he is not able to extract a glorious self-advertisement." A reference made near the editorial's conclusion to the National University of Dublin's

# THE AUTHOR'S PAYMASTER?

own sake. This means, I am afraid, that every case must be taken separately, and the decision left to the conscience of the individual writer.

### A Challenge to Advertisers
**Mr. Thomas Burke:**

Should authors engage in advertisement writing? Under present conditions of advertising, I think not, for the reason that all advertising has to be favourable to the firm or commodity advertised. Any author of repute, therefore, who engaged in such work, even if he could in complete honesty express a favourable opinion, would lie under suspicion of having sold his pen, so cynically does the public (and with justification) regard all advertising.

But if any commercial firm were bold enough to give an author a free hand, and permit him full liberty to express his honest opinion of the commodity in question, and if the public understood that it *was* his honest opinion, in no way influenced by the firm or the firm's money, there might be a change of attitude.

And I think that any advertiser who dared to pay for the services of an honest and independent critic of his wares, and to publish his opinions, whether favourable or adverse, would in time reap a benefit. The articles would attract wide attention; they would throw up critical ideas which might be of constructive value to the firm; the public would appreciate the advertiser's courage, and put faith in his advertisements; and the advertiser would stand out from his fellows as the first business man to give the world what it has often heard talked about, but never yet seen—truth in advertising.

### "Cutting" Mr. Wells
**Mr. C. Burnley-Jones:**

Authors should certainly *not* be encouraged to become paid copywriters. Most of them would be incompetent, and not worth the money they would expect to be paid.

Excepting the three selected by Harrods—with perhaps Edgar Wallace added—modern authors are a hundrum lot of craftsmen, who are able to make a popular appeal only through their own medium. Bennett, Shaw and Wells happen to be something more—they are provocative personalities who appeal to the public apart from their writings. This is what gives them special value as possible copywriters.

I must admit, however, that they all are tremendous writers of copy. Mr. Bennett has proved his ability by the way he sells books (for publishers who do not pay him) in the *Evening Standard*. What is an article that makes a best seller in a night ("Jew Suss," for example) but a piece of superlative copy? Mr. Wells is able to do what few can do: sell science and political theory to the millions. That takes some doing. While Mr. Shaw is the greatest master of personal publicity now living.

In a way, it is a great pity they cannot be caught. They would certainly add to the gaiety of the profession and it would be great fun handling them. Mr. Bennett would keep to the point, but would not

*Uncle Woodman finds Arnold, Herbert, and Bernard untippable, but Mother Public Opinion thinks he's such a kind gentleman, nevertheless*

surrender or curb his prejudices. He is and always will be a "Five Towns" Cosmopolitan. Mr. Wells' copy would have to be cut severely, and even then his first advertisement would probably fill a whole issue of the *Daily Mail*, while the only way to get Mr. Shaw to write a good piece of copy for Harrods would be to set him writing on Selfridges.

Still, I am glad they refused, and I agree with their reasons. It is well that the few men who have the ability to do it should tell the truth as they see it, not as they are paid to see it. If Mr. Shaw descended from the height on which he saw the vision of man and superman to hand out hucksterting patter in the market place—even at such a splendid stall as Harrods—he would certainly forfeit his authority as a prophet of our time, and I, for one, would feel that something sacred was smashed.

### Truth versus Fiction
**Mr. H. Stuart Menzies:**

Among all the advertising men who read the Bernard Shaw, Arnold Bennett and H. G. Wells letters to Harrods, I was perhaps the most interested owing to the enormous compliment paid to the commentaries I write for Fortnum and Mason in Bernard Shaw's letter.

Besides and apart from this, I, like everyone else, read the letters with pleasure and interest. The distinguished authors pointed out that they could not dream of writing advertisements for the public because they are prophets.

What great firm of publishers will now be enterprising enough to write to a number of distinguished advertising men, such as myself, asking us to write best sellers to the public? To which we would all instantly reply that we could not think of doing such a thing because, we, as advertising men write nothing but the truth while authors are well known to write fiction. Our replies will then be published with an immense splash in the Press, thus gaining quite as much publicity as anybody could desire so that everybody will be pleased. Which all

goes to show what fun life is when you look at it in the right way!

### "Yes, but Unsigned!"
**Mr. John Brophy** (who is both a copywriter and a novelist):

Should an author write advertisement copy? By all means—it will be good for him, and good for the advertising profession. But if he signs it, he is competing unfairly with other copywriters, just as a notorious divorcée, a jockey, or a politician who writes a novel is competing unfairly with professional novelists. Any piece of craftsmanship should succeed or fail by its own intrinsic merits, without being bolstered up by a reputation won in other fields.

My own experience may be interesting. I write serious novels for a small (but growing) public, which, I believe, cares for both thought and art. The commercial value of an author's books, for many years at least, is determined by other circumstances than literary merit, and if I were to attempt to live upon my royalties, I should be on the "dole." This is not to say that I entered advertising as a makeshift: my ignorance was first fascinated and my experience is now firmly and permanently interested.

What I did not realise was that advertising would help me in my writing, by pinning me down to a limited space and a definite object. It assures me of a steady income, so that I can take a year, or two years, or three over a novel, and write independently of fashion and popularity. It keeps me in touch with real life—not living in a tiny artificial world of "artistically minded!" people, as most authors with private incomes seem to do.

The extra expense of time and energy is negligible. I merely cut down my evening ration of conversation, bridge, and idling; this also is good for me in return; authorship improves my copy by giving me additional and different writing practice, and by keeping alive in me that faculty which a copywriter loses quickest —"human interest."

*(Continued on page 466)*

recent overwhelming vote against bestowing an honorary degree on Shaw reiterates the particular fear raised by one speaker at the hearing that Shaw would "refuse the honor or make it a subject for self-advertisement."[42] In both cases, the author suggested, "whether he got it or lost it all would be fish that came to his net." While it would seem that the writers' resistance was completely neutered with the store's choice to print, American publishing magnate Henry Robinson Luce observed cheekily that the series "gave Harrods a most excellent advertisement and furnished the three consecrated prophets with much incidental publicity."[43] Again, Shaw's letter was deemed the most proficient at doing so; *Printers' Ink* pointed out that Shaw, "that perennial bad boy of Europe," proved the most adept, managing to sink a barb into both Harrods (for making the offer) and Wells (as the only author's name Shaw used), so that the playwright "again had the last word in their perennial debates."[44] In any case, responses affirmed the cleverness of, as *Advertiser's Weekly* put it, "so emphatic an endorsement of the three writers' refusals to accept the invitation" and proffered "general praise for Messrs. Harrods' stage-management."[45]

In trade periodicals, the campaign also became a context within which the desirability of "celebrated men of letters [being] employed to write advertisements"[46] could be discussed, and many "commentators [were] quick to realize and to point out a distinction between copywriting as such and the 'copywriting' of the celebrity."[47] *Printed Salesmanship*, a monthly Chicago-based trade journal "for those who sell, produce, and use printing for sales purposes," published a feature piece on the campaign in May of 1929, entitled "Harrods of London Score the Biggest Scoop in Advertising History." F. McVoy, its author, quoted the majority of Shaw's letter and all of Wells's and Bennett's, indicating it "a very debatable point whether great authors would be able to write advertisements that would actually *sell* goods."[48] Rather than create copy, McVoy suggests, literary writers ought merely to endorse products. A copywriter who wrote to the London-based *Advertiser's Weekly* in response to the Harrods campaign made the same case that "literary men" have not yet had sufficient training to write copy since "an advertisement to be effective must interest by *matter* and not by *manner*." As such, he recommends they "dig deep into sales problems, and learn the angle of the appeal before their copy can serve."[49] Taking a slightly different tack, George Rowell, in his famous *Printers' Ink* column "The Little Schoolmaster's Classroom," reproduced excerpts from all three letters and lauded Harrods for its inventiveness yet felt that the three authors "deserve sympathy":

> But for the sad accident that they were born in the British Isles they might quite easily lend their pens to the cause of advertising at a great many dollars per word and not even be forced to the trouble of writing their own testimonials. ... [Plus,] a number of well-known American writers have quite legitimately lent their pens to commerce with no loss of prestige or apparent diminution of fame. Can it be that the three eminent Englishmen are perhaps taking themselves and their calling a bit too seriously?[50]

Stoking the debate, *Advertiser's Weekly*, self-styled the "organ of British advertising," invited a variety of prominent writers (including Storm Jameson and J. B. Priestley), public figures, and advertising professionals to share their views, finding only one—an Anglican reverend—who supported the writing of advertisements by established authors. Many contributors echo points made by Wells and Shaw concerning conflicted loyalties and the challenges posed by the commercial arrangement to honesty and intellectual freedom. C. Burnley-Jones, an advertising executive, conceded that Wells, Bennett, and Shaw "are provocative personalities who appeal to the public apart from their writings[, giving] them special value as possible copywriters."[51] To him, Shaw was "the greatest master of personal publicity now living," although "the only way to get [him] to write a good piece of copy for Harrods would be to set him writing on Selfridges." In the end, though, Burnley-Jones affirms Shaw's reasoning:

> If Mr. Shaw descended from the height on which he saw the vision of man and superman to hand out huckstering patter in the market place – even at such a splendid stall as Harrods – he would certainly forfeit his authority as a prophet of our time, and I, for one, would feel that something sacred was smashed.

Other correspondents made the claim that authors were unskilled in the practice of copywriting: "the psychology and viewpoint of such men are not suited for the commercial business of advertising which I interpret as only another definition of printed salesmanship."[52] As such, the authors' participation was deemed unfair to professional copywriters: "Any piece of craftsmanship should succeed or fail by its own intrinsic merits without being bolstered up by a reputation won in other fields."[53] H. Stuart Menzies, longtime copywriter for the Fortnum and Mason catalogue, playfully queried, "What great firm of publishers will now be enterprising enough to write a number of distinguished advertising men, such as myself, asking us to write best sellers to the public?"[54] With the advent of personality testimonial, copywriters found themselves facing total effacement behind product and celebrity. As Lears puts it, in response, "yearnings for autonomy surfaced in the trade press as early as the 1920s, when copywriters demanded the right to sign their ads – and agency executives indignantly refused, observing that the ad was meant to represent the client's 'personality,' not the copywriter's."[55]

Even Shaw, despite allegedly having worked himself as a copywriter early in his career, exhorted the "commercial houses [to continue to] engage skilled but nameless scribes ... to write their advertisements."[56] The conversation around the campaign thus provided an opportunity for industry scribes to surrender their anonymity, define their craft separately from the authors', and affirm themselves publicly as artisans within the business of commerce. In 1911, a *Printers' Ink* piece by James C. Moffett addressed the issue of signed advertisements, citing a trend in both British and American journals, magazines, and reviews of including signatures from and even biographical blurbs about their copywriters. Moffett draws a contrast between literary authors and copywriters, indicating that, in the past, using the names of contributors such as "Dickens or Thackeray ... was done because of its advertising value to the magazines [in that they] attracted attention to their publications." Even though "no editor [can] be made to understand how [disclosing the name] of an unknown writer would increase the circulation," the piece nonetheless advocates an "increase in the numbers of signed advertisements [because it] may do much to strengthen the confidence of the public in advertising."[57] Just as the industry explores how personalizing copy can help authenticate its appeal, copywriters, like the High Modernists, seized upon the turn towards personality marketing to contrive a distinct professional identity.

On the other hand, some proclaimed much overlap between the two professions, with again Shaw creeping into the discussion. A 1920 anthology entitled *The Literature of Business* excerpts a speech given in 1916 by John B. Obdycke that eventually formed the basis two years later for a book entitled *Advertising and Selling Practice*:

> Ours is a tabloid time [in which] the similarity between the English of Literature and the English of Advertising and Selling is startlingly true. ... The spirit of an age was never more highly reflected in its expression than at present. Wilde, Bennett, Galsworthy, Shaw, Chesterton, O. Henry – who are these but advertisers and sellers? ... All of these writers are so electrifying that one cannot tell for the life of him whether he would rather write advertising as Shaw writes literature, or literature as Shaw writes advertising![58]

E. McKenna, in a 1920 *Printers' Ink* essay goes even further, claiming, "the advertiser may usefully take a leaf from the playwrights notebook" and citing Shaw as the only model. Conspicuously appropriating the concept of a "drama of ideas" in his title ("The Dramatization of Advertising Ideas"), he introduces his central thesis with an example:

> It is perhaps not generally known that George Bernard Shaw earned his first money by writing patent medicine advertisements. These compositions are probably not to be found now, but if they could be, it is possible that it could be shown that young Mr. Shaw dramatized his appeal and did it successfully.[59]

McKenna goes on to argue that, like playwrights, "the organization of ideas and their shaping toward a climax ... is the essential business of" the copywriter.[60] Nevertheless, the distinction remains that, although "modern copywriting engages in the same work of the modernist author," it does so "without asserting authorship of any kind,"[61] and *Advertiser's Weekly* was rightly skeptical Harrods would have been successful in convincing Wells, Shaw, and Bennett to participate had the store "exercised the superhuman self-denial of publishing their 'copy' as anonymously as that of their own copywriters."[62] Neither Harrods nor the authors would be much interested in such self-effacement that effectively nullifies the publicity value for both.

Another oddity of the campaign was pointed out by *Printers' Ink*: "Why was a typically British store using large space in New York City?"[63] In response to a "flood of American cables asking whether Harrods is opening a New York shop," Charles Wildes maintained there was no intention to do so but that the "New York campaign was planned in the hope that American excitement over so unusual a testimonial campaign would reverberate [in Britain] and also appeal to American tourists."[64] The campaign did indeed catch the attention of American agencies, used to viewing British advertising as perpetually lagging behind, and they were particularly struck by the creation of a new promotional subgenre. According to Wildes, Harrods' risk in "printing the pictures [and letters] of these eminent authors who rejected the gold which had been offered them" created "not testimonial copy but something which looked like it." As such, the invention of this "new type of near-testimonial, or something, was handed to the advertising men for discussion."[65] In *Time*, a few weeks later, Luce noted that the "ingenious" campaign which made "three excellent testimonials out of three refusals to give testimonials [commanded] the instant admiration of U.S. advertising men, to whom British advertising is often a source of amusement."[66] He went on to state that the ads were "posted on the bulletin board" at the J. Walter Thompson Co., an industry powerhouse since the turn of the century and pioneer in the modern practices of celebrity-based copy and trademark branding.

Even other fields noticed. A regular column called "London Letter" in *Photo-Era Magazine: The American Journal of Photography* covered the campaign and paraphrased the letters ("their answers were not put as plainly as this"), bemoaning that, although it "commands many of the most skilled workers," photography has "failed to press the most important literary lights into its service."[67] On the continent, the September 1929 edition of avant-garde design magazine *Gebrauchsgraphik: International Advertising Art* included a feature that reproduced all three letters with commentary, entitled "The Tables Turned or Harrods and the Three Great English Authors." Its author, H. F. J. Kropff, speaks to what he calls the "unsolved problem" in Europe that "wide circles of the public, including artists, authors, and publishers, tend to reject advertising."[68] Particularly in Germany, he goes on, even when "publisher and author – whether moved by political enthusiasm or erroneous economic conclusions, allow themselves to be persuaded to lend their personalities to any cause, ... usually the thing is a failure" (47). In contrast, Kropff argues, with proficient authors behind them, "these three negative replies were a great success for Harrods' – 'the greatest advertising trick of recent times', an American said" (47). He urges readers to "recognize the gulf that yawns between normal German advertising copy and the high achievement of many a German commercial artist" and that "the consciously cultivated copywriter is an essential of commercial art" (51). Citing Shaw's response as the "most interesting" and "most biting" (47), Kropff uses the Harrods campaign to make a case for the importance of high-quality copywriting and for creating university courses of study in Germany to train writers in the "psychology of advertising" and "the art of salesmanship" (51). Similar to many of the *Advertiser's Weekly* respondents, McVoy, in his *Printed Salesmanship* piece, goes further, arguing that merely being a good journalist or writer with a university degree isn't enough, that

> the most successful copy writers of the future as far as securing result-bringing advertisements and sales-creating literature generally are concerned, will be men who have actually ... had to sell goods or services himself. ... Nine advertisements out of ten today are not as productive of business as they might be ... because they lack salesmanship.[69]

Again and again, the objection is raised that literary authors were venturing "into an expert profession with their inexpert methods, offering in the place of trained skill in writing 'selling' copy their fame won in another field."[70] Just as it did for copywriting as a trade, the campaign provided an occasion for advertising to assert its integrity and status as a legitimate professional field; as *Advertiser's Weekly* put it, "advertising cannot but be gratified that its status has risen so vastly that it is possible for such a question to be put and that three eminent writers can bring themselves to write on the subject in so sympathetic a manner."[71]

In the midst of extensive discussion about the efficacy of the endorsement technique in general and the appropriateness of using literary authors as copywriters, some trade publications went to prominent *American* writers to provide *anti*-testimonial testimonials. In their May 1929 issue, the Chicago-based *Magazine of Business* carried a piece by James Thurber, who would later go on to provide illustrations for advertising campaigns. "Now that testimonial writing has become a greater sport than baseball," the author claims it "high time that some rules for the game were adopted" and advocates for the creation of a National Rules Committee "to establish a board of censorship to edit testimonials before they are printed." Seeing little chance that the advertisers or profitable endorsements will cease, Thurber proposes a compromise since, "apparently, it doesn't make a difference in sales what the [personality] says, as long as he keeps the name of the product before the people." He envisions a cigarette ad in which a famous athlete encourages children not to smoke and expresses his desire that the act be banned. "The children's admiration for their hero will be kept intact [and] the cigaret's sales will grow, because the elements in this great land which won't stand for the prohibition of anything will quietly buy the cigaret in large quantities."[72]

The American journal *Advertising & Selling* published a long missive by Sinclair Lewis in their May 15, 1929 issue against personality marketing in "these Advertised States of America."[73] Using Ford car ads as positive examples, Lewis praises copy that avoids "nauseating slush" (60) and provides "definite information" about "what [the product] costs" and what specific virtues ... it possesses" so as to provide "definite reasons why I, and not some snob celebrity should buy it" (60, 62). Extremely critical of the testimonial in all of its forms, he mockingly dissects a number of current campaigns that employ the technique, leaving aside "the more obvious and vulgar advertisements – the boisterous assertions that Douglas Fairbanks, Chief Officer Manning, George Gershwin, and a few score opera singers owe their success to smoking Lucky Strike Cigarettes" (66). He concludes,

> I want to protest, as a layman, against ... the testimonial advertisements which differ from the old-fashioned medical advertisements only in being printed on better paper [and] the snob advertisements which suggest that I must buy something because Mrs. Umptidink of Paris and Terre Haute has bought it. ... I know! My advertising-agency friends tell me that a lot of these accounts have hugely increased their sales by just the sort of advertising to which I object. ... But my hunch is that there are quite a few million people who resent the valet swankiness as much as I do. And it is not a hunch but a certainty that when you get twenty soaps or shoes or cars all advertising against one another on the snobbish-and-testimonial basis, they will all cancel out, and the successful advertiser will be the man who tells factually what he has to sell, at what price, and why, with no extraneous pictures or would-be smart copy. (66)

The Harrods campaign even had an afterlife in professional memory. Frank Swinnerton, the London correspondent for the *Chicago Daily Tribune*, noted in his column in early January of 1931 that Shaw's comments about the Fortnum & Mason catalogues had spawned the creation of a volume entitled *Let's Forget Business* by H. Stuart Menzies:

> A short time ago, Bernard Shaw, when invited to write an advertisement, said that he read with gusto, and made point of collecting, the little brochures issued every few weeks by a London firm of provision dealers. ... Mr. Shaw is not alone in this habit, and I foresee a day when the brochures will be valuable collectors' items. They represent a particularly Anglo-American type of nonsense, the kind that is illustrated by "Alice in

Wonderland," or, more simply, by certain of the old nursery rhymes, and because they are so entertaining, they must be good advertisements.

Following upon Shaw's puff, a collection has been made of these brochures for those who have not been on Messrs. Fortnum & Mason's mailing list for the last few years.[74]

Two months later, *Advertising & Selling* reran virtually all of Swinnerton's text in their "The 8pt. Page" column, arguing for the aesthetic quality of commercial advertising:

> some of this Fortnum & Mason advertising has been reproduced in A. & S. from time to time. Nothing else so good is being done on either side of the Atlantic, to my way of thinking. Fortnum & Mason "first editions" may well one day command fancy prices among collectors: they are literature of a high order.[75]

Five years after the original ads appeared, in 1934, Gerald Blake published a humorous essay in *Advertising & Selling* that evoked the memory of "one of the cleverest publicity stunts of the decade." Musing what some of the greatest canonical authors might have produced if they were "weak enough to succumb to temptation," Blake furnished copy from a "typical advertisement currently being run by a nationally known flour mill" and then imaginary variations on it produced in the style of Chaucer, Shakespeare, Thomas Carlyle, Dickens, Proust, G. K. Chesterton, Hemingway, and Gertrude Stein.[76] A decade later, in 1945, *Newspaper World & Advertising Review* issued a call for "somebody [to] take the trouble to find out and give details (possibly in anthology form) of advertising's associations with literature." As an example, the piece asks,

> Do you remember a gallant attempt made by a famous London store to induce writers of the eminence of Bernard Shaw, Arnold Bennett, and others to write advertisements on the store's behalf? No direct advertisements were forthcoming, but, when printed with the author's photograph, the graceful prose in which the invitations were declined made a much-talked-of series.[77]

When Wells died in 1946, *Printers' Ink* ran a eulogy of sorts that discussed his representation of the adman in his writings and concluded by recalling the Harrods series, "his one practical connection (or near-connection) with the art of copy writing" that helped produce "advertisements which were not only better than they would have been in the first place but also for free!"⁷⁸ The campaign even became part of Harrods mythology; in 1949, during the store's centenary celebrations, *The Newspaper World and Advertising Review* devoted two paragraphs in a feature entitled "How Advertising Has Helped to Build the House of Harrods" to that "daring prestige move in 1929" that resulted in "world-wide editorial publicity in addition to that obtained through the actual announcements."⁷⁹

Besides the profession, the campaign also created ripples in scholarly circles. Unusually, *Publishers' Weekly* took notice, quoting a paragraph from each author's letter and complimenting Harrods for gaining "for itself, and for department stores in general, excellent publicity by printing" them.⁸⁰ However, if the advertising world found the campaign innovative and game changing, literary critics felt it confirmed how out of step Wells, Bennett, and Shaw were with modern times. Francis Hackett begins in the present tense in his March 1930 essay entitled "The Post-Victorians": "I open a noted English paper, the Sunday *Observer*, to see three full-page advertisements, each with a huge familiar portrait, and each with a great literary name attached."⁸¹ He characterizes all three authors as "the most eminent of post-Victorians and anti-Victorians [who] have done the most to form the minds of our generation":

> And yet, eminent as they are, they are already merging with the past. The epoch is waning. A new epoch is arriving. ... We who owe most to them, who have been most formed by them who have been deepest in subjection to them, are obliged to be candid with ourselves as to the degree in which we are shedding them or trying to shed them. ... We must repudiate them in order to fulfill our own temperaments.⁸²

Hackett outlines a cycle in which each generation "must detach [their] allegiances and scrutinize [their] origins," eventually discarding the influences that governed their "years of immaturity" in favor of those who speak more resonantly to and from the present moment.⁸³ In the essay, he is nostalgically reverent, especially towards Shaw, that "Niagara of intellectual monologue," that "heroic giraffe who has pushed himself out of the mental undergrowth[,] elongating his neck until he could crop the heads of the tallest trees."⁸⁴ Nonetheless, in the end, "when it came to 1914–1918," the "attitudes" of Wells, Bennett, and Shaw "did not measure up to the war."⁸⁵ Pointedly deploying the language of commodity marketing, Hackett claims that Shaw "invented a sort of couch-by-day-and-bed-by-night, three-in-one, patent combination corkscrew-and-toothpick religion which has no alcoholic content and is half the price."[86]

Accordingly, the "crystal common sense" the playwright provided only works "from the chin up" and produces the "revolting experience" of being "cheated of tragedy":

> Shaw has allowed his vivid social sense to compel him to create a mask, an artificial, superficial personality, so that the writing man and the real man have never tragically merged. [That is to say,] the one person whom Bernard Shaw never seems to have seen in his nakedness is Bernard Shaw.[87]

From the outside looking in, Hackett maintains, the creation of G.B.S. cost Shaw his humanity, and, after the upheaval of the war, he turns to another Irish writer whom he feels truly "bared himself":

> No Irishman ... has succeeded in relating himself to the human adventure with complete emotional absorption until the coming of James Joyce [whose] heartrending cries [reveal far more] than Bernard Shaw's firework display. The blackness after Shaw's dazzling is worse than ever, while in even a little of *Ulysses* you first gaze into the horror and stagger into daylight afterwards.[88]

The essay argues that, because "the anti-Victorians ... were in the heroic niches without being sufficiently heroic[,] out with them."[89] For Hackett, the authors' appearance in the Harrods advertisement seemingly confirms their seminal importance only so that it may be disavowed as prewar enthusiasm, conferring upon them the perishability of an expired shelf life.

Thirty years later, Stephen Spender, in his book *The Struggle of the Modern*, draws upon the same campaign ("an almost forgotten episode of the late 1920's [that] fascinated [him as] a boy") to demonstrate further why the three authors cannot be considered Modernists.[90] To him, the overlap of literature and commerce embodied by the campaign reveals a crucial difference in sensibility. Shaw, Wells, and Bennett all understand a writer's obligation to "accept responsibility to the world of public interests and materialist values even if they oppose the economic system as such."[91] Spender finds "something innocently disingenuous" about the authors' refusals that he sees as "really disguised acceptances" in that all three knew that they would eventually be printed.[92] All three conceive of themselves as members of the marketplace, producing wares and competing for public consumption; even if "the principles of Wells and Shaw were not the same as those of Harrods ... they were those of business (if publicly owned)."[93] In contrast, Spender argues,

> the "moderns," Joyce, Lawrence, Eliot, Woolf would feel that their responsibility towards themselves was *as artists* [and] would have treated [Harrods' offer] sniggeringly if they did not repudiate it disgustingly [out of an obligation to] a past which had been degraded by commerce, a past of realer values betrayed by advertising.[94]

Jackson Lears suggests that Spender's "division is a little too neat [since] technocratic modernists were not always uncritical celebrants of commerce [and often offered] a plainspoken critique of commercial chicanery."[95] Nonetheless, the Harrods campaign becomes essential for both Hackett and Spender in reifying that larger authorial program of *im*personality marketing as constitutively Modernist at the expense of writers formerly known as modern. Indeed, such demarcation between authors like Eliot, Pound, and Wyndham Lewis and authors like Shaw and Wells who forged authorial personae via popular media and testimonial commerce in the name of public advocacy becomes a tipping point in literary history.

> I suppose men such as Ford, Edison and Marconi were landed for the Simmons [mattress] campaign because those gentlemen were told they would be doing humanity a good turn if they preached the gospel of more and better sleep.—Anonymous ad executive, 1931[96]

Luce's essay in *Time*, recognizing the transatlantic success of the Harrods campaign, concluded with a sentence assuring its readers that, despite dipping a toe in the commercial pond, "the honor of literature was preserved, and the purity of what Harrods termed 'three of our greatest Masters of the Written Word' remained unsullied." Following the statement, an asterisk appears, disclosing the caveat that "Mr. Wells has allowed his picture and a little sermon on Sleep to appear in testimonial advertisements for Simmons Beds" and adroitly undercutting the writers' claims of separation from commerce.[97] His reference is to a November 1928 ad for Beautyrest mattresses that featured Wells and his views on sleep and insomnia. Less than a month after the Harrods ads ran, in May of 1929, Shaw too appeared in the same series, entitled "Making the World 'Sleep Conscious': Fifteen famous men talk on sleep through Simmons Advertising." Shaw and Wells are the only two literary authors included on a list of "distinguished sleepers" alongside Henry Ford, Gordon Selfridge, Harvey Firestone, Thomas Edison, Guglielmo Marconi, and Com. Richard Byrd, among others.[98] All, according to the JWT staff newsletter, "for the past two years, in behalf of the Simmons Company," were asked about their slumber habits and "have allowed their answers to be published in Simmons advertising."[99] The article makes clear that

> in this series of advertisements our distinguished men do not endorse Simmons products. They tell how important a factor sleep has been in maintaining their health, poise, and vitality, and in attaining success and even wealth! ... [Alongside their remarks] appear small captioned illustrations of Simmons famous Beautyrest Mattress and Ace Box Spring. A paragraph of Simmons institutional matter is inserted, but disassociated from the interview, and the Simmons logotype is used.[100]

Similar to what they had famously done on behalf of Pond's Cold Cream, the agency's prior work for Simmons involved recruiting "such high-profile targets as Mrs. Franklin Delano Roosevelt, Mrs. Charles Tiffany, and Mrs. Morgan Belmont" and had been another triumph of testimonial promotion with their trademark approach of bestowing "otherwise commonplace goods with an aura of glamor and sophistication, appealing to the average consumer's desire to read about other people and emulate their lifestyles and shopping habits."[101]

Shaw's appearances in product campaigns would fit into a larger tradition of endorsements that stretched back to patent medicine promotion in the nineteenth century but, via the Women's Editorial Department at JWT, were a staple of modern marketing technique and layout employed in that notorious Pond's campaign:

> Signed testimonials were displayed in the advertisements, and photographs of the women were reproduced. Interviews with the endorsers were reported in a narrative, with a careful style deemed appropriate to the particular woman being written up – gracious and dignified for one, vivacious

for another. Detailed descriptions of their houses, their personality, their social activities were a prominent and important part of the interviews. More than simply product ads, these endorsements were miniature ventures into "lifestyles of the rich and famous" and presented the creams as just one element in a whole way of life that the everyday consumer could ostensibly share.[102]

Evidently, Shaw could see the opportunity via a testimonial to extend the readers' vision far beyond the product; in this way, the contemporary form evolved from the utopic salubrious future broadly encouraged by patent medicine adverts to a specific lifestyle glimpsed through the lens of personality. The prophet sharing potential of such a platform is quite apparent.

The company's stated rationale for the "Celebrated Men on Sleep" campaign concentrated on expanding the demographic across the gender divide:

> Since 1927 the women's magazines have carried the message that bedrooms should be beautiful as well as comfortable, and that, furnished with the luxury of Simmons Beds and Beautyrest Mattresses, they will be both! Simmons-equipped bedrooms of distinguished women have been shown to prove it. But in 1928 we felt we could, with profit, through the pages of *The Saturday Evening Post* and *Time*, also address the men of the country with "sermons on sleep" preached by men outstandingly successful. Our aim was to make modern American men, most of whom will tell you "they can sleep as well on a board as on a bed," conscious that there is *quality* in sleep, that it's the *kind*, as well as the *quantity*, that matters!

And that *quality* has much to do with achievement in one's chosen field of action.[103] Accordingly, each interview strives "to paint a vivid picture of the personality of the man by placing under or near his photograph a caption which plays up his individuality and accomplishments and stresses any of his habits which are unusual and interesting."[104] The company newsletter goes on to say that

> widespread interest in the "Simmon's men's campaign on sleep" has been noted throughout the country, and it has been especially popular among Simmons' dealers. The ads have been hung in offices and stores, the dealers taking great pride in the connection of "big" men with their product.[105]

Coinciding with the American advent of sleep research, the campaign puts forth another form of "near-testimonial" in which personalities advocate healthy sleep habits alongside information about the Simmons mattress. For instance, under the headline "H.G. Wells disagrees with Napoleon on sleep," the Wells ad is divided into three columns, the first containing his interview answers to two questions on the importance of sleep alongside a center column photograph of the author. The right column is devoted to information about the company and the product. The Shaw Simmons ad also deliberately mimics a periodical feature by announcing itself in bold type as "A philosopher's ideas about Sleep" via "An interview with Bernard Shaw." The ostensible interlocutor, Irish nationalist writer and activist Eimar O'Duffy,[106] describes the playwright "at seventy, with that buoyant step and fresh complexion which men in their twenties might envy" and provides the platform for three paragraphs containing Shaw's thoughts about the importance of slumber because he "obviously sleeps well o'nights." O'Duffy opines that "perhaps it comes to us as something of a shock, or perhaps it is only natural, to find that Bernard Shaw needs his full portion of sleep like any ordinary man [because] his glorious evolutionary theory in 'Back to Methuselah' of sleep as an infantile habit, still remains a dream." Following the interview, in the lower right corner, are two italicized blurbs. The top serves as a caption to a picture of Shaw: "the sage of Adelphi Terrace, philosopher, novelist, essayist, scientist, playwright, vegetarian. Toppler of ideas, satirist, wit and speaker – his revolutionary teachings have astonished the world for two generations!" The bottom supplements two adjacent photographic images of a mattress and box spring and reframe the text, indicating that "the views on sleep expressed by a man with the rare intellectual capacity of Mr. Shaw are full of significance for all" and redirect the reader's focus to their "sleep equipment which gives complete relaxation and induces healthful sleep" and "extraordinary comfort ... within reach of every income."[107]

Less direct than in their Harrods' responses, Wells and Shaw never explicitly endorse the product, yet again the latter in particular uses the opportunity as a vehicle to promote subtly his own ideas and persona:

> Once in every thirty years or so I have a dream in which I am so extraordinarily happy and everything is so beautiful – as it is when one is in love – that it throws a light on what life may one day come to be. But for

workaday purposes you may take it that I am an ordinary sleeper. Some day we shall grow out of it; but for the present we must take our eight hours and make the best of them.

Here, Shaw is in "prophet" mode, modeling a present lifestyle with an eye on an evolved future.[108] The idea behind "Personality Advertising," according to Stanley Resor, was again what he called the "spirit of emulation" in which consumers "want to copy those whom we deem superior to us in taste, knowledge or experience." A 1910 *Printers' Ink* column pronounces that the "consumer nearly always purchases in unconscious obedience to what he or she believes to be the dictates of an authority which is anxiously consulted and respected."[109] Generally speaking, Shaw's participation in advertising follows the same line of thought, an outgrowth of what Spender refers to as his "faith [that he] will direct the powers of the surrounding world from evil into better courses through the exercise of the superior social or cultural intelligence of the creative genius, the writer prophet" (Fig. 4.2).[110]

Some responses to the Harrods campaign surfaced public hostility towards celebrity testimonials as a promotional practice; as one reader who wrote to *Advertiser's Weekly* asked, "What on earth can any one of these writers know about Harrods stores which entitled them to force their views on the general public?"[111] The specter of fiscal compensation had also haunted the technique for decades. *Advertising Copy*, a manual for copywriters published in 1924, contains a caution:

> Testimony [that is bought and paid for] is intrinsically worthless. ... Manufactured evidence of this kind is not only unethical but is valueless in convincing intelligent people. Unfortunately, the testimony of prize fighters for medicines and tonics and of moving picture actresses for cosmetics still has the power to convince a large percentage of the unintelligent and unsophisticated.[112]

The Simmons and Harrods "near-testimonial" campaigns were staged against the backdrop of industry disquiet in the mid-1920s over the efficacy of personality marketing, their atypical methodology a response to widespread concerns within the field over "insincere copy" and an apparent dwindling of public faith in advertising. In February 1929, the National Better Business Bureau, in response to repeatedly "receiving insistent demands for an expression of its attitude in the current

Fig. 4.2   Simmons advertisement, *Time* 13:18 (May 6, 1929), p. 29

controversy," sent out a questionnaire to nearly five thousand American advertisers and agencies in order to "ascertain the sentiment of the industry."[113] Those surveyed felt "decisively" that tainted testimonials were "destroying the effectiveness of a valuable advertising appeal" and that "prostitution of the testimonial [was] bringing all advertising under the shadow of disrepute."[114] In March, the Association of National Advertisers sent a statement to its membership and another to the members of the American Association of Advertising Agencies recognizing the "developing controversy" over testimonial techniques:

> No one would deny that testimonial copy is a time-honored and worthwhile form of advertising. The present discussion has arisen not because of objections to the use of testimonials, but rather because of the manner in which they have been used and because of the devices by which they have been obtained.[115]

In a 1929 *Printer's Ink* article, Roy Dickinson assesses the "sad plight of that former respectable citizen of the advertising world, the testimonial, [who has] fallen from its former high estate since and sincere attempts have been made to lay down rules indicating how the tainted testimonial may be spotted after careful investigation."[116] To balance the views of industry insiders, Dickinson interviewed consumers on the street, discovering they held "definite views" and needed no "length explanation" of the question. Their responses revealed that this "small cross-section of the general consuming public ... likes to take its advertising as it takes its fiction" and that this "modern, cynical, what-of-it attitude" is "a bad thing for advertising" and "certainly hasn't been helped by exaggerated copy, by pseudo-scientific copy, or by the tainted testimonial."[117] The industry faced a formidable crisis with a consuming public wary and suspicious of the veracity of promotional claims. In 1911, the first order of business for the newly formed Associated Advertising Clubs of America had been to set in motion a truth-in-advertising movement that sought to criminalize promotional exaggeration and misrepresentation and (again, like Shaw in his Harrods letter) re-brand advertisers as public advocates rather than salesmen. As one convention speaker put it, "*advertising is not to sell, but to help people buy.* ... We stand in the shoes of the customer. We are *outside*, not behind the counter. We are counselors for the public."[118] Considering the skeptical attitudes expressed by consumers at the end of the 1920s, the initiative had not worked.

Entitled "Who is Going to Clean Up This Testimonial Mess?" the main article in the same issue of *Printers' Ink* that covered the Harrods campaign strongly advocates for measures to end "testimonial abuses."[119] The article expresses the perspectives of O. C. Harn, Managing Director of the Audit Bureau of Circulations and former president of the A.N.A., who assesses various methods "through which the evil can be eradicated," from intervention by the Better Business Bureau and the Advertising Commission to the creation of an International Advertising Association czar through which all ads would be vetted. (Incidentally, the latter idea, which Harn calls "preposterous," anticipates a Shavian proposition outlined in the preface to *Farfetched Fables* for a Ministry of Statistics.[120]) Harn levels the blame squarely upon the economic system, arguing that "misuse of testimonials comes primarily from the exigencies of competition and not at all because astute merchandisers have suddenly parted company with their brains."[121] Again, Shaw in that 1889 Fabian lecture mentioned in chapter one also had decried commercial demagoguery as another by-product of capitalism and advertising's leveraging of "shameless lies" to dupe uncritical consumers to purchase their products.[122] In the end, with great faith in the benevolence of advertisers and publishers, Harn proposes the remedy be "educational rather than generally coercive" and subsequent action to come from "voluntary undertakings rather than from legal pressure."[123] He appeals to the A.A.A.A. and the A.N.A. create a "code covering the proper use of testimonials" that "would become the basis for agreements with specific industries which could operate the same as actual police power in routing out wrongful use of testimonial advertising as well as other reprehensible selling practices which are brought on by competition."[124] Perhaps surprisingly, the Fabian qualities of Harn's vision evoke Webb's utopian manifesto.

At the June 1929 convention of the A.N.A., a resolution was passed in which "the so-called paid testimonial" was formally viewed "with disapproval."[125] However, the session took the form of a debate rather than a consensus. The opposition to testimonial copy, in the person of the president of the G. Lynn Sumner Company, maintained that the negative public perception of it had already triumphed, warning that

> no matter how unquestioned the integrity of the advertiser may be, no matter how good his intentions, when he uses the personality element he

thereby opens the way for skepticism. It is not sufficient that advertising merely be true; it must *appear* to be true. If it is true and not believed, then the effect on sales is just as bad as if it were untrue.

A defense of the practice was mounted by George S. Fowler, vice president of the Simmons Company, American manufacturer of beds, box springs, and mattresses. *Printers' Ink* found Fowler a fair choice since "the use of testimonials in connection with the merchandising of Simmons beds is familiar to all students of advertising" and recounted his remarks for its readership as:

> This is the age of autobiography. ... And this same influence is what causes newspapers to run so much into personalities. People are interested in other people – what they are doing and what they think. ... The advertiser who uses testimonials should place an absolute ban upon anything that is unfair, untruthful or in bad taste. ... With this sort of standard, personalities can be used properly and profitably; and failure to use them ... would be to ignore one of the most fruitful methods of creating increased consumer acceptance.

That Fowler's characterization of the zeitgeist should dovetail so closely with Stanley Resor's fashioning of his advertising agency's new ethos three months earlier, mentioned at the beginning of this chapter, is not coincidental, considering that the Simmons account at the time was held by the J. Walter Thompson Company. Together, the two men had already launched a major personality-centered initiative, that would include Shaw and Wells on its roster of celebrity participants and provide another variation on the "near-testimonial."

The innovative merging of product testimonial with the names and lifestyles of cultural luminaries, a JWT specialty, was the brainchild of Helen Lansdowne, one of the industry's first female executives: "Her first coup, in 1924, involved persuading Mrs. O.H.P. Belmont, a New York socialite, to endorse Pond's cold cream in exchange for a hefty donation to a charity of her choice."[126] With tremendous "market insight as well as natural copywriting flair," Lansdowne was essential to JWT's success, especially since a lion's share of the clients manufactured products for women.[127] Resor, who inherited the company from Thompson in 1916 and remained its president during much of the twentieth century's first half, is credited with innovations in copy style that employed cinematic techniques (including the close-up) and with recognizing the promotional potential in linking products/brands with celebrities. An industry leader in the development of multimedia campaign design and market research, JWT "devoted considerable resources to attracting testimonials from reputable people for everything from mattresses and yeast to laundry detergent and face cream."[128] According to Stephen Fox, their success with testimonials "pushed the agency's total annual billings from $10.7 million in 1922 to $20.7 million in 1926 and $37.5 million by the end of the decade."[129] A retrospective on the company's "Personality Department" in a 1946 issue of the *J.W.T. News*, adorned with famous facsimile signatures, proclaimed that

> For 22 years, JWT has been the unquestioned leader in testimonial advertising. The agency pioneered in the first organized use of celebrated personalities for testimonials back in 1924. Through the advertising of Pond's Creams, millions of readers learned the beauty secrets of such noted women as Queen Marie of Roumania, Mrs. Marshall Field, Sr., Mrs. O.H.P. Belmont, the Queen of Spain, and Alice Roosevelt Longworth. The JWT "Personality" Department that contacts these personalities and arranges for the use of their names reaches around the world.[130]

In the feature, Shaw and Wells are again the sole literary writers on "a full list of JWT's 'testimonial personalities'" that includes Thomas Edison, Joan Crawford, Lou Gehrig, and the Archbishop of Canterbury and "reads like a roll call of the world's most famous people," all "names that are by-words in their fields." In May 1929, Corey Ford satirized this trend in a piece for the *New Yorker* entitled "A Meeting of the Endorsers' Club," in which one member remarks, "The advertising sections of our magazines practically amount to a *Social Register*. Everybody who is *anybody* has been photographed at least beside a jar of Pond's Cold Cream, or a Simmons Mattress."[131]

The testimonial technique though was not without its potential pitfalls and systemic criticisms (some of which Shaw had pointed out in his Harrods letter), and the formidable ongoing debate over the ethics of testimonial advertising ensured that both the Harrods and Simmons campaigns with which the authors were affiliated would be considered in its light for some time to come. For instance, a March 1929 *Printer's Ink* article, entitled "When is the Testimonial Tainted?" already had the Simmons campaign in its sights (albeit indirectly) as a "troubling" example:

Suppose that a writer like G.K. Chesterton is approached by a manufacturer of an exercising machine, and is asked for a short article on the importance of exercise, and is paid for the article. Mr. Chesterton does not say that he uses the exercising machine. He merely points out the importance of exercise. Is that a "testimonial," and therefore something to be banned, if paid testimonials are to be banned? Or is it simply a piece of journalism by a journalist, and therefore something which can properly be paid for?[132]

Even three decades later, in *The Story of Advertising* (1958), James Playsted Wood uses both campaigns as poster children for the troubled torrent of testimonial advertising in the 1920s:

A London department store published letters by Bernard Shaw, H.G. Wells, and Arnold Bennett, together with pictures of the popular writers, saying that they could not and would not lend their names to product endorsements. The advertisements worked as well as if the novelist and playwright had testified with the same earnestness as Douglas Fairbanks or Ty Cobb. A mattress manufacturer used testimonials and photographs of Henry Ford, Guglielmo Marconi, Shaw, and others, presumably in praise of his products. The letters were in favor, not of the mattress, but of sleep.[133]

A seemingly unshakeable legacy from advertising's early decades, apprehensiveness over "insincere copy" and the loss of public faith (especially in celebrity testimonials) continued to be widespread. The profession needed to better figure out how to ensure best practices in the field but also how to rehabilitate consumer perception of its rhetoric and navigate around what Shaw, in his Harrods letter, had condemned as "the last depravity of corruption in literature."[134]

In any case, on or about December 1924, American advertising executive and novelist Walter O'Meara declared in *The J. Walter Thompson News Bulletin* that the nature of marketing had changed:

For the advertisement has, in a few decades, developed characteristics quite as distinctive and definite, in their way, as those of the lyric, drama or novel. ... The advertisement of today is, by all the critical standards, a unique literary form. It produces, or seeks to produce, a single definite effect. It has its own laws of structure. Like the motion picture, it is *sui generis*.[135]

Just as High Modernists mimicked their publicity tactics to produce a new template for authorial personality, advertising agencies sought the prestige and influence of the literary to enhance their clients' commodities and their work in promoting them. Both attempting to capitalize literary authors, the Harrods and Simmons campaigns appear at the end of a decade of significant maturation for the industry that saw "the international consolidation of advertising interests, as well as important national mergers that produce the mega-agencies" and occasion "the coalesce of techniques, technologies, business styles, and economic change that translate into the modern advertising apparatus."[136] Both campaigns indicate how these new corporate entities sought to sidestep increasing public suspicion towards testimonial advertising and set the parameters for the concept of modern celebrity, even helping to shape the contours of High Modernism. For Shaw, the page space presented another opportunity to articulate the rationale for his presence in the media. As he wrote to Mabel Shaw in 1928, for him, "the question of becoming a professional writer is a pretty deep one when the intention behind it extends to becoming a prophet."[137]

## NOTES

1. James W. Egbert. "Making the Testimonial Worth More." *Printers' Ink* 77.8 (23 November 1911): 76–8. 76.
2. Michael Holroyd. *Bernard Shaw: The One Volume Definitive Edition*. New York: Random House, 1997. 466–7.
3. T. R. Nevett. *Advertising in Britain: A History*. London: The History of Advertising Trust, 1982. 145.
4. Kerry Segrave. *Endorsements in Advertising: A Social History*. Jefferson, NC: McFarland & Company, Inc., Publishers, 2005. 23–4.
5. Ibid., 14.
6. James Playsted Wood. *The Story of Advertising*. New York: The Ronald Press Company, 1958. 392, 394.
7. Ibid., 393, 394.
8. H. S. Gardner. "The Paid Testimonial Is Taking the Cure." *Advertising & Selling* 13.12 (17 April 1929): 17–18, 46. 17.
9. Jackson Lears. "Uneasy Courtship: Modern Art and Modern Advertising." *American Quarterly* 39.1 (Spring 1987): 133–54. 143.
10. Jonathan Goldman. "Celebrity." In *George Bernard Shaw in Context*. Ed. Brad Kent. Cambridge: Cambridge University Press, 2015. 255–64. 255.
11. Helen Powell. "Advertising Agencies and Their Clients." In *The Advertising Handbook*, 3rd edition. Eds. Helen Powell, Jonathan Hardy, Sarah Hawkin, and Iain MacRury. London: Routledge: 2009. 13–23. 14.

12. Stanley Resor. "Personalities and the Public: Some Aspects of Testimonial Advertising." *The J. Walter Thompson News Bulletin* 138 (April 1929): 1–7. 1.
13. Ibid., 5.
14. "Mr. Resor Leads Discussion on Personality Advertising." *The J. Walter Thompson News Letter* 10.8 (13 April 1928): 137–50. 139. Resor explicitly rejected the term "testimonial advertising" which not only must have sounded old-fashioned but also carried with it the taint of turn-of-the-century controversies over fraudulent patent medicine marketing.
15. Ibid., 140.
16. Quotes appropriated from canonical literary works had been staples in periodical advertisements for decades, and companies had actively sought before to make connections between famous living authors and their products. In the late nineteenth century, manufacturers seized upon references to brand name products in novels, plays, and even poetry and courted their authors for endorsements. For their part, literary writers on both sides of the Atlantic were far from averse to lending their likeness or approbation to commodity advertisements, one of the most notorious being J. M. Barrie's association with Craven Tobacco in the 1890s which was savaged in the pages of *Punch*. See Phillip Waller. *Writers, Readers, & Reputations: Literary Life in Britain 1870-1918*. Oxford: Oxford University Press, 2006. 329–63.
17. Aaron Jaffe. *Modernism and the Culture of Celebrity*. New York: Cambridge University Press, 2005. 16.
18. Jonathan Goldman. *Modernism Is the Literature of Celebrity*. Austin: University of Texas Press, 2011. 3.
19. In addition to Jaffe's *Modernism and the Culture of Celebrity* and Goldman's *Modernism Is the Literature of Celebrity*, Mark Morrisson's *The Public Face of Modernism*, Lawrence Rainey's *Institutions of Modernism*, and *Marketing Modernisms*, edited by Kevin Dettmar and Stephen Watt, are all cornerstone texts in this area.
20. Michael L. Ross. *Designing Fictions: Literature Confronts Advertising*. Montreal: McGill-Queen's University Press, 2015. 23. In addition to Ross, the task of charting the broader contours of a sometimes adversarial, sometimes dialectical discursive relationship between literature and advertising has been taken up by critics such as Theodor Adorno, Jean Baudrillard, Simone Weil Davis, Jennifer Wicke, and Raymond Williams.
21. "Should the Advertiser Be the Author's Paymaster?" *Advertiser's Weekly* 61.824 (15 March 1929): 440–1, 466–7. 440.
22. F. McVoy. "Harrods of London Score the Biggest Scoop in Advertising History." *Printed Salesmanship* 53.3 (May 1929): 214–5, 274–6. 214.
23. "Why London Department Store Advertised in New York." *Printers' Ink* 146.12 (21 March 1929): 73–4.

24. Ibid., 73.
25. "Arnold Bennett and Harrods." *The Pittsburgh Post-Gazette* (19 March 1929): 16.
26. "H. G. Wells and Harrods." *The New York Times* (14 March 1929): 15.
27. "Bernard Shaw and Harrods." *The New York Times* (15 March 1929): 15.
28. Alice McEwan. "Commodities, Consumption, and Connoisseurship: Shaw's Critique of Authenticity in Modernity." *SHAW: The Journal of Bernard Shaw Studies* 35.1 (November 2015): 46–85. 62.
29. Gordon Honeycombe. *Selfridges: Seventy-Five Years, The Story of the Store, 1909–1984.* London: Park Lane Press, 1984. 172.
30. Elizabeth Outka. *Consuming Traditions: Modernity, Modernism, and the Commodified Authentic.* Oxford: Oxford University Press, 2009. 192n32.
31. "Bernard Shaw and Harrods." *The New York Times* (15 March 1929): 15.
32. Lears, "Uneasy Courtship," 134.
33. McEwan, 77.
34. C. H. Sandage and Vernon Fryburger. *Advertising Theory and Practice*, 7th edition. Homewood, IL: Irwin, 1967. 31.
35. Sidney Webb. "Introduction." G. W. Goodall, *Advertising: A Study of a Modern Business Power*. London: Constable & Co., 1914. ix–xvii. xvi–xvii.
36. Archibald Henderson. *George Bernard Shaw: Man of the Century*, vol. 2. New York: Da Capo Press, 1972. 762.
37. John Strachan and Claire Nally. *Advertising, Literature and Print Culture in Ireland, 1891–1922*. New York: Palgrave Macmillan, 2012. 24.
38. A single-page version of the ad containing all three letters continued to run in regional American newspapers.
39. *Advertiser's Weekly* 61.824 (15 March 1929): 441.
40. "Why London Department Store Advertised in New York," 73.
41. "Ingenious Advertising." *New York Times* (15 March 1929): 18.
42. "Irish Refuse to Give a Degree to Shaw." *New York Times* (13 March 1929): 4.
43. Henry Robinson Luce. "Holy Ghost." *Time* 13.12 (25 March 1929): 51.
44. "Why London Department Store Advertised in New York," 74.
45. "Should the Advertiser Be the Author's Paymaster?," 440.
46. "Copywriting or Paid Testimonial?" *Advertiser's Weekly* 61.823 (8 March 1929): 393.
47. "Should the Advertiser Be the Author's Paymaster?," 440.
48. McVoy, 276.

49. "Authors as Copywriters." *Advertiser's Weekly* 61.814–26 (1929): 490.
50. George Rowell. "The Little Schoolmaster's Classroom." *Printers' Ink* 146.12 (21 March 1929): 200, 202. 202.
51. "Should the Advertiser Be the Author's Paymaster?," 441.
52. Ibid., 441.
53. Ibid., 441.
54. Ibid., 441.
55. Lears, "Uneasy Courtship," 138.
56. "Bernard Shaw and Harrods," 15.
57. James C. Moffett. "Should Advertisements Be 'Signed,' Like Articles." *Printers' Ink* 76.1 (6 July 1911): 58, 60–1. 58, 60, 61.
58. Alta Gwinn Saunders and Herbert LeSourd Creek, eds. *The Literature of Business*. New York: Harper & Brothers Publishers, 1920. 467.
59. E. McKenna. "The Dramatization of Advertising Ideas." *Printers' Ink* 112.8 (19 August 1920): 93–6. 93.
60. Somewhat disappointingly, McKenna ultimately seems more to advocate the structure of melodrama rather than the drama of ideas as a model; the "well-built advertisement" for him should be "based upon a struggle between contending forces or a triumph won over obstacles" (93, 96).
61. Rod Rosenquist. "Copywriting Gertrude Stein: Advertising, Anonymity, Autobiography." *Modernist Cultures* 11.3 (2016): 331–50. 341.
62. "Should the Advertiser," 440.
63. "Why London Department Store Advertised in New York," 73.
64. Ibid., 73.
65. Ibid., 73, 74.
66. Luce, 51.
67. Carine and Will Cadby. "London Letter." *Photo-Era Magazine: The American Journal of Photography* 62 (January 1929–June 1929). Wolfeboro, New Hampshire: The Photo-Era Publishing Company, Inc. 334.
68. H. F. J. Kropff. "The Tables Turned or Harrods and the Three Great English Authors." Trans. E. T. Scheffauer. *Gebrauchsgraphik: International Advertising Art* 6.9 (1 September 1929): 47–51. 47.
69. McVoy, 276.
70. "Should the Advertiser Be the Author's Paymaster?," 466.
71. "Copywriting or Paid Testimonial," 393.
72. James Thurber. "Let's Have a Set of Rules for Our Testimonial Industry." *The Magazine of Business* 55 (May 1929): 538.
73. Sinclair Lewis. "Sinclair Lewis Looks at Advertising." *Advertising & Selling* 13.2 (15 May 1929): 17–18, 60, 62, 64–66. 64. The choice to go to Lewis is not necessarily a surprise. In 1922, *Printers' Ink* ran a

book review of *Babbitt* that exclaimed it was a novel "every advertising man ought to read" because of how "the fabric of advertising is [so] skillfully interwoven" (89). Earnest Elmo Calkins. "A Ballyhoo for Babbitt." *Printers' Ink* 121 (12 October 1922): 89–90, 93.
74. Frank Swinnerton. "British Schools Hit by Teacher's Novel; Shaw Boosts 'Ads'." *Chicago Daily Tribune* (10 January 1931): 10.
75. Odds Bodkins. "The 8pt. Page." *Advertising & Selling* 16.9 (4 March 1931): 46.
76. Gerald Blake. "Un-sinned Sins." *Advertising & Selling* 23.2 (24 May 1934): 22, 24. 22.
77. "Advertising and Literature." *Newspaper World & Advertising Review* 2453 (13 January 1945): 19.
78. "H. G. Wells on Advertising." *Printers' Ink* 216.8 (23 August 1946): 126.
79. "How Advertising Has Helped to Build the House of Harrods." *The Newspaper World and Advertising Review* 2674 (23 April 1949): 113–4. 113.
80. "Authors as Advertisers." *The Publishers' Weekly* 115.14 (6 April 1929): 1674.
81. Francis Hackett. "The Post-Victorians." *The Bookman* 71.1 (March 1930): 20–6. 20.
82. Ibid., 20.
83. Ibid., 21, 22.
84. Ibid., 22, 23.
85. Ibid., 23.
86. Ibid., 23.
87. Ibid., 23, 24. 23.
88. Ibid., 24.
89. Ibid., 24.
90. Stephen Spender. *The Struggle of the Modern*. Oakland: University of California Press, 1963. 73. His views on the Harrods campaign initially appeared in a short essay in *The Listener* (11 October 1962) entitled "Moderns and Contemporaries" (555–6).
91. Ibid., 75.
92. Ibid., 75.
93. Ibid., 75.
94. Ibid., 76.
95. Jackson Lears. *Fables of Abundance: A Cultural History of Advertising in America*. New York: Basic Books, 1994. 300. Building upon early work by Andreas Huyssen, recent scholarship by (among others) Elizabeth Outka, Thomas Strychacz, Kevin J. H. Dettmar, and Stephen Watt has also problematized this binary understanding of the relationship between Modernists and the commercial marketplace.

96. Quoted in Segrave, 14.
97. Luce, 51.
98. Interestingly, at a moment when High Modernists are hastily propping up distinctions of highbrow and middlebrow and also consolidating an elite authorial identity category, it is striking how in the Harrods campaign authors that might be considered of different "brows" are grouped together and how in the Simmons campaign they appear alongside figures from other fields, both "high" and "low." Their value for campaigns is determined solely by the notoriety of their brand.
99. Esther Eaton. "Making the World 'Sleep Conscious': Fifteen famous men talk on sleep through Simmons Advertising." *JWT Company News Letter* 11.47 (1 December 1929): 1, 3. 1.
100. Ibid., 1.
101. Marlis Schweitzer and Marina Moskowitz, eds. *Testimonial Advertising in the American Marketplace: Emulation, Identity, Community*. New York: Palgrave Macmillan, 2009. 9.
102. Denise H. Sutton. *Globalizing Ideal Beauty: How Female Copywriters of the J. Walter Thompson Advertising Agency Redefined Beauty for the Twentieth Century*. New York: Palgrave Macmillan, 2009. 86.
103. Eaton, 1.
104. Ibid., 3.
105. Ibid., 3.
106. Eaton's newsletter piece oddly identifies O'Duffy as a "young English novelist" although he actually was an Irish writer and activist, newly living in England after becoming disillusioned by the resurgence in conservative nationalism after the Easter Rising. At the time of his "interview" with Shaw, O'Duffy was fresh from publishing the second novel in his satirical utopic trilogy (*The Spacious Adventures of the Man in the Street*); the first novel in that series included a scene set in 1950s Ireland at a Shaw centenary celebration run by Andrew Undershaft types.
107. "A philosopher's Ideas About Sleep." *Time* 13.18 (6 May 1929): 29.
108. Michael Schudson. *Advertising, the Uneasy Persuasion: Its Dubious Impact on American Society*. New York: Basic Books, 1984. 215.
109. John Lee Mahin. "Advertising—A Form of Organized Salesmanship." *Printers' Ink* 70 (30 March 1910): 5.
110. Spender, 72.
111. "Authors as Copywriters," 490.
112. George Burton Hotchkiss. *Advertising Copy*. New York: Harper and Brothers, 1949. 98.
113. "What the Advertising Industry Thinks of Purchased Testimonials." *Printers' Ink* 146.12 (21 March 1929): 148–9. 148.

114. Ibid., 148–9.
115. "Advertisers' Association Issues Testimonial Suggestion." *Printers' Ink* 146.12 (21 March 1929): 182, 184.
116. Roy Dickinson. "What the Consumer Thinks of the Modern Testimonial." *Printers' Ink* 146.13 (28 March 1929): 17–20. 17.
117. Ibid., 19.
118. Joseph Appel. *Growing Up with Advertising*. New York: The Business Bourse, 1940. 149.
119. O. C. Harn. "Who Is Going to Clean Up This Testimonial Mess?" *Printers' Ink* 146.12 (21 March 1929): 3–6, 181–7. 3.
120. Bernard Shaw. "Preface" to *Farfetched Fables*. In *Complete Plays with Prefaces*, vol. 6. New York: Dodd, Mead & Company, 1963. 455–90. 482.
121. Harn, 6.
122. Bernard Shaw, *Essays in Fabian Socialism, Major Critical Essays* 30. New York: Wm. H. Wise & Company, 1932.
123. Harn, 4.
124. Ibid., 6, 181
125. "A.N.A. Declares Against Paid Testimonial Advertising." *Printers' Ink* 147.10 (6 June 1929): 73–80. 73.
126. Michelle Hilmes. *Hollywood and Broadcasting: From Radio to Cable*. Champaign: University of Illinois Press, 1999. 87.
127. Mark Tungate. *Ad Land: A Global History of Advertising*. London: Kogan Page, 2007. 26.
128. Schweitzer and Moskowitz, 7.
129. Stephen Fox. *The Mirror Makers: A History of American Advertising and Its Creators*. New York: William Morrow and Company Inc., 1984. 90.
130. *J.W.T. News* 1.29 (16 December 46): 4.
131. Corey Ford. "A Meeting of the Endorsers' Club." *The New Yorker* (11 May 1929): 19–20. 20.
132. Raymond Rubicam. "When Is the Testimonial Tainted?" *Printers Ink* 146.11 (14 March 1929): 17–20. 18.
133. Wood, 393–4.
134. "Bernard Shaw and Harrods," *The New York Times* (15 March 1929): 15.
135. Walter O'Meara. "On a Phase of Copy Style." *The J. Walter Thompson News Bulletin* 110 (December 1924): 11–3. 11.
136. Jennifer Wicke. *Advertising Fictions: Literature, Advertisement, and Social Reading*. New York: Columbia University Press, 1988. 172.
137. Letter from Shaw to Mabel Shaw (30 January 1928). Bernard Shaw. *Collected Letters*, vol. 4. Ed. Dan H. Laurence. New York: Viking, 1988. 90.

CHAPTER 5

# "Those Magic Initials, G.B.S.": Copywriting for the Irish Clipper

Shaw's articulation of his own prophet motive in 1929 mirrors moves made by the advertising industry during that decade to reboot their public image in a more altruistic vein with regard to the consumer. Attempting to distance themselves from their patent-medicine past and legitimate themselves professionally, advertisers in America "established the Associated Advertising Clubs of America and at their first meeting in 1911 they launched the truth-in-advertising movement [to reaffirm] their commitment to ideals of public opinion."[1] In a speech delivered at the 1911 convention, Joseph Appel insisted "advertising is not to sell, but to help people to buy ... We stand in the shoes of the customer. We are outside, not behind the counter. We are counselors for the public."[2] In any case, "the war marked the high tide of progressive faith in the beneficent powers of 'publicity'."[3]

When the market crashed at the end of the 1920s, the bottom fell out of advertising, and the industry in America would not return to the same expenditure levels until after the Second World War. At the same time, it found itself criticized during the Great Depression as the "public voice of industry and business [by] articulate customers organized into self-constituted vigilance committees [such as the National Consumers' League and the Consumers' Club] and from government."[4] In the 1930s, soon after the Wells and Shaw Simmons ads appeared, American agencies faced increased scrutiny over their compensation practices when

© The Author(s) 2018
C. Wixson, *Bernard Shaw and Modern Advertising*,
Bernard Shaw and His Contemporaries,
https://doi.org/10.1007/978-3-319-78628-5_5

133

the Federal Trade Commission (FTC) turned its attention toward the problem of "tainted testimonials," particularly false or fabricated testimonials and the practice of paying "widely known people" for their statements. What the public had assumed was a gift freely given to a company, an act of enthusiasm or goodwill, was now revealed to be a commodity exchange, a service rendered for a fee.[5]

The J. Walter Thompson agency in particular came under fire for a Simmons mattress campaign that preceded the one that involved the two authors. Historians Marina Moskowitz and Marlis Schweitzer characterize the campaign an "innovative take on the pyramid scheme" in which JWT enlisted

> the services of prominent society women to recruit their friends and relatives [and] received a commission ranging between $1,000 and $2,000, depending on the reputation and status of the endorsee, who was similarly paid between $1,000 and $5,000 for her statement. ... Not surprisingly, the J. Walter Thompson Company did not reveal to the public that these women had been compensated for their efforts, presumably hoping that readers would believe that such testimonial statements were spontaneous expressions of consumer delight.[6]

Unsurprisingly, much attention given to the Harrods campaign concerned the question of whether the authors were compensated for their appearances. The *Printers' Ink* London correspondent directly had inquired of the store "what was behind the copy," and Charles Wildes, director of Harrods, unequivocally claimed that the "three authors were genuinely unpaid" and went on to reassert that "no other authors were approached [and] no money or other inducement was given to either Wells, Shaw or Bennett. Two years ago, Bennett refused a 500 pound offer to write one large advertisement, made by a large London firm."[7] Skepticism continued to be directed towards both 1929 campaigns (and those like them) over endorser compensation so that the experimental "near-testimonial" for both Harrods and Simmons ultimately proved unsuccessful in allaying concerns over the technique.

In April of 1929, invoking both campaigns, H. S. Gardner wrote in *Advertising & Selling* that the innovation in testimonial form was proof that the technique was indeed on the wane:

> Possibly the perpetrators of these silly hoaxes are beginning to realize that they have been too blatant, for more subtle treatment is creeping in.

We now see sleep endorsed, instead of a certain make of beds. Since this endorsement of nature's great blessing appears in an advertisement of beds, no doubt the advertiser feels that a near endorsement is as good as a real one. This near endorsement of a product reached the heights of subtlety recently when three of the world's leading literary lights declined to sell their talents in the interest of commercialism, and yet permitted the advertiser to publish in advertisements their pictures and letters declining the offer. ... No doubt some of these testimonials were given without a price consideration, the desire for publicity being a sufficient reward – but how can the public discriminate? The sheep are all herded with the goats.... And who, pray, is being deluded, except the manufacturer who pays the bills? Certainly not the public—who merely laughs at such gross stupidity.[8]

After noting recent scandalous fraudulent testimonial exposures, Gardner concludes with a near-epitaph:

> This is all evidence that the prostituted advertisement is taking the cure. Complete recovery is certain to be effected if the patient is given big and frequent doses of well-deserved publicity. Lay on, MacDuff, and don't let up until there remains no copy theme chaser who has the temerity to submit a testimonial advertisement to a client. Honest testimonials will disappear with the paid ones, but one can always fall back on a simple statement of a product's merits and have an effective advertisement. After so much highly seasoned advertising, the public might like a little plain talk, if it has the ring of sincerity in it.[9]

It was clear that the testimonial would again have to fight for legitimacy and seek new ways to regain the public's attention and trust, and, late in his life, Shaw again becomes the linchpin of a campaign that sought to counteract the technique's beleaguered public reputation.

In September of 1930, *Advertising & Selling*'s European correspondent noted an "advertisement [that] occupied a generous space in the *New York Herald* of Paris" and served as "another illustration of the mass of international advertising appearing" on the continent. The travel advert repackaged a statement Shaw had made in 1929:

> Englishmen, Irishmen, Scots, Americans and holiday makers of all civilized nations, come in your millions to Yugoslavia. The people are everything you imagine yourselves to be and are not. They are hospitable, good humoured and very good looking. Every town is a picture and every girl is a movie star. Come quickly before they find us out: it is too good to last. Bernard Shaw.

In response, Amos Stote, entitling his piece "G.B.S. Joins Us," raves,

> Here's a testimonial advertisement, and a signed one, that I am all *for*. Just how the Ministry of Commerce of Yugoslavia got it I can't tell. But it must be authentic, and very spontaneous. [The text] certainly elevates G.B.S. to the exalted rank of copywriter, gives him an honest place among the world's workers, and shows what a testimonial advertisement can be.[10]

Shaw indeed belonged to those exalted ranks, having already been for decades his own best copywriter for print appearances in newspapers, periodicals, and advertisements. It was even commonplace for him discreetly to "touch up" interviews and articles about him before they went to press. Twenty years after the Harrods ads, though, his practice of producing copy took center stage, after he was approached again by the J. Walter Thompson agency, this time for permission to use a quote in an ad for Pan-American's Clipper air service from New York to Ireland. Having become in 1947 "the first [agency in America] to pass the US$100 million billings mark"[11] as well as the largest such company in Britain, JWT continued to creatively resuscitate celebrity endorsement as a lucrative marketing technique and decided to approach the promotion in an unusual way, heavily stressing Shaw's involvement in the copywriting process. When it appeared in 1948, the spot proved to be yet another international marketing event, one that not only foregrounded Shaw's savvy marketing but also illustrated once more how agencies could re-purpose "G.B.S." to suit their own interests.

Biographer Dan Laurence locates the campaign's genesis with JWT copywriter Gelston Hardy who, in 1946, "conceived the idea of promoting Pan American's Clipper service between the United States and Ireland by use of a Shaw quotation he had found in an Irish Tourist Association leaflet."[12] However, an interview with Hardy that appeared in *The New Yorker* in 1948 pushed the origin back to the fall of 1945 when

> [Hardy] was poking around for an idea to encourage flights by trans-atlantic Clipper and came across a statement by [Irish politician Éamon] De Valera that seemed to be ready-made for the purpose: "When you come to Ireland, a hearty welcome awaits you." [Despite obtaining de Valera's consent,] it didn't strike Pan American as cogent copy.[13]

Hardy then discovered and immediately realized the potential of the ITA leaflet blurb attributed to the playwright: "I was lost in dreams of Ireland; one cannot work in a place where there is such infinite peace."[14]

As a result of Helen Lansdowne's lucrative Pond's campaign, the Personality Department at J. Walter Thompson was created in the mid-1920s to identify, contact, and negotiate directly with prospective product endorsers without having to contract with companies who specialized in that service, and international company offices each had their own Personality staff. William M. Freeman, in his book *The Big Name* (1957), provides an overview of the solicitation and endorsement process:

> Once the campaign has been decided on and a huddle has produced the concept of a celebrity or an unknown, selected by occupation or background, as an endorser, the agency calls in the specialist who has on file a list of names of personalities who are appropriate to certain fields of endorsements. ... It is a matter of "good casting" – matching the right product to the right name. The specialist in the field, armed with a rough of the copy, ... makes the contact and goes ahead with the sometimes delicate negotiations. ... The honorarium varies considerably. The average "fee" may range from nothing all the way to $1,500, sometimes more. Quite often a celebrity will accept nothing at all with a mention of his latest picture or book or whatever it might be the only quid pro quo for the endorsement.[15]

Immediately after discovering the quotation, Hardy directed the London office to contact Shaw and attempt to persuade him for permission to use it.

For months, JWT heard nothing back from the playwright. In October 1946, though, a reply to their permission query arrived in which Shaw disavowed and denounced the quotation:

> I object most strenuously to the advertisement. I am quoted as saying what I never said, and [it] is not only manifest nonsense as to Ireland being a land of peace, but is most unlikely to stimulate tourist traffic, which is presumably your object. And will you please refer to me in public as Bernard Shaw and not George Bernard Shaw.
>
> I authorize you to substitute the following quotation:
>
> "There is no magic like that of Ireland.
> There are no skies like Irish skies.

> There is no air like Irish air.
> Two years in the Irish climate will make the stiffest and slowest mind flexible and faster for life."
>
> You can put my photograph and signature to this; but you must follow it, as from Airways, with: "And all this within two hours of luxurious travel from London instead of an uncomfortable sixteen."
>
> I should like to see a proof of the altered advertisements before it goes to press.
>
> Faithfully,<br>G. Bernard Shaw[16]

Unsurprisingly, JWT was thrilled at the unexpected contribution and reconceived the campaign around these "corrected" lines, visually supplemented by postcard images of Dublin and Ashford Castle.[17] Stumped as to what to do about the reference to Ireland's being only two hours from *London*, Hardy asked the British office to clarify for Shaw that Pan-American was pushing transatlantic travel. Then, he set about reworking the playwright's copy, smoothing out the confusion of that final line, rendering it as "And you can go on to London by luxurious Clipper in less than two hours now instead of an uncomfortable sixteen." Hardy also replaced "two years in the Irish Climate" with "two weeks in the Irish Climate," deemed a more appropriate length for tourism.

Unwilling to spend nearly $2000 on a proof of the four-color ad in case Shaw withdrew from the project, Hardy sent him a typewritten version of all the proposed copy (including captions for the images) in March of 1948. In a rapid response, as Dan Laurence puts it, "Shaw characteristically proceeded to revise not only his own contribution but everything else as well."[18] Alongside "Press as corrected, GBS," the emended copy read,

> There is no magic like that of Ireland.
> There are no skies like Irish skies.
> There is no air like Irish air.
> The Irish climate will make the stiffest and slowest mind flexible for life;
> And you can now go on to London by air in less than two hours instead of sixteen by rail and unquiet sea.[19]

Significantly, Shaw excised the explicit mention of the client in the last line, but Hardy affirmed "the old gentleman's" decision to remove "our commercial about 'luxurious Clipper' [since] we really wanted to be sincere about this thing."[20] As he had in the earlier Simmons campaign, Shaw is careful not specifically to endorse the product but rather rhapsodize about Ireland. The ad's final draft supplemented Shaw's text and signature with four images (the largest being of the playwright in the upper left corner), copy about the Clipper including their experienced crew and directions for fares and reservations, and the Pan-American World Airways logo in the lower left corner.[21] With layout and copy finalized, the campaign was ready for rollout in the summer of 1948, and the ad proliferated widely through a number of American periodicals, from June and July editions of *Time* and *The New Yorker* to the September issues of the *Princeton Alumni Weekly* (49:2) and *Cornell Alumni News* (51:2) (see Fig. 5.1).

The ad's appearance was preceded by a novel vanguard, a wave of promotional "articles" that emphasized Shaw's participation throughout the copywriting process as a strategy to infuse his copy with integrity and veracity. Appearing a month prior to the color ads, a *New York Times* article entitled "'Plug' for Airways Written by Shaw" announced in its opening sentence that "Bernard Shaw… has turned huckster" and that "Ireland was the theme that induced the irascible exile to take pencil in hand." The piece goes on to iterate what Shaw wrote and the changes he made to the ad's copy as does another short item that ran that same week in *Time* magazine entitled "Free Irish Air." *Editor & Publisher*, a trade publication for the newspaper industry, was the first to reproduce a facsimile of the copy typescript with Shaw's handwritten revisions in the June 19th issue (under the heading "Bernard Shaw Touches Up Agency Copy for Airline"). Even after the ad eventually appeared, supplemental notices continued to emerge, and the facsimile of Shaw's handwritten copy revisions from March resurfaced "especially reproduced from the original typescript for readers of *The Saturday Review*" in its July 17, 1948 issue (see Fig. 5.2). TSR dutifully directed its readers to "see the complete 4-color version" appearing "now on the newsstands."[22]

Within the industry as well, periodicals called attention to the campaign and its celebrity spokesman. For example, a short piece entitled "'As Corrected' By G.B.S." ran in *Tide: The News Magazine of Advertising, Marketing and Public Relations* (July 23, 1948) to relate how the *Saturday Review of Literature*, "proud of its burning interest in everything George Bernard Shaw does, sprang to action" upon hearing of the playwright's copy revision and asked permission from JWT to "run the actual proof in the magazine … with all the messy alterations, printers' symbols etc. … instead of the fancy finished product." *Tide* also noted that "it was the first time Pan Am ever advertised in *SRL*."[23]

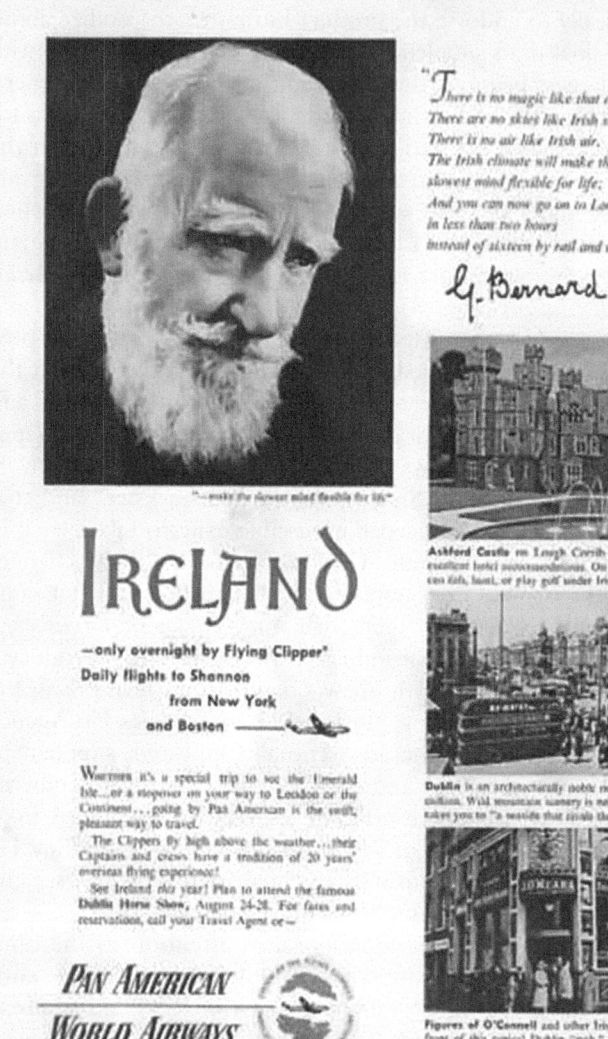

Fig. 5.1 Irish Clipper advertisement, *The New Yorker* (July 17, 1948)

5 "THOSE MAGIC INITIALS, G.B.S.": COPYWRITING FOR THE IRISH CLIPPER  141

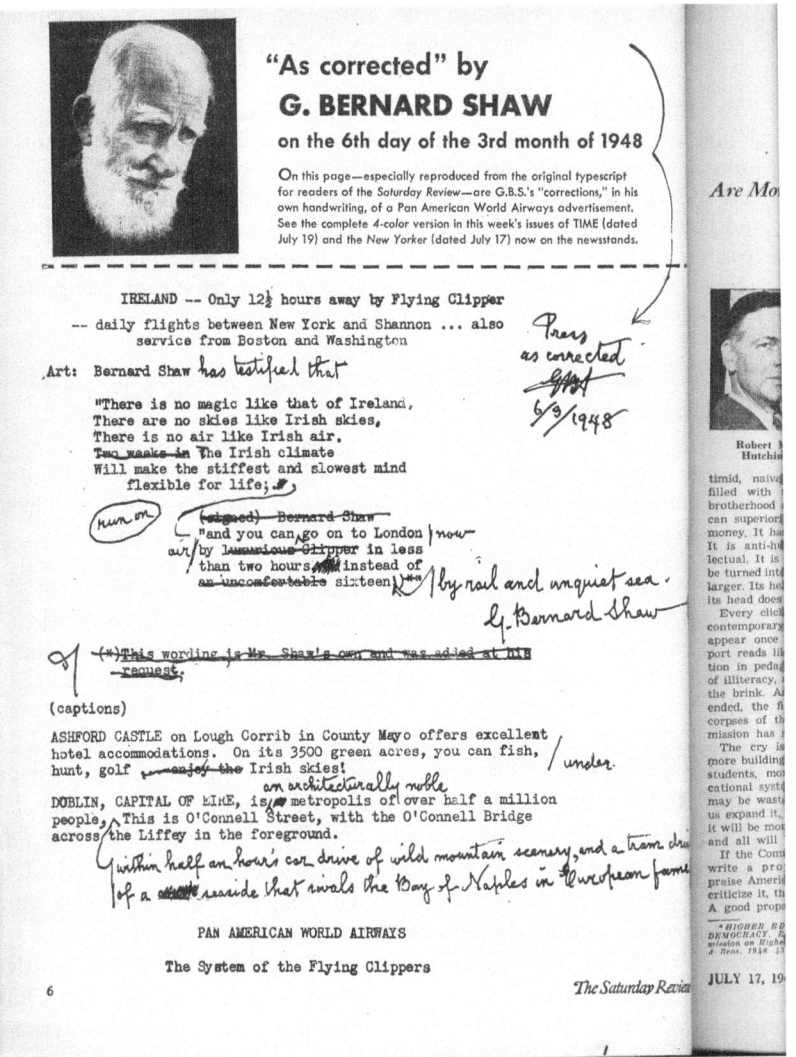

Fig. 5.2  Irish Clipper advertisement, *The Saturday Review* (July 17, 1948), p. 6

Within the agency, this flurry of promotional activity was recognized and celebrated in the June 21 edition of *The J.W.T. News*:

> PAN AMERICAN WORLD AIRWAYS (NY) began last week to reap – <u>double free</u> – newsprint benefits far beyond any publicist's wildest dreams from an advertisement scheduled to appear in July. New York City newspapers and wire services across the nation reported at length how advertising and literary and financial history had been made. George Bernard Shaw (pardon – "Bernard Shaw") had taken a fling at copywriting and – for free – had, on the solicitation of JWT, written an advertisement telling the pleasures of a flight to Ireland on Pan American Airways.[24]

A few weeks later, *The J.W.T. News* continued to trumpet the success of the supplemental notices:

> Advance publicity stories made much of the fact that George Bernard Shaw, at the request of JWT, wrote this advertisement to promote travel by air to Ireland. Clippings are still coming in to Pan Am from Los Angeles, Dallas, Kansas City, San Francisco, Milwaukee, Miami, New Orleans and Boston, as well as those already collected from New York City and the advertising press. "Nemo," the weather man on Station WOR (NY), used the Shaw statement, unsolicited, in an amusing radio interview on the subject of Irish weather. Dublin and London papers are also carrying the story.[25]

The piece also proudly directed its readers to "note that in this advertisement, G.B.S. says nothing at all about the product—the Clipper. He only 'testifies' about IRELAND; and thereby shows how true it is that 'names make news' even if they are only <u>associated</u> with the product or the client's name."[26] Nonetheless, as with the previous Simmons campaign, the issue of compensation again resurfaced.[27]

In a "Talk of the Town" piece from July of 1948 entitled "Copywriter," *The New Yorker* took up the subject of the campaign, most curious that the prominently featured "encomium by Bernard Shaw on his native land" had allegedly been provided *gratis*: "inasmuch as Shaw's fame as a writer is scarcely second to his fame as a shrewd and firm man with a pound or dollar, we have looked into this report."[28] In the piece, campaign "engineer" Gelston Hardy confirms that this account of the "unprecedented gift of words [that] shook J. Walter Thompson" is indeed accurate. A month prior, *Time*'s "Fresh Irish Air" enhanced its own retelling of the story of the negotiations with Shaw ("a hard man with a dollar") with an exchange between offices concerning payment. In Hardy's account, JWT's "London office thought Shaw's endorsement might be obtained by a 'combination of audacity and a large sum of money' ($4000 was suggested)" while "New York suggested London try 'audacity' ... leaving the money for him to bring up." The story concluded by indicating that "up to last week, with the ad ready to run, Copywriter Shaw had not even mentioned the matter of payment."[29] The *New York Times* article also emphasizes that Shaw produced this copywriting "for free" while *Editor & Publisher*'s piece recounts the anxious inter-office exchange over the issue of paying Shaw.[30] In the entire body of meta-publicity that surrounds the campaign, the story of Shaw's involvement is told and retold, always reproducing his lines about Ireland and usually interwoven, to a greater or lesser degree, with accounts of solicitation, remuneration, and copy revisions negotiations. If these clues suggest that the campaign with Shaw was part of a larger effort to restore credibility to personality advertising, who better than the prophet who demonized authors turning to commerce and refused Harrods' tempting advances to restore public faith in testimonial-based marketing? After the critical scrutiny it had received during the previous decade over its endorsement practices, JWT claimed it had "redoubled its efforts to verify all statements used in testimonial advertising, reexamined its practice of paying for statements, and opted to play it safe in situations where other advertising strategies could work just as well."[31] The extensive and unusual preemptive publicity blitz for the Irish Air campaign is interesting in this light, particularly its obsessive foregrounding of how the sausage is made. Indeed, the process garnered as much if not more attention than the product.

In addition to exposing Shaw at work drafting copy, the campaign also illuminated the "invisible hands" at the agency who were attracting publicity all their own. The mythology around the playwright's role grew to engulf even the staffers who orchestrated it, most protrusively Gel Hardy. In August 1948, *J.W.T. News* duly recognized the attention from the *New Yorker* with a blurb entitled "Claims to Fame": "Few of the famous – or infamous – make the New Yorker's "Talk of the Town" editorial feature, but JWT's Gel Hardy rated three columns last week [in which] Gel's activities on the now much-acclaimed G.B. Shaw, Pan Am. Advertisement were cited."[32] Likewise, the very *first* sentence of a December 1948 profile of Hardy in the weekly J. Walter Thompson staff newsletter reads, "One of Gel Hardy's recent Pan American advertisements was written in collaboration with George Bernard Shaw."[33]

More incredible is the degree to which Shaw's name became synonymous with that of Dorothea Campbell Blaker in JWT's London office, whom Hardy enlisted to contact the playwright initially for permission to use the leaflet quote.[34] The colorful Blaker came to the J. Walter Thompson agency in the late 1920s as a freelance worker on testimonial assignments initially and eventually rose to become head of the Legal and Personality Department where she handled "intransigent celebrities, would-be self-publicists, nervous housewives, and enthusiastic hypochondriacs alike with amazing charm and tact."[35] In 1947, Blaker was featured in the "How Well Do You Know Your JWT'ERS?" column of the weekly J. Walter Thompson staff newsletter. Accompanied by a sketch of the subject in profile, with close-cropped hair and a necktie, the piece began: "If you want an English film star signed up, or a Pond's beauty, or a celebrated footballer or any person of note (including George Bernard Shaw) you apply to the Personality Department, JWT-London. And there you will find 'Bill' Blaker."[36]

*Round the Square*, a monthly publication issued by the J. Walter Thompson London office, itself ran a profile of Blaker in 1953. It maintains that, for an affirmation of Blaker's motto ("It can't be done – but we'll do it."), "one can't do better than to study – on the wall of her room – a selection of the correspondence that passed between her office and that of the Sage of Ayot, which shows how Bill's department, after a wordy battle with the most indefatigable non-co-operator of them all, finally won for an advertisement the magic initials, G.B.S."[37]

Staffer Peter Yeo, in his memoirs published privately in 1988, remembered her at the agency's annual fête and gala, forsaking "her rather masculine, tweedy apparel for a regular evening gown [and intoning] in a deep contralto." Yeo goes on to note that Blaker's "biggest achievement was to get George Bernard Shaw, a fierce opponent of publicity, to sponsor an advertisement for Pan-American Airways" and recalled the "signed photograph of the great man hanging in her office."[38] Indeed, in a circa 1950 company photograph as well as in another photo published with her 1953 newsletter profile, two letters (matted, framed, and hung) flanking the signed photograph are visible behind Blaker, Shaw benevolently gazing down at the manager at work.[39]

The success of this promotion of staffers *and* personalities went on to become a series in 1949 for Pan-American, again featuring not only endorsements from Robert W. Service, Billy Rose, and Lowell Thomas but also accounts of the intrepid JWT agents committed to securing participation from difficult celebrities. According to the *JWT News*, "these advertisements are a far cry from typical 'testimonials' that read 'I like your clipper because …' and naturally they are hard to get. For the current advertisement, a well-known JWT copywriter interviewed pajama-clad Billy Rose for several hours to accomplish his mission."[40] After running its course through periodicals and newspapers, an initial printing of travel posters, and even a postage stamp, iterations of Shaw's image and lines continue to be emblazoned in travel-related guidebooks and on websites to this day, as occasionally does the erroneously attributed leaflet quote that engendered the campaign. On behalf of the Pan-American Clipper, JWT's ingeniousness at turning the workings of campaign creation inside-out not only created an enormous amount of incidental publicity but also infused the "personality" copy with much-needed authenticity and probity. The degree to which JWT had a hand in placing those preemptive notices in trade publications and outlets such as *Time* and *The New Yorker* (where suspiciously the ads would also eventually appear) is unknown, but the agency's canny involvement with cross-marketing practices is well documented.

To what degree Shaw was aware of the extent to which JWT would anchor their campaign around his participation is also unknown. Nonetheless, his extensive contributions exemplify how committed he was to striving for autonomy over his copy. Yet, his copywriting for the Clipper also reflects his ambivalence towards commodity culture and his sensitivity in particular to the difficulties of marketing Ireland. If Shaw's lines lack the usual impishness and bombast of Shavian rhetoric and, beyond a banal nod to generic mental fitness, don't exert their usual pull towards a lifestyle worthy of emulation, they nonetheless contain implicit echoes of three plays that span Shaw's playwriting career. The nod to flexibility of mind within the Irish climate seems to proceed from an exchange from *Back to Methuselah*:

> THE WOMAN: Have you been sent here to make your mind flexible?
> THE ELDERLY GENTLEMAN: What an extraordinary question! Pray do you find my mind noticeably stiff?
> THE WOMAN: Perhaps you do not know that you are on the west coast of Ireland, and that it is the practice among natives of the Eastern Island to spend some years here to acquire mental flexibility. The climate has that effect.
> THE ELDERLY GENTLEMAN [*haughtily*]: I was born, not in the Eastern Island, but, thank God, in dear old British Baghdad; and I am not in need of a mental health resort.[41]

Shaw's copy also evokes yet contradicts Larry Doyle's miasmic view of the Irish climate in *John Bull's Other Island*:

> DOYLE: My dear Tom, you only need a touch of the Irish climate to be as big a fool as I am myself. ... The dullness! the hopelessness! The ignorance! the bigotry!
> BROADBENT [matter-of-factly]: The usual thing in the country, Larry. Just the same here.
> DOYLE [hastily]: No, no: the climate is different. Here, if the life is dull, you can be dull too, and no great harm done. [*Going off into a passionate dream*] But your wits can't thicken in that soft moist air, on those white springy roads, in those misty rushes and brown bogs, on those hillsides of granite rocks and magenta heather. You've no such colors in the sky, no such lure in the distances, no such sadness in the evenings. Oh, the dreaming! the dreaming! the torturing, heartscalding, never satisfying dreaming, dreaming, dreaming, dreaming!⁴²

Shaw's negative characterization of the travel industry as a whole is perhaps most direct in Popsy's account of one consequence of her newfound wealth and independence in *Too True to Be Good*, to which his copy lines further lightly allude:

> I was devoured by parasites: by tourist agencies, steamboat companies, railways, motor car people, hotel keepers, dressmakers, servants, all trying to get my money by selling me things I don't really want; shoving me all over the globe to look at what they call new skies, though they know as well as I do that it is only the same old sky everywhere; and disabling me by doing all the things for me that I ought to do for myself to keep myself in health.⁴³

Sharply critical of an industry that serves what he calls in the play's preface a class a "vagrant rootless rich ... detached from work, from responsibility, from tradition, from every sort of prescribed routine,"⁴⁴ it perhaps is surprising that he agreed to participate in the Clipper campaign, beyond a sharp rebuke of the euphemistic misrepresentation of Ireland in the leaflet quote. The intertextual play between his copy and passages in the plays would most likely be lost on the ordinary reader, and the larger vision articulated by the ad as a whole seems uncomfortably close to what Broadbent imagines.

Travel marketing is indeed among the central preoccupations of *John Bull's Other Island*; in fact, the set design for the firm of Doyle and Broadbent calls for a "pictorial advertisement of a steamship company" to hang on the wall.⁴⁵ Kathleen Ochshorn has pointed out that Shaw's 1904 play "anticipates the international marketing of Ireland's beauty and the exploitation of its rural landscape [to further a] postcolonial economy based on tourism."⁴⁶ Guided by the rhetoric of Murray's guidebook, Broadbent plans to marshal available material resources towards an imaginative repackaging of Irishness as they "make a Garden city of Rosscullen" and render "the Round Tower ... thoroughly repaired and restored."⁴⁷ Shaw had, in an 1896 theatrical review, affirmed his commitment to "the saving work of reducing the sham Ireland of romance to a heap of unsightly ruins" but here as copywriter risks complicity with the commodification of a certain idyllic image of Ireland, repurposing sites like Ashford Castle for tourist consumption.⁴⁸ Like Tim Haffigan's act of "native impersonation" in *John Bull's Other Island*, Shaw's ad text is fraught with the danger of Ireland imitating "its own colonially coercive image for commercial ends."⁴⁹

Recent scholarly discussions have formulated tourism in colonial terms, situating "the contemporary marketing of 'Ireland' [within] a wider system of globalization in which cultural signifiers circulate at the behest and under the aegis of powerful national/corporate formations, replicating the earlier colonial heritage."⁵⁰ As Mark Phelan observes, *John Bull's Other Island* staged this nascent trend with an "implicit connection between tourism and colonialism ... explicitly articulated in Broadbent's closing vision of golf courses built on the west coast of Ireland: a conflation of imperial and tourist rhetoric that has proved astonishingly prescient."⁵¹ In the evolution of modern advertising, "copywriters ... shifted [focus] with the beginning of the century from the object for sale to the consumer's subjective associations and experiences"⁵² but also emphasized a notion of "authenticity," a concept central to current scholarly discussions of consumerist culture and modernism. Jennifer Outka recently has charted the late nineteenth-century advent of a "commodified authentic" in which "new objects and places were packaged and sold as mini-representations of supposedly noncommercial values: nostalgic evocations of an English rural past; appeals to an original, genuine article; and images of a purified aesthetic free from any taint of the mass market."⁵³ In *Too True to Be Good*, the Patient's account of her experience following her act one escape outlines the process through which virtues and the natural world are commodified and packaged as copy: "Popsy stole my necklace, and got me to run away with him by a wonderful speech he made about freedom and sunshine and lovely scenery. Sweetie made me write it all down and sell it to a tourist agency as an advertisement."⁵⁴

In similar ways, travel marketing often deployed discourse from an imperial past, and the tourist industry marks one intersection of Irish cultural representation and commodity capitalism within which what Colin Graham characterizes as the "peddling of the authentic in an explicit and populist way" becomes a potentially neo-imperialist act.[55] Since the early 1970s, sociologists have understood tourism as motivated by a desire for authenticity, a quality deemed a casualty of alienated, industrialized modernity,[56] and thus travel marketing invested in representing destinations as opportunities for encounters with "authentic" inhabitants and practices, especially what Nina Wang calls "ethnic, history or cultural tourism which involve the representation of the Other or the past."[57] Especially over as contested an ideological space as Ireland, though, this practice of "staging authenticity" has a much deeper resonance. Because "authenticity" is precisely what imperialism denies the colonized culture, decolonization engenders a quest for authenticity in which native inhabitants strive to recover and reclaim an authentic (in this case) "Irishness" apart from imperial ideological constructions. In the preface to the published version of the play, Shaw gauged the Abbey Theater's refusal to stage *John Bull's Other Island* to be a function of the play being "uncongenial to the whole spirit of the neo-Gaelic movement, which is bent on creating a new Ireland after its own ideal,"[58] suggesting Yeats and other members were perhaps as invested in commodifying the Irish "authentic" to further its ends as Broadbent was to further his. As Brad Kent has argued, "Yeats's decolonizing of Irish identity led to another form of colonization, a *re*colonization of Irish identity [so that] the constructs of both nationalists and imperialists, the fixed identities inherent in stereotypes, are two aspects of the same process of mummification," and *John Bull's Other Island* critiques "the dangerous essentialism of both the colonial and the emergent national constructs."[59]

While positing the desirability of being in Ireland, the text contained in the Pan-Am Clipper ad subtly avoids trading in either nationalist or imperialist constructions. The first three lines of copy each establish the uniqueness of Ireland without ever defining it (e.g. "There is no magic like that of Ireland"), and the final line asserts that the climate is restorative for the mind without indicating what about Ireland specifically engenders this effect. As such, particularized qualities of Irishness elude precise capture in the language of American marketing. Besides tinkering with Hardy's drafted copy, Shaw also modified both captions that were to appear underneath photographic images of Dublin and Ashford Castle in County Mayo. Hardy's initial draft of the Ashford Castle caption read as, "Ashford Castle on Lough Corrib in County Mayo offers excellent hotel accommodations. On its 3500 green acres, you can fish, hunt, golf, and enjoy Irish skies!" While retaining Hardy's straightforward list of generic activities one can do on the grounds, Shaw's only change is a significant one, amending the second sentence to become in the final copy, "On its 3500 green acres, you can fish, hunt, and play golf under Irish skies." As such, "Irish skies" are no longer a commodity to be consumed, no longer subject to the tourist's gaze and instead just a backdrop for leisurely pursuits. A number of contemporary sociologists problematize the claim that tourism is motivated solely by the need for authenticity by pointing to the concept's inadequacy in assessing "phenomena such as visiting friends and relatives, beach holidays, … fishing, hunting, or sports."[60] Shaw's modification to the line maintains its focus on activities rather than the "commodified authentic."

Similarly, Hardy's suggestion for the Dublin image caption read as, "Dublin, capital of Eire, is a metropolis of over half a million people. This is O'Connell Street, with the O'Connell Bridge across the Liffey in the foreground." In turn, Shaw supplemented Hardy's straightforward descriptiveness, calling Dublin an "architecturally noble metropolis" and suggesting an extension to the first sentence that indicated the city was "within half an hour's car drive of wild mountain scenery, and a tram drive of a seaside that rivals the Bay of Naples in European fame."[61] Again accenting *doing* as opposed to simply *seeing*, Shaw asserts the beauty and diversity of Ireland, sidestepping that system that objectifies and exoticizes according to "a particular mode of aesthetic *perception*— one which renders people, objects, and places strange even as it domesticates them, and which effectively manufactures otherness even as it claims to surrender to its imminent mystery."[62] The copy Shaw provides for the Clipper campaign (eventually condensed by Hardy with respect to the dictates of space) doesn't trade in what Griffiths calls the "mythologised and fetishised sign" of Irishness in the global market.[63] In avoiding both "nostalgic" tropes of Gaelic, pagan authenticity and any hint of colonial stereotype, Shaw's copywriting on the Pan-American campaign seems deliberately phrased and consistent with much of his other writing which, as McEwan has argued, "reveals the tensions that render authenticity an unstable category in modernity."[64]

Nevertheless, the copy Shaw wrote is counterbalanced by JWT copy that not only is explicit about the product, replete with Pan-American logo and motto ("World's Most Experienced Airline"), but treads dangerously close to the ideology of tourist marketing. The full facsimile of Shaw's handwritten changes (published in an August 1956 *Round the Square* feature) includes a third caption to accompany an image of a Dublin pub that remained mysteriously untouched by Shaw.[65] Indeed, it is the only section whose copy he did not amend in any way: "Figures of O'Connell and other Irish 'greats' decorate the front of this typical Dublin 'pub.' You can reach Dublin and other parts of Ireland by air, rail or bus from Shannon." In the first sentence, Irish culture is exotically paraded in quotation marks. Whether Shaw gave any specific blessing or offered revision to this caption cannot be determined but, considering the changes he made to the other captions and the torrent of changes he made to every piece of drafted copy sent to him, it is strange that it was left untouched. In any case, based on the surviving evidence, the playwright seems not to have responded to the other elements of what became the finished advertisement after it appeared; as *The New Yorker* later observed, "no kick from Shaw so far."[66]

To a degree, Shaw also is used implicitly as a "stage Irishman" of sorts by the campaign. Even as Shaw the copywriter works to disentangle the description from neo-imperialism, JWT appropriates "G.B.S." as a brand name endowed not only with authority as a writer but specifically as an *Irish* writer. Shaw thus is unable to remain apart from commodification; this issue arises most pointedly in a supplement produced in connection with the Pan-Am campaign. Simultaneous to the periodical appearance of the ads, "Pan American distributed to travel agents a redesigned and simplified display poster ... which contained a five-line abbreviation of Shaw's original eight-line statement."[67] The emerald-colored poster has at its center an image of Shaw's face (an airplane flying literally overhead) surrounded by Irish iconography (a harp, a cottage, a shamrock, and a castle; see Fig. 5.3). Hovering above Shaw's condensed blurb and a facsimile signature, the only other text is the centered heading ("Ireland By Clipper") and the client's name. Significantly, the revision to Shaw's blurb removes all reference to air travel, reconfiguring Ireland as the ostensible product, brought to the consumer "by" Pan-Am.

Evoking what Larry Doyle calls "all this top-o-the-morning and broth-of-a-boy and more-power-to your-elbow business," the design emphasizes recognizable signifiers of "Irishness," including Shaw's disembodied head. In the original ad, the image of Shaw (larger than the other three

5 "THOSE MAGIC INITIALS, G.B.S.": COPYWRITING FOR THE IRISH CLIPPER 151

Fig. 5.3 Irish Clipper travel poster, ca. 1940s

and situated in a visually dominant position) appears to the left of his text and signature at the top of the page. Oddly, the playwright's picture is captioned with an incomplete sentence, a quoted extract from his copy: "– make the slowest mind flexible for life." Typical of the choppy JWT copy on the left side of the ad (its ellipses and dashes standing in pointed contrast to the italicized flow of Shaw's texts), the blurb lacks a subject and, lopping off the "will" from the original, renders the verb inexplicably plural. As such, the copy is a grotesque version of the original, and there certainly is some deeper significance in eliminating the subject and the "will." Dwarfing the fragment in the travel poster version is the huge, green, stylized word "Ireland" directly beneath Shaw's picture. Overall, Shaw's presence in this campaign resembles the way in which Kent reads the representation of Irishness in *John Bull's Other Island* as both an expression of postcolonial resistance yet also paradoxically "bound up with [an] inevitability and might of multinationals and transnational capital."[68] That is to say, while Shaw manages in his own lines to avoid marketing in the key of Broadbent, the ad struggles to evade the imperialist undertones inherent to marketing discourse appealing to American tourists. As with the Harrods campaign, though, the Clipper ad provided another opportunity for agency and personality to renegotiate their relationship to one another and to the consuming public.

\*\*\*

> If we wished to bequeath to our best friend a MOTTO by which to regulate his efforts and to advance his interest, we would say ADVERTISE, ADVERTISE, ADVERTISE!
> — banner from the *Irish Weekly Advertiser* (March 25, 1863)[69]

On August 31, 1950, just a couple months before his death, a letter from Shaw appeared in *The Times* in which he discusses the necessity of promotion:

> The Soviet State beats us all to nothing in the matter of advertisement, which is a more effective method of propaganda than war, however victorious, can ever be. For over 40 years the Kremlin has been flooding Europe with splendid illustrated magazines in all languages, boosting its extraordinary achievements. ... Meanwhile, what have we to show for our own Communism? Plenty. But we never show it. ... Our propaganda of plutocracy is incessant. We call it freedom and private enterprise. The future is to the countries that carry Communism farthest and advertise it most

effectually. The Labour slogan used to be Educate, Agitate, Organise. As nobody disputes this nowadays, I propose the addition of Advertise, Advertise, Advertise.[70]

Despite the playwright's fervent belief in both Communism and marketing, he seems perhaps unable to resist infusing into his advice an undercurrent of Shavian paradox via the implicit echo of the hapless George Robinson in Anthony Trollope's satirical novel about the field of advertising, *The Struggles of Brown, Jones, and Robinson* (1870). In it, Robinson declares,

> Different great men have promulgated the different means by which they have sought to subjugate the world. "Audacity – audacity – audacity," was the lesson which one hero taught. "agitate – agitate – agitate," was the counsel of a second. "register – register – register," of a third. But I say – Advertise, advertise, advertise! And I say it again and again – Advertise, advertise, advertise!

When reading this passage, it is hard not to see the contours of Shaw's modus operandi with G.B.S., carving the brand into the zeitgeist with audacity, agitation, and advertisement. In any case, a week later, always attuned to G.B.S.'s missives and their potential to serve the practice, the trades made mention. The *World's Press News and Advertisers' Review* reproduces nearly the entirety of the letter, framing it with the premise that

> George Bernard Shaw is unlikely to find any advertising men who will agree with him that the future lies with those countries which "carry Communism farthest and advertise it most effectively" – or even that Britain is, in reality, red right through. However, he will have plenty of his support for his argument that our way of life, whatever we care to call it, needs an efficient promotional backing if others are to be persuaded that it is a good thing.[71]

It concludes by affirming Shaw's "Advertise, Advertise, Advertise" to be "a proposition which clearly has the makings of a simple, down-to-fundamentals rallying cry for next year's advertising conference."

London agency Samson Clark & Co., Ltd. also jumped on the quote, running notices with the all-caps headline "ADVERTISE! ADVERTISE! ADVERTISE" weeks later in (among other places) *The Economist* and *The Spectator* that read,

These words conclude a recent letter to "The Times" from Mr. George Bernard Shaw. Although Mr. Shaw was advocating national propaganda, his sage advice applies with equal force to commerce. Sound and sustained advertising – such as is produced by Samson Clarks – is the gateway to growth and greater prosperity.[72]

Just as the makers of Formamint four decades earlier had seized upon his casual mention of their product in an editorial piece, once again, Shaw's words become repurposed as promotional copy, this time to underscore the imperative of commercial advertising as a whole. That the industry, time and again, turns to him for copy is an indication of the vitality and viability of Shaw's brand.

Executive H. S. Gardner observed in a 1929 *Advertising & Selling* piece that "the modern way of handling [endorsements] is different [in that] now the advertiser doesn't make the celebrity – the celebrity makes the advertiser."[73] This trajectory is mirrored in how Shaw initially brokered advertising to "make" G.B.S. and how later the industry returned to him after the brand was established to assist not only in selling wares but in professionalizing their techniques in doing so. Indeed, Shaw's progenitive marketing and endorsement practices pioneered the practice "in today's multimedia and cross-promotional marketplace [through which] celebrities from David Beckham and Michael Jordan to Gwyneth Paltrow and Beyoncé construct their own images through the products they endorse or (to borrow a term from Naomi Klein) 'co-brand'."[74]

Across the perpetually evolving media landscape since Shaw's death, the testimonial has not only endured but ferociously thrives. After significant stumbles in its early decades, nowadays, "the money … celebrities receive for product endorsements often surpasses their other income, making them financially dependent on promotional contracts. … In fact, the financial remunerations sometimes offered for such endorsements have fostered a new industry unto itself."[75] One major difference, for Schweitzer and Moskowitz, is that these compensations, about which contemporary consumers have no illusions, do not seem to harm the efficacy of the endorsements as they did in previous eras:

> Even in the media-saturated twenty-first century, in which magazine readers know that the familiar faces looking up at then from print ads are likely being handsomely recompensed and favorite television commercials featuring "on the street" testimony are replayed on YouTube, testimonial advertising remains big news and big business.[76]

## 5 "THOSE MAGIC INITIALS, G.B.S.": COPYWRITING FOR THE IRISH CLIPPER

Soon after Shaw's death, British advertising experienced a game changer with the arrival of commercial television, "capable of building nigh on 100 per cent public awareness of a new product or campaign in a matter of days" and whose "intrusion into people's homes changed the relationship of advertisers with the public, and the public with advertisers, [and] transformed the nature of advertising creativity and of agency creative departments."[77] During the economic boom in America of the late 1950s, Chicago agency executive William D. Tyler heralded the return of what he refers to as the "image-projection concept" in marketing:

> It was used with tremendous success the last time around when we had rollicking prosperity in the land. That was during the'twenties. In those days, it was known as snob appeal. It did not take the deepest kind of thought to come up with the concept that lots of people want to use the kind of product that the people whom they admire, envy, and emulate use. This was the first writhing in the primeval ooze of the image-projection concept in advertising. ... It became so universally used that research seems to indicate that it was losing its potency. This does not imply that emulation, as a motivation, is on the wane, but just the straight-face celebrity-testimonial expression of it.[78]

He argues that personality advertising can only succeed when you "take the people into the act with you":

> You have to let them know your tongue is in your cheek, and that you are just asking them to go along with the gag [rather than] insult their intelligence with headlines like "Marilyn Monroe bakes all her seven-layer cakes with Pillsbury's Best."[79]

The impish meta-sensibility that Tyler valorizes perfectly characterizes Shaw's "near-testimonial" performances in commercial ad campaigns but perhaps is equally applicable to any G.B.S. print appearance. As Fintan O'Toole suggests, "the most breathtaking part of the game was that Shaw always let his audience know precisely that it was a game."[80]

In a July 1895 piece for the *Saturday Review*, Shaw made the case for personality endorsement while at the same time demarcating the media space G.B.S. would inhabit for the next half century:

> People do not trust advertisements: the more concerned they are with the benefits held out by the advertiser, the more anxious they are to have the opinion of a disinterested expert as to whether the advertisement can be trusted.[81]

A year earlier, he had articulated his method of creating just such a "disinterested expert":

> Very recently the production of a play of mine in New York led to the appearance in the New York papers of a host of brilliant critical and biographical studies of a remarkable person called Bernard Shaw. I am supposed to be that person; but I am not. There is no such person; there never was any such person; there never will or can be any such person. You may take my word for this, because I invented him, floated him, advertised him, impersonated him, and am now sitting in my dingy second floor lodging in a decaying London Square, breakfasting off twopenn'orth of porridge and giving this additional touch to his makeup with my typewriter.[82]

Of course, being Shaw, he could be disingenuous when doing so served his purposes. Ambivalent about participating in a radio program about personal achievement, for example, he declared in a 1932 letter to John Reith, "I never advertised: advertisement, like success, has been shoved on me."[83] In truth, his campaign was so effective that, in a 1940 letter to his American publisher Dodd, Mead & Co., Shaw advises that "there is no need to spend anything worth mentioning on advertisement: my publicity advertises itself."[84]

Less than a year before his death, *Newspaper World & Advertising Review* noted the reboot of the periodical *Public Opinion* under the auspices of *The Daily Mirror*. The January 1950 premiere issue "follow[ed] the style of the political weeklies" with content that "cover[ed] political and current affairs with special features on films, books, television, and the open air." On the front page,

> what was described as a letter of the week ... stated that George Bernard Shaw stood out like a sore thumb from the ruck of contemporary publicists because he preserved "the unaffected, lucid, vigorous style of the uninhibited Victorian." The question is then asked: "Can Public Opinion

in 1950 regain the tone and get away from the mealy mouthed pomposity that distinguishes the 'serious' half of the Press today from the mindlessness that is foisted on us as the popular style?" The editor's footnote comments: "Let the shining past be the guide to the future. We can but hope to learn."[85]

Coincidentally, Shaw's very first publication (in April 1875) appeared "in the correspondence column of *Public Opinion*, a London weekly news digest" at the time.[86]

Combining sustained public visibility in the earliest forms of modern mass media with shrewd cultivation of his persona, Shaw's branding of "G.B.S." was part of the vanguard of

> this concept of celebrity as commodity when highly visible people who were known for their creations – whether as artists, poets, writers or performers – received orchestrated publicity ... to popularize their outputs and enhance the extent to which they could be monetized [as part of] the emergence also of an increasingly "commoditized" cultural environment that characterized capitalist societies.[87]

During the period that Shaw was directly participating in product marketing,

> advertisers found that initially many established celebrities from the world of film, stage, and even television were reluctant to "lower" themselves to making public appearances as brand promoters [due to] a deeply ingrained feeling among stars of the 1930s, 1940s, and 1950s that their public image could be damaged if they lent their names as endorsers of commercial products.[88]

Throughout his career, Shaw modeled a different relationship to the marketplace and public media, one that anticipated the proliferation of celebrity endorsement in the second half of the twentieth century into itself a multi-trillion dollar-a-year industry staged across a staggering array of media platforms. The lucrative profit margin of its evolution though has regretfully obscured what for Shaw was the central actuating force of his campaign: the prophet motive.

## Notes

1. Jackson Lears. *Fables of Abundance: A Cultural History of Advertising in America*. New York: Basic Books, 1994. 204, 205.
2. Quoted in Lears, 205.
3. Lears, 219.
4. James Playsted Wood. *The Story of Advertising*. New York: The Ronald Press Company, 1958. 418.
5. Marlis Schweitzer and Marina Moskowitz. "Introduction." In *Testimonial Advertising in the American Marketplace: Emulation, Identity, Community*. Eds. Marlis Schweitzer and Marina Moskowitz. New York: Palgrave Macmillan, 2009. 9.
6. Ibid., 9.
7. "Why London Department Store Advertised in New York." *Printers' Ink* 146.12 (21 March 1929): 73–4. 74.
8. H. S. Gardner. "The Paid Testimonial Is Taking the Cure." *Advertising & Selling* 13.12 (17 April 1929): 17–18, 46. 17, 46, 18.
9. Ibid., 46.
10. Amos Stote. "G.B.S. Joins Us." *Advertising & Selling* 15.10 (17 September 1930): 32.
11. Mark Tungate. *Ad Land: A Global History of Advertising*. London: Kogan Page, 2007. 26.
12. Dan H. Laurence. *Bernard Shaw: A Bibliography*, vol. 1. Oxford: Clarendon Press, 1983. 252.
13. "Copywriter." *The New Yorker* (31 July 1948): 13–14. 13.
14. The misattributed quote proliferates, from *Holiday Haunts in England, Wales and Channel Islands: The Official Guide to the Holiday Resorts Served by the Great Western Railroad* (1928) to Brendan Lehane's *The Companion Guide to Ireland* (2001).
15. William M. Freeman. *The Big Name*. New York: Printers' Ink Books, 1957. 38.
16. Ibid., 14. Also: "'Plug' for Airways Written by Shaw." *New York Times* 28.4 (17 June 1948): 28.
17. Ibid., 14.
18. Laurence, 252.
19. "Copywriter," 13–14.
20. Ibid., 14.
21. Bizarrely, in *Fifty in 40: The Unofficial History of JWT London, 1945–1995*. Rayfield Writers, 1996, Tom Rayfield puzzles over the gap of time between Shaw's initial letter (dated 16 October 1946) and his copy correction letter (dated 20 October 1948), noting the insertion date of March 1948. He concludes that "it seems unlikely that it took the Testimonial Department two years to get final approval, but rather that

the 90 (or 92)-year-old author may have been a bit confused as to the year" (39).
22. *The Saturday Review* 31 (17 July 1948): 6.
23. "'As Corrected' By G.B.S." *Tide: The News Magazine of Advertising, Marketing and Public Relations* (23 July 1948): 17.
24. *The J.W.T. News* 3.25 (21 June 48): 1. The piece ends with a teaser, that "the story of how the copy and free endorsement were obtained, together with a reproduction of the original manuscript as personally revised and inscribed by GBS will be reported next week." However, it doesn't seem as if a follow-up appeared, perhaps because the "story" was so prominently and publically recounted elsewhere.
25. *The J.W.T. News* 3.28 (12 July 1948): 1.
26. Ibid., 1.
27. Another odd detail that pops up in various reviews of the campaign (both within the industry and outside of it) is the claim that Shaw was brand new to the world of commerce. *Editor & Publisher* proclaimed that, "so far as is known, Mr. Shaw has never associated himself with a commercial service or product before" (24). The *New York Times* article, in its final paragraph, also emphasizes that "Pan American believes this is the first time Mr. Shaw has lent his name to a commercial product or venture" (28). These statements, perhaps intended to boost the credibility of the product via Shaw's participation belie the playwright's previous and prominent participation in commodity advertising.
28. "Copywriter," 13.
29. "Free Irish Air." *Time* 51.25 (21 June 1948): 90.
30. "'Plug' for Airways Written by Shaw." *New York Times* 28.4 (17 June 1948): 28.
31. Moskowitz and Schweitzer, 9.
32. *J.W.T. News* 3.31 (2 August 1948): 5.
33. "How Well Do You Know Your JWT'ERS?: 'Thumb-Nail Sketch' of Gelston Hardy." *The J.W.T. News* 3.49 (6 December 1948): 6.
34. Even before her encounter with Shaw, "Bill" Blaker's life was quite extraordinary. Born in the fall of 1886, she spent much of her childhood in British Columbia, and her young adulthood was marked by dramatic shifts in professional focus with stints as a barrow-girl, owner/operator of a nursing home, a secretary, and a ballet/fencing instructor in Brussels. During the first world war, she was one of the first to join the Women's Volunteer Reserve, beginning her journey to becoming Major and Adjutant. During the second world war, Blaker became second-in-command of the Auxiliary Territorial Service while still continuing work in the streets with the Fire Service and the Red Cross. Blaker retired from her *JWT* position in 1954 and died in 1976.

35. *Round the Square* 3.2 (1953): 6.
36. "How Well Do You Know Your JWT'ERS?: 'Thumb-Nail Sketch' of Dorothea Campbell Blaker (London)." *The J.W.T. News* 2.43 (27 October 1947): 6.
37. *Round the Square*, 6.
38. Peter Yeo. *Reflections on an Agency*. Published Privately, 1988. 24.
39. In the image, the reflected glare from the camera flash on the Shaw display indicates its contents are under glass in contrast to the materials on the corkboard immediately behind the seated Blaker.
40. *JWT News* 4.34 (8/22/49): 1.
41. Bernard Shaw. *Back to Methuselah*. In *The Bodley Head Bernard Shaw: Collected Plays with Their Prefaces*, vol. 5. London: The Bodley Head, 1971. 340–684. 496. The Elderly Gentleman's characterization of Ireland as a "mental health resort" itself seems slightly to adapt tourist rhetoric, and "British Baghdad" has a theme park sense to it.
42. Bernard Shaw. *John Bull's Other Island*. In *The Bodley Head Bernard Shaw: Collected Plays with Their Prefaces*, vol. 2. London: The Bodley Head, 1971. 893–1027. 909.
43. Bernard Shaw. *Too True to Be Good*. In *The Bodley Head Bernard Shaw: Collected Plays with Their Prefaces*, vol. 6. London: The Bodley Head, 1971. 429–528. 510.
44. Bernard Shaw. "Preface" to *Too True to Be Good*. In *The Bodley Head Bernard Shaw: Collected Plays with Their Prefaces*, vol. 6. London: The Bodley Head, 1971. 399–428. 409.
45. Shaw, *John Bull's Other Island*, 893–4.
46. Kathleen Ochshorn. "Colonialism, Postcolonialism, and the Shadow of a New Empire: *John Bull's Other Island*." *SHAW: The Annual of Bernard Shaw Studies* 26 (2006): 180–93. 192, 181.
47. Shaw, *John Bull's Other Island*, 1015.
48. Bernard Shaw. "Dear Harp of My Country." In *Dramatic Opinions and Essays*, vol. 1. New York: Brentano's, 1906. 326–32. 330.
49. Colin Graham. *Deconstructing Ireland: Identity, Theory, Culture*. Edinburgh: Edinburgh University Press, 2001. 171.
50. Ibid., 166–7.
51. Mark Phelan. "'Authentic Reproductions': Staging the 'Wild West' in Modern Irish Drama." *Theatre Journal* 61.2 (May 2009): 235–48. 245.
52. Rod Rosenquist. "Copywriting Gertrude Stein: Advertising, Anonymity, Autobiography." *Modernist Cultures* 11.3 (2016): 331–50. 341.
53. Elizabeth Outka. *Consuming Traditions: Modernity, Modernism, and the Commodified Authentic*. Oxford: Oxford University Press, 2009. 4.
54. Shaw, *Too True to Be Good*, 510.
55. Graham, 144.

56. See Dean MacCannell. *The Tourist: A New Theory of the Leisure Class.* Berkeley: University of California Press, 1999.
57. Ning Wang. "Rethinking Authenticity in Tourism Experience." *Annals of Tourism Research* 26.2 (1999): 349–70. 349–50.
58. Bernard Shaw, *John Bull's Other Island.* London: Constable, 1927. v.
59. Brad Kent. "Shaw's Everyday Emergency: Commodification in and of *John Bull's Other Island.*" *SHAW: The Annual of Bernard Shaw Studies* 26 (2006): 162–79. 164.
60. Wang, 349–50.
61. The final version of the caption was: "Dublin is an architecturally noble metropolis of over half a million people. Wild mountain scenery is nearby—and a tram drive takes you to a seaside that rivals the Bay of Naples."
62. Graham Huggan. *The Post-colonial Exotic: Marketing the Margins.* London: Routledge, 2001, 13.
63. Gareth Griffiths. "The Myth of Authenticity: Representation, Discourse and Practice." In *De-scribing Empire: Post-colonialism and Textuality.* Eds. Chris Tiffin and Alan Lawson. London: Routledge, 1994. 70–85. 71.
64. Alice McEwan. "Commodities, Consumption, and Connoisseurship: Shaw's Critique of Authenticity in Modernity." *SHAW: The Journal of Bernard Shaw Studies* 35.1 (November 2015): 46–85, 78.
65. "Focus: The Legal and Personality Department." *Round the Square* (August 1956): 7–9. The originals of these documents have not survived, framed or otherwise. They are not contained among the Pan-American materials within the JWT London client account files (held by the History of Advertising Trust in Norfolk), and any separate records kept by the JWT London Legal & Personality department itself were not retained.
66. "Copywriter," 14.
67. Laurence, 253. This variation on Shaw's copy is also cited on page 863 in volume two of Archibald Henderson's *George Bernard Shaw: Man of the Century.* New York: Da Capo Press, 1972. Henderson also indicates that the text was provided "gratuitously."
68. Kent, 175.
69. Cited in John Strachan and Claire Nally. *Advertising, Literature and Print Culture in Ireland, 1891–1922.* New York: Palgrave Macmillan, 2012. 19. The blurb also appears as the heading of the "Index to Advertisements" at the back of W. F. Wakeman's *Dublin: What's to Be Seen, and How to See It,* 2e. Dublin: Hodges and Smith, Grafton Street, 1853.
70. "Story of British "Communism": Mr. Shaw on the Need to Advertise." In *The Letters of Bernard Shaw to "The Times."* Ed. Ronald Ford. Dublin: Irish Academic Press, 2007. 286–7.

71. "Advertising Angle." *World's Press News and Advertisers' Review* 44.1121 (8 September 1950): 12.
72. "ADVERTISE! ADVERTISE! ADVERTISE!" *The Economist* 159 (1950): 590.
73. Gardner, 17–18.
74. Marlis Schweitzer and Marina Moskowitz, 5.
75. Ibid., 5.
76. Ibid., 19.
77. Winston Fletcher. *Powers of Persuasion: The Inside Story of British Advertising.* Oxford: Oxford University Press, 2008. 27, 22.
78. William D. Tyler. "The Image, the Brand, and the Consumer." *Journal of Marketing* 22.2 (October 1957): 162–5. 163.
79. Ibid., 163.
80. Fintan O'Toole. *Judging Shaw: The Radicalism of GBS.* Dublin: Prism, 2017. 96.
81. Bernard Shaw. "Criticism on the Hustings." In *Bernard Shaw: The Drama Observed*, vol. 2 (1895–1897). Ed. Bernard F. Dukore. University Park: Pennsylvania State University Press, 1993. 395–401. 397.
82. Bernard Shaw. "How to Become a Man of Genius." In *Selected Non-dramatic Writings of Bernard Shaw.* Ed. Dan H. Laurence. Boston: Houghton Mifflin Company, 1965. 341–6, 344–5.
83. Bernard Shaw. *Collected Letters*, vol. 4 (1926–1950). Ed. Dan H. Laurence. New York: Viking, 1988. 290.
84. Bernard Shaw, *Collected Letters*, vol. 4, 560–3. 562.
85. "An Addition to the Journals of Opinion." *Newspaper World & Advertising Review* 2712 (12 January 1950): 43.
86. A. M. Gibbs. *A Bernard Shaw Chronology.* New York: Palgrave Macmillan, 2001. 33.
87. Barrie Gunter. *Celebrity Capital: Assessing the Value of Fame.* New York: Bloomsbury, 2014. 3–4.
88. Ibid., 61.

# Bibliography

"Advertisers' Association Issues Testimonial Suggestion." *Printers' Ink* 146.12 (21 March 1929): 182, 184. Print.
"Advertising and Literature." *Newspaper World & Advertising Review* 2453 (13 January 1945): 19. Print.
"Advertising Angle." *World's Press News and Advertisers' Review* 44.1121 (8 September 1950): 12. Print.
"A.N.A. Declares Against Paid Testimonial Advertising." *Printers' Ink* 147.10 (6 June 1929): 73–80. Print.
"An Addition to the Journals of Opinion." *Newspaper World & Advertising Review* 2712 (12 January 1950): 43. Print.
Appel, Joseph. *Growing Up with Advertising*. New York: The Business Bourse, 1940. Print.
Arlington, Lauren. "The Censorship of 'O'Flaherty V.C.'." *SHAW: The Annual of Bernard Shaw Studies* 28 (2008): 85–106. Print.
"Arnold Bennett and Harrods." *The Pittsburgh Post-Gazette* (19 March 1929): 16. Print.
"'As Corrected' By G.B.S.." *Tide: The News Magazine of Advertising, Marketing and Public Relations* (23 July 1948): 17. Print.
"Authors as Advertisers." *The Publishers' Weekly* 115.14 (6 April 1929): 1674. Print.
"Authors as Copywriters." *Advertiser's Weekly* 61.814–26 (1929): 490. Print.
Beegan, Gerry. *The Mass Image: A Social History of Photomechanical Reproduction in Victorian London*. New York: Palgrave Macmillan, 2008. Print.

"Bernard Shaw and Harrods." *The New York Times* (15 March 1929): 15. Print.
Bertolini, John A. *The Playwrighting Self of Bernard Shaw*. Carbondale: Southern Illinois University Press, 1991. Print.
Biggs, Murray. "Shaw's Recruiting Pamphlet." *SHAW: The Annual of Bernard Shaw Studies* 28 (2008): 107–11. Print.
Blake, Gerald. "Un-sinned Sins." *Advertising and Selling* 23.2 (24 May 1934): 22, 24. Print.
Bodkins, Odds. "The 8pt. Page." *Advertising & Selling* 16.9 (4 March 1931): 46. Print.
Brecht, Bertolt. "Ovation for Shaw." Trans. Gerhard H. W. Zuther. *Modern Drama* 2.2 (Summer 1959): 184–7. Print.
"British Trade Can Win Through—By Constructive Advertising." *Commercial Art* 9.54 (1 December 1930) and 10.56 (1 February 1931): 8. Print.
Cadby, Carine, and Will. "London Letter." *Photo-Era Magazine: The American Journal of Photography* 62 (January–June 1929): 334. Print.
Calkins, Earnest Elmo. "A Ballyhoo for Babbitt." *Printers' Ink* 121 (12 October 1922): 89–90, 93.
"A Case of Poisoning by Formamint Tablets." *The British Medical Journal* 2.2494 (17 October 1908): 1224. Print.
Chappelow, Allan, ed. *Shaw the Villager and Human Being: A Biographical Symposium*. London: Charles Skilton Ltd., 1961. Print.
Chesterton, G. K. *George Bernard Shaw*. London: John Lane, 1910. Print.
"Chesterton on Shaw." *The Nation* (21 October 1909): 375. Print.
Church, Roy. "Advertising Consumer Goods in Nineteenth-Century Britain: Reinterpretations." *The Economic History Review* 53.4 (November 2000): 621–45. Print.
Colbourne, Maurice. *The Real Bernard Shaw*. New York: Dodd, Mead & Company, 1940. Print.
"Copywriter." *The New Yorker* (31 July 1948): 13–14. Print.
"Copywriting or Paid Testimonial?" *Advertiser's Weekly* 61.823 (8 March 1929): 393. Print.
Davis, Tracy. "Shaw's Interstices of Empire: Decolonizing at Home and Abroad." In *The Cambridge Companion to Bernard Shaw*. Ed. Christopher Innes. Cambridge: Cambridge University Press, 1998. 218–39. Print.
Dickinson, Roy. "What the Consumer Thinks of the Modern Testimonial." *Printers' Ink* 146.13 (28 March 1929): 17–20. Print.
Doyle, Arthur Conan. *The Final Adventures of Sherlock Holmes*. New York: Heritage Press, 1957. 1330. Print.
Duba, Frank. "'The Genuine Pulpit Article': The Preface to *Man and Superman*." *SHAW: The Annual of Bernard Shaw Studies* 25 (2005): 221–40. Print.

*Dublin Journal of Medical Science* 125 (January–June 1908). Dublin: Fannin & Company Ltd., 1908. 239–40. Print.

Eaton, Esther. "Making the World 'Sleep Conscious': Fifteen Famous Men Talk on Sleep Through Simmons Advertising." *JWT Co. News Letter* 11.47 (1 December 1929): 1, 3. Print.

Egbert, James W. "Making the Testimonial Worth More." *Printers' Ink* 77.8 (23 November 1911): 76–8. Print.

———. "What Makes a Good Testimonial." *Printers' Ink* 77. 2 (12 October 1911): 44, 46. Print.

"An Epitome of Current Medical Literature." *The British Medical Journal* 2 (1908): 40. Print.

Ervine, St. John. *Bernard Shaw: His Life, Work and Friends.* New York: William Morrow & Company, 1956. Print.

Eveleigh, David J. *Bogs, Baths, and Basins: The Story of Domestic Sanitation.* Thrupp: Sutton Publishing, 2002. Print.

Everding, Robert G. "Shaw and the Popular Context." In *The Cambridge Companion to George Bernard Shaw.* Ed. Christopher Innes. Cambridge: Cambridge University Press, 1998. 309–33. Print.

"Fifty Years 1888–1938." *Printers' Ink* 184.4 (28 July 1938): Section Two. Print.

Fletcher, Winston. *Powers of Persuasion: The Inside Story of British Advertising: 1951–2000.* Oxford: Oxford University Press, 2008. Print.

"Focus: The Legal and Personality Department." *Round the Square* (August 1956): 7–9. Print.

Ford, Corey. "A Meeting of the Endorsers' Club." *The New Yorker* (11 May 1929): 19–20. Print.

Ford, Ronald, ed. *The Letters of Bernard Shaw to "The Times."* Dublin: Irish Academic Press, 2007. Print.

"Formaldehyde Lozenges." *Journal of the American Medical Association* 73.14 (4 October 1919): 1077. Print.

"Formamint." *Journal of the American Medical Association* 65.9 (28 August 1915): 816–19. Print.

"Formamint: The So-Called Germ-Killing Throat Tablet." *Journal of the American Medical Association* 58.8 (24 February 1912): 572. Print.

Fox, Stephen. *The Mirror Makers: A History of American Advertising and Its Creators.* New York: William Morrow and Company Inc., 1984. Print.

"Free Irish Air." *Time* 51.25 (21 June 1948): 90. Print.

Freeman, William M. *The Big Name.* New York: Printers' Ink Books, 1957. Print.

Gainor, J. Ellen. "Bernard Shaw and the Drama of Imperialism." In *The Performance of Power: Theatrical Discourse and Politics.* Eds. Sue-Ellen Case and Janelle G. Reinelt. Iowa City: University of Iowa Press, 1991. 56–74. Print.

Gardner, H. S. "The Paid Testimonial Is Taking the Cure." *Advertising & Selling* 13.12 (17 April 1929): 17–18, 46. Print.

"German Patents and Trademarks in England." *Scientific American* 3.20 (14 November 1914): 402. Print.

Gibbs, A. M. *Bernard Shaw: A Life*. Gainesville: University Press of Florida, 2005. Print.

———. *A Bernard Shaw Chronology*. New York: Palgrave MacMillan, 2001. Print.

———, ed. *Shaw: Recollections and Interviews*. London: Macmillan, 1990. Print.

Goldman, Jonathan. "Celebrity." In *George Bernard Shaw in Context*. Ed. Brad Kent. Cambridge: Cambridge University Press, 2015. 255–64. Print.

———. *Modernism Is the Literature of Celebrity*. Austin: University of Texas Press, 2011. Print.

Graham, Colin. *Deconstructing Ireland: Identity, Theory, Culture*. Edinburgh: Edinburgh University Press, 2001. Print.

Gregory, James. *Of Victorians and Vegetarians: The Vegetarian Movement in Nineteenth-Century Britain*. London: Tauris Academic Studies, 2007. Print.

Grene, Nicholas, and Dan. H. Laurence, eds. *Shaw, Lady Gregory, and the Abbey*. Gerrards Cross: Colin Smythe, 1993. Print.

Gruber, L. Fritz. "Englische Schaufenster (English Shop Windows)." *Gebrauchsgraphik: International Advertising Art* 15.11 (1 November 1938): 57–63. Print.

Gunter, Barrie. *Celebrity Capital: Assessing the Value of Fame*. New York: Bloomsbury, 2014). Print.

Griffiths, Gareth. "The Myth of Authenticity: Representation, Discourse and Practice." In *De-scribing Empire: Post-colonialism and Textuality*. Eds. Chris Tiffin and Alan Lawson. London: Routledge, 1994. 70–85. Print.

"H. G. Wells and Harrods." *The New York Times* (14 March 1929): 15. Print.

"H. G. Wells on Advertising." *Printers' Ink* 216.8 (23 August 1946): 126. Print.

Hackett, Francis. "The Post-Victorians." *The Bookman* 71.1 (March 1930): 20–6. Print.

Hamon, Augustus. *Bernard Shaw: The Twentieth Century Molière*. Trans. Eden and Cedar Paul. New York: Frederick A. Stokes Company Publishers, 1916. Print.

Harn, O. C. "Who Is Going to Clean Up This Testimonial Mess?" *Printers' Ink* 146.12 (21 March 1929): 3–6, 181–7. Print.

Hegglund, Jon. "Defending the Realm: Domestic Space and Mass Cultural Contamination in *Howards End* and *An Englishman's Home*." *English Literature in Transition 1880–1920* 40.4 (1997): 398–423. Print.

Henderson, Archibald. *George Bernard Shaw: Man of the Century*. New York: Da Capo Press, 1972. Print.

Hilmes, Michelle. *Hollywood and Broadcasting: From Radio to Cable.* Champaign: University of Illinois Press, 1999. Print.
Holroyd, Michael. *Bernard Shaw: The One Volume Definitive Edition.* New York: Random House, 1997. Print.
———. *Bernard Shaw, Volume One: 1856–1898: The Search for Love.* New York: Vintage Books, 1988. Print.
———. *Bernard Shaw, Volume Two: 1898–1918: The Pursuit of Power.* New York: Vintage Books, 1989. Print.
Honeycombe, Gordon. *Selfridges: Seventy-Five Years, The Story of the Store, 1909–1984.* London: Park Lane Press, 1984. Print.
Hotchkiss, George Burton. *Advertising Copy.* New York: Harper & Brothers Publishers, 1924. Print.
"How Advertising Has Helped to Build the House of Harrods." *The Newspaper World and Advertising Review* 2674 (23 April 1949): 113–14. Print.
"How Well Do You Know Your JWT'ERS?: 'Thumb-Nail Sketch' of Gelston Hardy." *The J.W.T. News* 3.49 (6 December 1948): 6. Print.
"How Well Do You Know Your JWT'ERS?: 'Thumb-Nail Sketch' of Dorothea Campbell Blaker (London)." *The J.W.T. News* 2.43 (27 October 1947): 6. Print.
Huggan, Graham. *The Post-colonial Exotic: Marketing the Margins.* London: Routledge, 2001. Print.
Hurd, Charles W. "How Price Maintenance of One Article Helps Another." *Printers' Ink* 83.2 (10 April 1913): 65–6, 69. Print.
"Ingenious Advertising." *New York Times* (15 March 1929): 18. Print.
Ionesco, Eugène, and Jack Undank. "The Tragedy of Language: How an English Primer Became My First Play." *The Tulane Drama Review* 4.3 (March 1960): 10–13. Print.
"Irish Refuse to Give a Degree to Shaw." *New York Times* (13 March 1929): 4. Print.
Jaffe, Aaron. *Modernism and the Culture of Celebrity.* New York: Cambridge University Press, 2005). Print.
Jennings, H. R. *Our Homes and How to Beautify Them.* London: Harrison & Sons, 1902. Print.
*The J.W.T. News* 1.29 (16 December 1946): 4. Print.
*The J.W.T. News* 3.25 (21 June 1948): 1. Print.
*The J.W.T. News* 3.28 (12 July 1948): 1. Print.
*The J.W.T. News* 3.31 (2 August 1948): 5. Print.
*The J.W.T. News* 4.34 (22 August 1949): 1. Print.
Kandela, Peter. "The Rise and Fall of the Turkish Bath in Victorian England." *Journal of Dermatology* 39 (2000): 70–4. Print.
Kaplan, Joel H., and Sheila Stowell. *Theatre and Fashion: Oscar Wilde to the Suffragettes.* Cambridge: Cambridge University Press, 1994. Print.

Kellogg, J. H. "Are We a Dying Race?" *Good Health: A Journal of Hygiene* 33.1 (January 1898): 1–4. Print.

Kent, Brad. "Bernard Shaw, the British Censorship of Plays, and Modern Celebrity." *English Literature in Transition, 1880–1920* 57.2 (2014): 231–53. Print.

———. "Shaw's Everyday Emergency: Commodification in and of *John Bull's Other Island*." *SHAW: The Annual of Bernard Shaw Studies* 26 (2006): 162–79. Print.

Kinder, John. "Marketing Disabled Manhood: Veterans and Advertising Since the Civil War." In *Phallacies: Historical Intersections of Disability and Masculinity*. Eds. Kathleen M. Brian and James W. Trent, Jr. Oxford: Oxford University Press, 2017. 93–125. Print.

Kropff, H. F. J. "The Tables Turned or Harrods and the Three Great English Authors." Trans. E. T. Scheffauer. *Gebrauchsgraphik: International Advertising Art* 6.9 (1 September 1929): 47–51. Print.

Laurence, Dan H. *Bernard Shaw: A Bibliography*. Oxford: Clarendon Press, 1983. Print.

Lears, Jackson. *Fables of Abundance: A Cultural History of Advertising in America*. New York: Basic Books, 1994. Print.

———. "Uneasy Courtship: Modern Art and Modern Advertising." *American Quarterly* 39.1 (Spring 1987): 133–54. Print.

Lewis, Sinclair. "Sinclair Lewis Looks at Advertising." *Advertising & Selling* 13.2 (15 May 1929): 17–18, 60, 62, 64–66. Print.

Lister, Harold. "Health for Intellectuals." *The New Age* 13.9 (26 June 1913): 228. Print.

"The London Education Act 1903: How To Make the Best of It." Fabian Tract No. 117. London: The Fabian Society, February 1904. Print.

Long, Helen C. *The Edwardian House: The Middle-Class Home in Britain 1880–1914*. Manchester: Manchester University Press, 1993. Print.

Loving, Pierre. "Autumn." *The Drama* 13 (November 1922): 61–3. Print.

Luce, Henry Robinson. "Holy Ghost." *Time* 13.12 (25 March 1929): 51. Print.

Lynd, Robert. *Old and New Masters*. New York: Charles Scribner's Sons, 1919. Print.

MacCannell, Dean. *The Tourist: A New Theory of the Leisure Class*. Berkeley: University of California Press, 1999. Print.

Mahin, John Lee. "Advertising—A Form of Organized Salesmanship." *Printers' Ink* 70 (30 March 1910): 5. Print.

Marchand, Roland. *Advertising the American Dream: Making Way for Modernity, 1920–1940*. Berkeley: University of California Press, 1985. Print.

Martin, Gustavo A. Rodríguez. "'I Often Quote Myself' (and Others): Modified Quotations in the Plays of Bernard Shaw." *SHAW: The Annual of Bernard Shaw Studies* 31 (2011): 192–206. Print.

McKenna, E. "The Dramatization of Advertising Ideas." *Printers' Ink* 112. 8 (19 August 1920): 93–6. Print.
McKenzie, Malcolm. "Jaeger: Health Gospel of 1884, Fashion Movement of 1937." *Commercial Art* 23.134 (1 August 1937): 42–57.
McEwan, Alice. "Commodities, Consumption, and Connoisseurship: Shaw's Critique of Authenticity in Modernity." *SHAW: The Journal of Bernard Shaw Studies* 35.1 (November 2015): 46–85. Print.
———. "George Bernard Shaw and His Writing Hut: Privacy and Publicity as Performance at Shaw's Corner." *Interiors* 2.3 (2011): 333–56. Print.
———. "'The 'Plumber-Philosopher': Shaw's Discourse on Domestic Sanitation." *SHAW: The Annual of Bernard Shaw Studies* 34 (2014): 75–107. Print.
McVoy, F. "Harrods of London Score the Biggest Scoop in Advertising History." *Printed Salesmanship* 53.3 (May 1929): 214–15, 274–6. Print.
Michalos, Alex C., and Deborah C. Poff, eds. *Bernard Shaw and the Webbs*. Toronto: University of Toronto Press, 2002. Print.
Mills, John A. *Language and Laughter: Comic Diction in the Plays of Bernard Shaw*. Tucson: University of Arizona Press, 1969. Print.
Minney, R. J. *The Bogus Image of Bernard Shaw*. London: Leslie Frewin, 1969. Print.
Moffett, James C. "Should Advertisements Be 'Signed,' Like Articles." *Printers' Ink* 76.1 (6 July 1911): 58, 60–1. Print.
Morgan, Margery M. *A Drama of Political Man: A Study in the Plays of Harley Granville Barker*. London: Sidgwick and Jackson, 1961. Print.
"Motor-Car Posters: Selections from Different Nations." *Commercial Art* Vol. 1. London: The Studio Limited, 1926. 208–13. Print.
"Mr. Bernard Shaw on Formamint." *Collier's* 53 (5 December 1914): 26. Print.
"Mr. Charles Chassé Investigates Bernard Shaw's Philosophy." *New York Times* (13 December 1908): SM4. Print.
"Mr. Resor Leads Discussion on 'Personality Advertising'." *The J. Walter Thompson News Letter* 10.8 (13 April 1928): 137–50. Print.
Nevett, T. R. *Advertising in Britain: A History*. London: The History of Advertising Trust, 1982. Print.
Ochshorn, Kathleen. "Colonialism, Postcolonialism, and the Shadow of a New Empire: *John Bull's Other Island*." *SHAW: The Annual of Bernard Shaw Studies* 26 (2006): 180–93. Print.
O'Meara, Walter. "On a Phase of Copy Style." *The J. Walter Thompson News Bulletin* 110 (December 1924): 11–13. Print.
Orman, Felix. "Picture Advertising Is 'Flash' Advertising." *Advertising & Selling* 28.28 (15 March 1919): 11. Print.
O'Toole, Fintan. *Judging Shaw: The Radicalism of GBS*. Dublin: Prism, 2017. Print.

Outka, Elizabeth. *Consuming Traditions: Modernity, Modernism, and the Commodified Authentic*. Oxford: Oxford University Press, 2009. Print.
Palmer, John. "George Bernard Shaw: Harlequin or Patriot?" *The Century Magazine* 89 (November 1914–April 1915): 768–82. Print.
Peters, Sally. "Shaw's Life: A Feminist in Spite of Himself." In *The Cambridge Companion to George Bernard Shaw*. Ed. Christopher Innes. Cambridge: Cambridge University Press, 1998). 3–24. Print.
Phelan, Mark. "'Authentic Reproductions': Staging the 'Wild West' in Modern Irish Drama." *Theatre Journal* 61.2 (May 2009): 235–48. Print.
Phillips, Terry. "Shaw, Ireland, and World War 1: 'O'Flaherty V.C.', An Unlikely Recruiting Play." *SHAW: The Annual of Bernard Shaw Studies* 30 (2010): 133–46. Print.
"A Philosopher's Ideas About Sleep." *Time* 13.18 (6 May 1929): 29. Print.
"Plug for Airways Written by Shaw." *New York Times* 28.4 (17 June 1948): 28. Print.
Powell, Helen. "Advertising Agencies and Their Clients." In *The Advertising Handbook*, 3rd edition. Eds. Helen Powell, Jonathan Hardy, Sarah Hawkin, and Iain MacRury. London: Routledge: 2009. 13–23. Print.
"The Power of Heat: Turkish Baths at Home." Century Thermal Bath Cabinet Company Booklet @1901. Special Collections, Cambridge University Library.
"The Press, the Quacks, and the Public." *British Medical Journal* 1726 (27 January 1894): 208. Print.
"Pride." *The New Yorker* (18 November 1950): 42. Print.
Prior, Edward S. "Upon House-Building in the Twentieth Century." In *Modern British Domestic Architecture and Decoration*. Ed. Charles Holme. London: Offices of the Studio, 1901. 9–14. Print.
"Purchase of the Santogen Company." *The Journal of the American Medical Association* 67.25 (16 December 1916): 1861–2. Print.
Rayfield, Tom. *Fifty in 40: The Unofficial History of JWT London, 1945–1995*. Rayfield Writers, 1996. Print.
Resor, Stanley. "Personalities and the Public: Some Aspects of Testimonial Advertising." *The J. Walter Thompson News Bulletin* 138 (April 1929): 1–7. J. Walter Thompson Information Center Records, Box 4, Testimonial Advertising, 1928–1977. John W. Hartman Center for Sales, Advertising, and Marketing History, Rare Book, Manuscript and Special Collections Library, Duke University.
Richards, Thomas. *The Commodity Culture of Victorian England: Advertising and Spectacle 1851–1914*. Stanford: Stanford University Press, 1990. Print.
Rosenquist, Rod. "Copywriting Gertrude Stein: Advertising, Anonymity, Autobiography." *Modernist Cultures* 11.3 (2016): 331–50. Print.
Ross, Michael L. *Designing Fictions: Literature Confronts Advertising*. Montreal: McGill-Queen's University Press, 2015. Print.

*Round the Square* 3.2 (1953): 6. Print.
Rowell, George. "The Little Schoolmaster's Classroom." *Printers' Ink* 146.12 (21 March 1929): 200, 202. Print.
Rubicam, Raymond. "When Is the Testimonial Tainted?" *Printers' Ink* 146.11 (14 March 1929): 17–20. Print.
Sandage, C. H., and Vernon Fryburger. *Advertising Theory and Practice*, 7th edition. Homewood, IL: Irwin, 1967. Print.
Saunders, Alta Gwinn, and Herbert LeSourd Creek, eds. *The Literature of Business*. New York: Harper & Brothers Publishers, 1920. Print.
Schudson, Michael. *Advertising, the Uneasy Persuasion: Its Dubious Impact on American Society*. New York: Basic Books, 1984. Print.
Schweitzer, Marlis. "'The Mad Search for Beauty': Actresses' Testimonials, the Cosmetics Industry, and the 'Democratization of Beauty'." *The Journal of the Gilded Age and Progressive Era* 4.3 (July 2005): 255–92. Print.
Schweitzer, Marlis, and Marina Moskowitz, eds. *Testimonial Advertising in the American Marketplace: Emulation, Identity, Community*. New York: Palgrave Macmillan, 2009. Print.
Segrave, Kerry. *Endorsements in Advertising: A Social History*. Jefferson, NC: McFarland & Company, Inc., Publishers, 2005. Print.
Selden, Charles A. "Shaw Tells Critics They're Never Good." *New York Times* (12 October 1929): 7. Print.
Shaw, Bernard. *Back to Methuselah*. In *The Bodley Head Bernard Shaw: Collected Plays with Their Prefaces*, vol. 5. London: The Bodley Head, 1971. 340–684. Print.
———. *Candida*. In *The Bodley Head Bernard Shaw: Collected Plays with Their Prefaces*, vol. 1. London: The Bodley Head, 1971. 513–94. Print.
———. Collected Letters, vol. 1–4. Ed. Dan H. Laurence. New York: Viking, 1965–1985. Print.
———. "Criticism on the Hustings." In *Bernard Shaw: The Drama Observed*, vol. 2 (1895–1897). Ed. Bernard F. Dukore. University Park: Pennsylvania State University Press, 1993. 395–401. Print.
———. "Dear Harp of My Country." In *Dramatic Opinions and Essays*, vol. 1. New York: Brentano's, 1906. 326–32. Print.
———. *The Devil's Disciple*. In *The Bodley Head Bernard Shaw: Collected Plays with Their Prefaces*, vol. 2. London: The Bodley Head, 1971. 51–141. Print.
———. *Doctors' Delusions*. In *The Collected Works of Bernard Shaw*, vol. 22. New York: Wm. H. Wise & Company, 1932. 1–170. Print.
———. *The Doctor's Dilemma*. In *The Bodley Head Bernard Shaw: Collected Plays with Their Prefaces*, vol. 3. London: The Bodley Head, 1971. 321–436. Print.
———. *Dramatic Opinions and Essays with an Apology from Bernard Shaw*, vol. 2. New York: Brentano's, 1928. Print.

———. *Essays in Fabian Socialism. Major Critical Essays* 30. New York: Wm. H. Wise & Company, 1932. Print.

———. *Everybody's Political What's What*. London: Constable and Company, 1944. Print.

———. *Fanny's First Play*. In *The Bodley Head Bernard Shaw: Collected Plays with Their Prefaces*, vol. 4. London: The Bodley Head, 1971. 347–441. Print.

———. *Getting Married*. In *The Bodley Head Bernard Shaw: Collected Plays with Their Prefaces*, vol. 3. London: The Bodley Head, 1971. 547–662. Print.

———. "How to Become a Man of Genius." In *Selected Non-dramatic Writings of Bernard Shaw*. Ed. Dan H. Laurence. Boston: Houghton Mifflin Company, 1965. 341–6. Print.

———. *The Intelligent Woman's Guide to Socialism and Capitalism*. New York: Wm. H. Wise & Company, 1931. Print.

———. *John Bull's Other Island*. In *The Bodley Head Bernard Shaw: Collected Plays with Their Prefaces*, vol. 2. London: The Bodley Head, 1971. 893–1027. Print.

———. "The Life Force: Mr. Bernard Shaw's Reply to Mr. Campbell." *The Christian Commonwealth* (3 July 1912): 655. Print.

———. *Major Barbara*. In *The Bodley Head Bernard Shaw: Collected Plays with Their Prefaces*, vol. 3. London: The Bodley Head, 1971. 67–185. Print.

———. *The Millionairess*. In *The Bodley Head Bernard Shaw: Collected Plays with Their Prefaces*, vol. 6. London: The Bodley Head, 1971. 882–969. Print.

———. *Misalliance*. In *The Bodley Head Bernard Shaw: Collected Plays with Their Prefaces*, vol. 4. London: The Bodley Head, 1971. 143–253. Print.

———. *Mrs. Warren's Profession*. In *The Bodley Head Bernard Shaw: Collected Plays with Their Prefaces*, vol. 1. London: The Bodley Head, 1971. 272–356. Print.

———. "The Music-Cure." In *The Bodley Head Bernard Shaw: Collected Plays with Their Prefaces*, vol. 4. London: The Bodley Head, 1971. 877–94. Print.

———. "Notes to *Caesar and Cleopatra*." In *The Bodley Head Bernard Shaw: Collected Plays with Their Prefaces*, vol. 2. London: The Bodley Head, 1971. 293–305. Print.

———. "O'Flaherty V.C." In *The Bodley Head Bernard Shaw: Collected Plays with Their Prefaces*, vol. 4. London: The Bodley Head, 1971. 983–1014. Print.

———. "Postscript" to the "Preface" of *How He Lied to Her Husband*. In *John Bull's Other Island and Major Barbara: Also How He Lied to Her Husband*. London: Archibald Constable & Co. Ltd., 1907. 119–24. Print.

———. "Preface" to *Androcles and the Lion*. In *The Bodley Head Bernard Shaw: Collected Plays with Their Prefaces*, vol. 4. London: The Bodley Head, 1971. 455–579. Print.

———. "Preface" to *The Doctor's Dilemma*. In *The Bodley Head Bernard Shaw: Collected Plays with Their Prefaces*, vol. 3. London: The Bodley Head, 1971. 225–320. Print.

———. "Preface" to *Farfetched Fables*. In *The Bodley Head Bernard Shaw: Collected Plays with Their Prefaces*, vol. 7. London: The Bodley Head, 1971. 381–428. Print.

———. "Preface" to *Heartbreak House*. In *The Bodley Head Bernard Shaw: Collected Plays with Their Prefaces*, vol. 5. London: The Bodley Head, 1971. 11–58. Print.

———. "Preface" to *Major Barbara*. In *The Bodley Head Bernard Shaw: Collected Plays with Their Prefaces*, vol. 3. London: The Bodley Head, 1971. 15–63. Print.

———. "Preface" to *Man and Superman*. In *The Bodley Head Bernard Shaw: Collected Plays with Their Prefaces*, vol. 2. London: The Bodley Head, 1971. 493–532. Print.

———. "Preface" to *Misalliance*. In *The Bodley Head Bernard Shaw: Collected Plays with Their Prefaces*, vol. 4. London: The Bodley Head, 1971. 13–142. Print.

———. "Preface" to "O'Flaherty V.C." In *The Bodley Head Bernard Shaw: Collected Plays with Their Prefaces*, vol. 4. London: The Bodley Head, 1971. 985–7. Print.

———. "Preface" to *On the Rocks*. In *The Bodley Head Bernard Shaw: Collected Plays with Their Prefaces*, vol. 6. London: The Bodley Head, 1971. 573–628. Print.

———. "Preface" to *Pygmalion*. In *The Bodley Head Bernard Shaw: Collected Plays with Their Prefaces*, vol. 4. London: The Bodley Head, 1971. 659–64. Print.

———. "Preface" to *Three Plays for Puritans*. In *The Bodley Head Bernard Shaw: Collected Plays with Their Prefaces*, vol. 2. London: The Bodley Head, 1971. 11–48. Print.

———. "Preface" to *Too True to Be Good*. In *The Bodley Head Bernard Shaw: Collected Plays with Their Prefaces*, vol. 6. London: The Bodley Head, 1971. 399–428.Print.

———. "Preface" to *Mrs. Warren's Profession*. In *The Bodley Head Bernard Shaw: Collected Plays with Their Prefaces*, vol. 1. London: The Bodley Head, 1971. 231–266. Print.

———. *Pygmalion*. In *The Bodley Head Bernard Shaw: Collected Plays with Their Prefaces*, vol. 4. London: The Bodley Head, 1971. 669–819. Print.

———. *The Quintessence of Ibsenism*. In *Selected Non-dramatic Writings of Bernard Shaw*. Ed. Dan H. Laurence. Boston: Houghton Mifflin Company, 1965. 205–306. Print.

———. "The Revolutionist's Handbook." In *The Bodley Head Bernard Shaw: Collected Plays with Their Prefaces*, vol. 2. London: The Bodley Head, 1971. 739–80. Print.

———. *Shaw's Music*. Ed. Dan H. Laurence. London: The Bodley Head, 1981. Print.

———. *Sixteen Self-Sketches*. New York: Dodd, Mead, & Company, 1949. Print.

———. *Too True to Be Good*. In *The Bodley Head Bernard Shaw: Collected Plays with Their Prefaces*, vol. 6. London: The Bodley Head, 1971. 429–528. Print.

———. *What Shaw Really Wrote About the War*. Eds. J. L. Wisenthal and Daniel O'Leary. Gainesville: University Press of Florida, 2006. Print.

———. *Widowers' Houses*. In *The Bodley Head Bernard Shaw: Collected Plays with Their Prefaces*, vol. 1. London: The Bodley Head, 1971. 33–121. Print.

———. *You Never Can Tell*. In *The Bodley Head Bernard Shaw: Collected Plays with Their Prefaces*, vol. 1. London: The Bodley Head, 1971. 667–794. Print.

"Should the Advertiser Be the Author's Paymaster?" *Advertiser's Weekly* 61.824 (15 March 1929): 440–1, 466–7. Print.

Simonson, Lee. "Mobilizing the Billboards." *New Republic* 13 (10 November 1917): 41–43. Print.

Spender, Stephen. *The Struggle of the Modern*. Oakland: University of California Press, 1963. Print.

Stafford, Tony. "Postmodern Elements in Shaw's *Misalliance*." *SHAW: The Annual of Bernard Shaw Studies*, vol. 29 (2009): 176–88. Print.

Stote, Amos. "G.B.S. Joins Us." *Advertising & Selling* 15.10 (17 September 1930): 32. Print.

Strachan, John, and Claire Nally. *Advertising, Literature and Print Culture in Ireland, 1891–1922*. New York: Palgrave Macmillan, 2012. Print.

Sutton, Denise H. *Globalizing Ideal Beauty: How Female Copywriters of the J. Walter Thompson Advertising Agency Redefined Beauty for the Twentieth Century*. New York: Palgrave Macmillan, 2009. Print.

Swinnerton, Frank. "British Schools Hit by Teacher's Novel; Shaw Boosts 'Ads'." *Chicago Daily Tribune* (10 January 1931): 10. Print.

Thurber, James. "Let's Have a Set of Rules for Our Testimonial Industry." *The Magazine of Business* 55 (May 1929): 538. Print.

Toye, Richard. *The Labour Party and the Planned Economy, 1931–1951*. Woodbridge: Royal Historical Society, Boydell Press, 2003. Print.

"Trade Notes." *The Chemist and Druggist* 60.2 (11 January 1902): 45. Print.

Tungate, Mark. *Ad Land: A Global History of Advertising*. London: Kogan Page, 2007. Print.

"Turkish Baths at Home." Supplement to *Pall Mall Magazine* 43.192 (April 1909): 14. Print.

Turner, E. S. *Taking the Cure*. London: Michael Joseph, 1967. Print.
Tyler, William D. "The Image, the Brand, and the Consumer." *Journal of Marketing* 22.2 (October 1957): 162–5. Print.
Ueyama, Takahiro. *Health in the Marketplace: Professionalism, Therapeutic Desires, and Medical Commodification in Late-Victorian London*. Palo Alto, CA: The Society for the Promotion of Science and Scholarship, 2010. Print.
Ugolini, Laura. "Men, Masculinities, and Menswear Advertising, c.1890–1914." In *A Nation of Shopkeepers: Five Centuries of British Retailing*. Eds. John Benson and Laura Ugolini. London: I.B. Tauris, 2003. 80–104. Print.
Vanbrugh, Irene. *To Tell My Story*. London: Hutchinson, 1950. Print.
Waller, Phillip. *Writers, Readers, & Reputations: Literary Life in Britain 1870–1918*. Oxford: Oxford University Press, 2006. Print.
Wang, Ning. "Rethinking Authenticity in Tourism Experience." *Annals of Tourism Research* 26.262 (1999): 349–70. Print.
Webb, Sidney. "Introduction." In *Advertising: A Study of a Modern Business Power*. G. W. Goodall. London: Constable & Co., 1914. ix–xvii. Print.
"What the Advertising Industry Thinks of Purchased Testimonials." *Printers' Ink* 146.12 (21 March 1929): 148–9. Print.
"Why London Department Store Advertised in New York." *Printers' Ink*, 146.12 (21 March 1929): 73–4. Print.
Wicke, Jennifer. *Advertising Fictions: Literature, Advertisement, and Social Reading*. New York: Columbia University Press, 1988. Print.
Wisenthal, J. L. *The Marriage of Contraries: Bernard Shaw's Middle Plays*. Cambridge, MA: Harvard University Press, 1974. Print.
Wood, James Playsted. *The Story of Advertising*. New York: The Ronald Press Company, 1958. Print.
Yde, Matthew. *Bernard Shaw and Totalitarianism: Longing for Utopia*. New York: Palgrave Macmillan, 2013. Print.
Yeo, Peter. *Reflections on an Agency*. Published Privately, 1988. Print.
Zweiniger-Bargielowska, Ina. "Building a British Superman: Physical Culture in Interwar Britain." *Journal of Contemporary History* 41.4 (October 2006): 595–610. Print.

# Index

**A**
Advertising
  and First World War, 76
  history of, 16, 86, 105
  and theatre, 10
*Advertising & Selling*, 63, 111, 112, 134, 135, 154
American Medical Association (AMA), 71, 73, 76, 77
Appel, Joseph, 133
Arlington, Lauren, 81, 82

**B**
Barker, Harley Granville, 37
Barrie, J.M., 127n16
Beegan, Gerry, 60
Bennett, Arnold, 23, 98, 99, 101–103, 105, 106, 108, 112–114, 125, 134
Bertolini, John, 19
Biggs, Murray, 83
Blake, Gerald, 112

Blaker, Dorothea Campbell, 144, 159n34, 160n36
Brecht, Bertolt, 16
British Medical Association (BMA), 34, 38
*British Medical Journal*, 38, 70, 77
Burbidge, Woodman, 103
Burnley-Jones, C., 106

**C**
Campbell, Reginald John, 72
Carnegie, Andrew, 53n20
Celebrity testimonial, 21, 23, 24, 68, 79, 84, 98, 119, 125
Century Thermal Bath Cabinet Company, 38
Chesterton, G.K., 15, 19, 108, 112, 125
*Christian Commonwealth*, 72, 73
Church, Roy, 1
Colbourne, Maurice, 15

## D
Dickinson, Roy, 121
Downing, E.P., 69, 72, 88n46
Doyle, Arthur Conan, 56n67
Duba, Frank, 17

## E
*The Editor & Publisher*, 139, 143
Egbert, James W., 65, 93
Eliot, T.S., 115
Ervine, St. John, 53n20

## F
Fabian, 2, 16, 17, 50, 52, 101, 122
Faversham, William, 7
Ford, Corey, 124
Formamint, 12, 22, 69–73, 75–77, 81, 88n46, 89, 93, 154
Fowler, George S., 123
Fox, Stephen, 124
Freeman, William M., 65, 137
French, John, 81

## G
Gainor, J. Ellen, 36, 37, 47, 48
Gardner, H.S., 95, 134, 135, 154
Gibbs, A.M., 78
Goldman, Jonathan, 61, 65, 86n6, 95, 97
Graham, Colin, 148
Gregory, James, 34
Griffiths, Gareth, 149
Gruber, L. Fritz, 20

## H
Hackett, Francis, 113–115
Hamon, Augustus, 15, 78
Hardy, Gelston, 136–138, 142–144, 148, 149

Harn, O.C., 122
Harrods, 12, 22, 23, 36, 85, 94, 95, 98–103, 105, 106, 108, 109, 112, 115, 119, 122, 125, 128–132n98, 134, 136, 143, 152
Henderson, Archibald, 31, 32, 102
High Modernism, 97, 126
Holroyd, Michael, 16, 51, 61, 81
Hubbard, Elbert, 31

## I
Ionesco, Eugène, 41

## J
Jaeger, 19, 20
Jaffe, Aaron, 97
Jones, Henry Arthur, 79
Joyce, James, 97, 114, 115

## K
Kandela, Peter, 37
Kaplan, Joel H., 66
Kent, Brad, 2, 148, 152
Kropff, H.F.J., 109
Kyllman, Otto, 2

## L
*The Lancet*, 34, 39
Langtry, Lily, 39
Lansdowne, Helen, 123, 137
Laurence, Dan H., 31, 32, 78, 136, 138
Lears, Jackson, 20, 33, 101, 107, 115
Lewis, Sinclair, 111, 129n73
Loving, Pierre, 76
Luce, Henry Robinson, 105, 109, 115
Lynd, Robert, 16

## M

*The Madras House*, 37
Mann, W.A., 103
Marchand, Roland, 22
Martín, Gustavo A. Rodríguez, 51, 57n75
McEwan, Alice, 3, 33, 45, 47, 73, 75, 100, 149
McKenna, E., 32, 52, 108, 129n60
McKenzie, Malcolm, 19
McNulty, Matthew Edward, 51
McVoy, F., 105, 110
Menzies, H. Stuart, 107, 111
Mills, John A., 41
Moffett, James C., 107
Morgan, Margery M., 35, 37, 43, 54n27
Moskowitz, Marina, 134, 154
Mussolini, Benito, 21

## N

Nally, Claire, 80
Nathan, Matthew, 81
Near testimonial, 22–24, 94
Nevett, T.R., 2, 33, 94
*The New Age*, 75
*The New Yorker*, 1, 124, 136, 139, 140, 142, 143, 145, 150
*The New York Times*, 73, 103, 128n27, 132, 143, 159

## O

Obdycke, John B., 107
Ochshorn, Kathleen, 147
O'Duffy, Eimar, 118, 131n106
O'Leary, Michael John, 80–82, 86
O'Meara, Walter, 125
Orman, Felix, 63
Outka, Elizabeth, 35, 100, 147
O'Toole, Fintan, 16, 28, 30n99, 53, 85, 89, 91, 155, 162

## P

Palmer, John, 1, 14
Pan-American, 12, 22, 24, 94, 136, 138, 139, 144, 145, 149, 150
Patent medicine, 3, 8, 11, 16, 31–34, 38, 45, 46, 48, 52, 62, 64, 65, 67–69, 71, 80, 81, 85, 93, 95, 108, 116, 117
Patti, Adelina, 87n30
Pearson, Hesketh, 31
Personality, 64, 107, 124, 145
Personality advertising, 73, 86, 96, 119, 143, 155
Peters, Sally, 16, 51
Phelan, Mark, 147
Phillips, Terry, 83, 84, 89, 90n77
Physical culture, 36
Portable Turkish Bath, 22, 36, 52
Pound, Ezra, 97, 115
*Printers' Ink*, 22, 32, 52, 65–67, 70, 71, 88, 93, 95, 103, 105–108, 112, 119, 122, 123, 127, 129–132, 130n73, 134, 158
Public personality, 2, 24, 85

## R

Radford, George, 32
Rayfield, Tom, 158n21
Reith, John, 156
Resor, Stanley, 21, 29, 86, 91, 96, 119, 123, 127n14
Richards, Thomas, 35, 39, 46
Rosset, B.C., 31
*Round the Square*, 144, 150
Rowell, George, 106
Roycroft book, 31
Ruskin, John, 21

## S

*The Saturday Review of Literature*, 139
Schweitzer, Marlis, 68, 69, 134, 154

Scribner's, 1, 3
Secret Remedies, 34, 35, 51
Selfridge, Gordon, 35, 49, 55n46, 100, 116
Shakespeare, William, 5, 15, 41, 61, 112
Shaw, Bernard
  as copywriter, 3, 18, 109, 143, 150
  and First World War, 5, 80
  and G.B.S., 1–3, 13, 19, 21, 22, 30n99, 33, 51, 61, 65, 153–155, 157
  and patent medicine, 8, 16, 32, 69, 95
  as playwright, 14, 52, 60, 78, 79, 114, 137, 139
Shaw, Bernard (dramatic and fictional works)
  *Androcles and the Lion*, 8
  *Back to Methuselah*, 13, 118, 145
  *Caesar and Cleopatra*, 13
  *Candida*, 7
  *Cashel Byron's Profession*, 5
  *The Devil's Disciple*, 6
  *The Doctor's Dilemma*, 11, 19, 31, 33, 35
  *Fanny's First Play*, 11
  *Farfetched Fables*, 11, 12, 16, 122
  *Getting Married*, 6
  *Heartbreak House*, 16
  *How He Lied to Her Husband*, 9
  *The Irrational Knot*, 5
  *John Bull's Other Island*, 146–148, 152
  *Love among the Artists*, 5
  *Major Barbara*, 7, 8, 14
  *Man and Superman*, 6, 17, 63, 106
  *The Millionairess*, 7, 26n30
  *Misalliance*, 3, 7, 11, 13, 22, 31, 35, 36, 39, 41, 42, 44, 45, 48–52, 59, 69
  "The Music-Cure", 7
  "O'Flaherty, V.C.", 22, 80, 81, 85, 90n76, 93
  *Pygmalion*, 7, 13, 48
  *On the Rocks*, 13
  *The Revolutionist's Handbook*, 8, 31, 52
  *Three Plays for Puritans*, 18
  *Too True to Be Good*, 146, 147
  *Mrs. Warren's Profession*, 6, 10
  *Widowers' Houses*, 6
  *You Never Can Tell*, 6
Shaw, Bernard (non-fictional works)
  *Common Sense about the War*, 78, 85, 93
  *Doctors' Delusions*, 31
  *Everybody's Political What's What*, 9, 12
  *The Intelligent Woman's Guide to Socialism and Capitalism*, 9
  *The Quintessence of Ibsenism*, 57n71
  *Sixteen Self-Sketches*, 32
Shaw, Charlotte Payne-Townshend, 45, 72
Shaw, Mabel, 126
Simmons, 12, 22, 23, 85, 94–96, 98, 115–120, 123, 124, 126, 131n98, 133, 134, 139, 142
Spender, Stephen, 19, 114, 115, 119
Stafford, Tony, 41
Stalin, Joseph, 21
Stote, Amos, 136
Stowell, Shelia, 66
Strachan, John, 80
Sweet, Henry, 7
Swinnerton, Frank, 111, 112

## T

Testimonial endorsement, 20, 22, 23, 64, 94, 97
*The J. Walter Thompson News Bulletin*, 125
*The J. Walter Thompson News Letter*, 96
*The J.W.T. News*, 124, 142
Thompson, J. Walter (agency), 22, 84, 86, 136, 144
Thurber, James, 110
*Tide*, 22, 139
*Time*, 109, 115, 117, 120, 139, 142, 145
Tomalin, H.R., 19
Tourist marketing, 150
Trollope, Anthony, 153
Turkish bath, 3, 4, 7, 36–39, 47–50, 70
Turner, E.S., 3
Tyler, William D., 155

## W

Wang, Nina, 148
Webb, Beatrice, 50
Webb, Sidney, 17, 101
Wells, H.G., 23, 56n69, 98, 99, 101–103, 105, 106, 108, 112–116, 118, 123–125, 128, 130, 133, 134
Whiteley, William, 53n20
Wicke, Jennifer, 40
Wilde, Oscar, 14, 19, 97
Wildes, Charles, 98, 99, 108, 109, 134
Williams, Raymond, 1, 9, 33
Winsten, Stephen, 31
Wisenthal, J.L., 41, 44
Wood, James Playsted, 94, 125
W.S. Crawford Ltd., 20

## Y

Yeo, Peter, 144

The manufacturer's authorised representative in the EU is Springer Nature Customer Service Centre GmbH, Europaplatz 3, 69115 Heidelberg, Germany. If you have any concerns regarding our products, please contact ProductSafety@springernature.com

Printed and bound by CPI Group (UK) Ltd, Croydon, CR0 4YY
23/03/2026
02076736-0001